"This lively update of Jonathan Edwards's classic
Treatise Concerning Religious Affections is a masterful analysis for today of reality in the spiritual life.
Well set out and vividly illustrated, it was clearly a
labor of love for its author, and I predict that many are
going to thank God for it. I wish it could be made
compulsory reading in every evangelical congregation."

J. I. PACKER
Sangwoo Youtong Chee Professor of Theology
Regent College

"*Seeing God* uses the skeleton and outlook of Jonathan
Edwards's *Religious Affections* to revisit the question
of spiritual reality. To Edwards's effort this book adds
modern terminology, a careful use of written
sources recounting the spiritual experience of saints in
former eras, and a wide range of experiences
from individuals known personally by the author. The
result is as welcome as it is refreshing."

MARK A. NOLL
McManis Professor of Christian Thought
Wheaton College

"This is a book of wisdom that reminds us that some of
the most unreliable signs of our salvation
often look very religious indeed and some of the
most reliable signs of our salvation are
so common we can easily miss them."

STANLEY HAUERWAS
Gilbert T. Rowe Professor of Theological Ethics
Duke Divinity School

"Edwards's *Religious Affections* is a mountain of
Christian spirituality to which Gerry McDermott is
an able guide. Readers not quite ready to
scale the contours of Edwards's thought by themselves
will have McDermott ready to present the chief
peaks and valleys in all their splendor. And, like the best
guides, McDermott adds his own colorful
illustrations and hard-won insight both to lighten each
step and to illuminate each principle."

JOHN G. STACKH(
Associate Professor of I
University of Mani

D0819303

Other books by Gerald R. McDermott:

One Holy and Happy Society: The Public Theology of Jonathan Edwards
Living with Cancer: A Medical and Spiritual Guide (with William A. Fintel, M.D.)

SEEING GOD

Twelve Reliable Signs of TRUE Spirituality

Gerald R. McDermott

InterVarsity Press
Downers Grove, Illinois

131326

InterVarsity Press® is the book-publishing division of InterVarsity Christian Fellowship®, a student movement active on campus at hundreds of universities, colleges and schools of nursing in the United States of America, and a member movement of the International Fellowship of Evangelical Students. For information about local and regional activities, write Public Relations Dept., InterVarsity Christian Fellowship, 6400 Schroeder Rd., P.O. Box 7895, Madison, WI 53707-7895.

Scripture quotations, unless otherwise noted, are from the New Revised Standard Version of the Bible, copyright 1989 by the Division of Christian Education of the National Council of the Churches of Christ in the U.S.A., and are used by permission.

Cover photograph: Carr Clifton

ISBN 0-8308-1616-X

Printed in the United States of America ∞

Library of Congress Cataloging-in-Publication Data

McDermott, Gerald R. (Gerald Robert)
    Seeing God: twelve reliable signs of true spirituality/Gerald
R. McDermott.
        p.   cm.
    Includes bibliographical references.
    ISBN 0-8308-1616-X (pbk.: alk. paper)
        1. Spirituality.   2. Apologetics.   3. Emotions—Religious aspects—
Christianity.   4. Edwards, Jonathan.   1703-1758.   Treatise
concerning the religious affections.   I. Title.
BV4501.2.M2236   1995
248.2—dc20   95-25286
                                                                                                                    CIP

21   20   19   18   17   16   15   14   13   12   11   10   9   8   7   6   5   4   3   2   1

12   11   10   09   08   07   06   05   04   03   02   01   00   99   98   97   96   95

To Jean,
a living illustration
of the twelve reliable signs

*O WORSHIP THE LORD
IN THE BEAUTY OF HOLINESS.*
(PSALM 96:9)

*BLESSED ARE THE PURE IN HEART,
FOR THEY SHALL SEE GOD.*
(MATTHEW 5:8)

*ALL WHO SEE THE SON
AND BELIEVE IN HIM HAVE ETERNAL LIFE.*
(JOHN 6:40)

Preface

Shortly after I entered graduate school, I read a book that opened up a whole new world for me. It gave me a new way of seeing God, and as a result, a new way of looking at my walk with God. That book was Jonathan Edwards's *Religious Affections*.

Reading the *Affections* felt like undergoing (spiritual) open-heart surgery. Edwards seemed to understand my secret thoughts and feelings better than I understood them myself. But more important, I began to see God's beauty, and it started to transform my life. It's not as if I had seen nothing of God's beauty before this. From the very beginning of my Christian life I had been struck by God's beauty. But I didn't understand it or have words for it. And because I had never been shown its importance, I didn't press on to see and enjoy more of that beauty. I had thought of my Christian life more as a grateful response to what Jesus had done for me on the cross. Or as doing my duty to a God who seemed somewhat removed from my daily experience.

When I read the *Affections,* God's beauty became more real, and my enjoyment of that beauty suddenly exploded. The Christian life for me changed from dutiful response to delighted enjoyment. Because my motivation became based more on awe and love, obedience was less painful and forced. I found myself becoming more like the person I wanted to be.

The *Affections* also helped me make sense of the confused tangle of spiritualities on the American scene. It dispelled much of the bewilderment I felt when trying to understand why so many people who seemed to be Christians had lost their faith or horribly compromised their testimonies. It also helped me identify which teachers and authors I could learn from, and which I should ignore.

Several years ago I became convinced that it was time to make Edwards's insights available to a broad audience. I gave a series of lectures on spiritual discernment to pastors and professors at Faculdade Batista (a Baptist seminary in São Paulo, Brazil) and used the arguments from the *Affections* as my outline. These men and women said that my material spoke to their needs like nothing they had heard and asked how they could get more of it in written form. They lived and worked in a different culture, but I was convinced that Edwards's insights were transcultural. I trust you will see that they are.

This book has been fun to write. My youngest son, Sean (age eight), is a model of enthusiasm. When he's happy, which is most of the time, he is excited about nearly everything that he encounters. Finding a new library book on animals, for instance, can send him into ecstasy. So can the prospect of playing baseball with Dad. Writing this book has given me something of the pleasure that I see in Sean so much of the time. It has also given me an opportunity to share with a popular audience insights that have been restricted for the most part to scholarly students of Jonathan Edwards. It is my hope that more people in the pew will be enriched by encountering this treasure of spiritual wisdom.

Another reason I've enjoyed writing this book has been the friends who have offered their criticisms and suggestions. I am deeply grateful to the following friends and colleagues who have taken time to read and comment on the manuscript: my pastor Quigg Lawrence, Alan and Melody Pieratt, Robert Benne, John and Joan McDermott, Art Thomas, Everett Kier, Greg Scharf, Howie Dahl, Jay Steinke and Mark Seifrid. Of special help have been two physicians: Bill Fintel, who has provided many illustrations and much inspiration, and Bob Williams, who helped sharpen both text and title. My editor and critic of first resort has been my wife, Jean. Her penetrating discernment has saved me from things that would later embarrass me. Throughout, she has prodded me to make my prose more interesting for a nonacademic audience. She's also thankful that this year I won't be writing another book! Finally, thanks are due to John G. Stackhouse Jr., whose meticulous reading produced a host of extremely helpful suggestions, and Rodney Clapp, a terrific editor who has become a friend.

Part One

· · · · ·

Introduction

1
· · · · ·

Spiritual Confusion

*DON'T QUENCH THE SPIRIT. AND DON'T DESPISE PRO-
PHETIC UTTERANCES. BUT TEST EVERY SO-CALLED
MOVING OF THE SPIRIT. HOLD ON TO WHAT PROVES
TO BE GOOD, AND STAY AWAY FROM
ANYTHING THAT TURNS OUT TO BE EVIL.*
PAUL

THE DASHING YOUNG MINISTER HAD A CAPTIVATING PERSONALITY.
Educated at a prestigious college, this brilliant heir to a distinguished
family was a magnetic preacher. When spiritual awakening came to his
area of New England, he gathered his congregation together for a
special meeting. Incredibly, they listened to him speak for twenty-four
hours—until he collapsed. From then on he called those he regarded
as truly Christian "brother" or "sister," the rest "neighbor."

When speaking as a guest preacher in a Connecticut city, he concluded his address by sauntering down the center aisle crying out,
"Come to Christ! Come to Christ! Come away [from the world]!" Then
he went into a pew of women and stood singing and praying intermittently. Women joined in with him, some fainting and others erupting
in hysterics. This continued into the evening, when he marched off
through the streets singing at the top of his lungs.

Spiritual confusion is not new. This young minister carried on not in late-twentieth-century America but in mid-eighteenth-century New England. His name was James Davenport (1716-1757), and before his self-appointed mission had ended, he was arrested for disturbing the peace, indicted for slander and judged by a grand jury to be insane. His religious antics caused Christian believers living 250 years ago to question both the claims of their religious leaders and their own ability to discern authentic religious teachings.

Four Cultural Trends

Many modern Christians are asking similar questions. Today, however, the questions are more searching because of four enduring trends in American culture. Perhaps the most noticeable is *declining trust in religious leaders*. In the 1980s we were bombarded with media stories about TV preachers who paid for sex, misused their supporters' money and lied to their audiences. Jonestown and Waco are now household words that remind us that a group of dedicated religious people can become a dangerous cult. In the early 1990s the Roman Catholic Church was rocked by allegations that priests had sexually molested children in their congregations. It is no wonder that public confidence in the clergy has dropped precipitously. According to Gallup polls conducted before 1988, Americans trusted the integrity of clergymen more than that of any other profession. But in 1993 public esteem for the clergy ranked fourth, behind pharmacists (first), college teachers (second) and engineers (third).

Second, there is growing *disenchantment with organized religion*. Many associate organized religion with the sex and money scandals of the 1980s and believe that it interferes with our right to develop a personal religion of our own. The "Sheilaism" made famous by sociologist Robert Bellah's *Habits of the Heart* illustrates this anti-institutional trend perfectly: "I believe in God. I'm not a religious fanatic. I can't remember the last time I went to church. My faith has carried me a long way. It's Sheilaism. Just my own little voice."[1] Like Sheila, many individuals today want to make up their own religion as they go along. They resent the notion that it is necessary or even helpful to join an organized religious group.

A third cultural pressure causing spiritual confusion is *religious pluralism*. Many different religions are now competing for our attention and devotion. Catholics and Protestants, Pentecostals and Baptists, "high church" Episcopalians and "low church" nondenominational sects all claim to have a better or truer form of Christianity than their rivals. To further complicate things, Zen Buddhists and Muslims are also telling us that they have the final truth.

Religious pluralism is nothing new. The early church preached the gospel in a Roman Empire which boasted a bewildering array of competing religions. What *is* new is a pluralistic mindset, which says that truth is relative and therefore there can be no final truth. This is the mindset that Allan Bloom called "openness" in his *The Closing of the American Mind:*

> Openness—and the relativism that makes it the only plausible stance in the face of various claims to truth and various ways of life and kinds of human beings—is the great insight of our times. The true believer is the real danger. The study of history and of culture teaches that all the world was mad in the past; men always thought they were right, and that led to wars, persecutions, slavery, xenophobia, racism, and chauvinism. The point is not to correct the mistakes and really be right; rather it is not to think you are right at all.[2]

In the face of this dominant cultural attitude (and it *is* dominant; I have discovered, as did Bloom, that the majority of my college students walk into class with this approach to truth), it is not surprising that American Christians are hesitant to declare that they have found *the* truth. They know that academics and cultural commentators tend to treat religion as a useful fiction or regard the world religions as equally valid paths to God.

Finally, American Christians have been influenced by our culture's promotion of *intellectual autonomy.* This is the attitude that I am not intellectually mature if I permit other persons, or particularly the institutional church, to influence my thinking. Michael J. Donahue of the Search Institute discovered in a major survey of six Protestant denominations that one-third of adult church members affirm the following propositions: "All spiritual truth and wisdom is within me" and "An individual should arrive at his or her own religious beliefs independent of any church."[3] According to this attitude, we should not affirm the truth of any religious group because it violates our own intellectual autonomy.

All of these cultural pressures—mistrust of religious leaders, suspicion of institutional religion, religious pluralism and emphasis on intellectual autonomy—contribute to a sense of spiritual confusion among Christians today. Christians believe that Jesus is God, but the cultural milieu I have described discourages many from speaking with any conviction about the finality of this truth.[4] And more important, they don't know how to evaluate competing *Christian* claims to true religion. That is, they don't know how to judge between different Christian groups, leaders or teachings.

A More Basic Problem

Some Christians have a more fundamental problem. They wonder how they can know if their own spiritual experiences are genuine. Scott, for example, was a philosophy major at an elite college in Minnesota. He had the tanned and shaggy look of a slightly cleaned-up hippie. A certain odor suggested that he didn't bathe often. But it was his eyes that struck me. They were crystal blue and glittered like twinkling stars.

Scott was a seeker. He'd already gone the route of the late-sixties counterculture looking for truth, beauty and love in drugs, nature and sex. After some opiated hash terrified him with unstoppable hallucinations one night, he concluded that drugs could do more harm than good. But his search had not been entirely unfruitful. He had sensed a certain mystical beauty in the arboretum down the road from the college, and he felt he had tasted love in a passionate relationship with a young woman who had since departed for Colorado. These faint stirrings of his spirit persuaded him that the answers he was seeking could be found in the spiritual realm. But they also convinced him that nature and human love could introduce him to only the outermost fringes of the spiritual world.

In the fall of his second year at college Scott became a Christian. Or so he thought. The campus Christian fellowship was experiencing a revival of sorts that was led by the son of a Pentecostal preacher and a Catholic freshman. There were healings and tongues and prophecies. Scott was intrigued by the strange hybrid he observed in the leaders: though intellectually sharp, they spoke of spiritual experiences with passionate conviction. They quoted the Bible, but without the wooden literalism of fundamentalists he knew. They distinguished between the

Bible's perennial truths and the cultural baggage in which those truths were carried. For instance, they said that though Paul told women to cover their heads at all times, he did so because in his culture women without head coverings were considered sexually promiscuous. The timeless truth intended by Paul was that sexual immorality should be discouraged.

One Friday night John, the Pentecostal minister's son, spoke on the baptism of the Holy Spirit. He described it as immersion in the Spirit of God, an experience of God's power and love. Scott was touched. Although the emotional fervor of this group had at first made him wary, their sincerity and transparent happiness attracted him. Perhaps it had something to do with the broken home in which he had been raised. His father had divorced his mother when Scott was five. Ever since, Scott had felt incomplete. In his most vulnerable moments he accused himself of causing his parents' separation. But he usually reminded himself that it wasn't his fault his dad had left, that his parents just didn't get along. Recently he had concluded that his mother must have felt deeply rejected. Maybe this was why she had rarely hugged Scott and seemed to find it hard to verbalize her love for him. Perhaps it even explained why he continued to feel unworthy despite the accolades of teachers and being elected vice president of his class at Madison High School.

When John came to the end of his talk, he suggested that students pray for "the baptism." Some started praying out loud; others bowed their heads and closed their eyes. Scott felt uncomfortable. He didn't like being told what to pray for. Yet as he closed his eyes and heard others praying in the background—and some exclaiming as if they were feeling or seeing something delightful—he found himself praying, "God, give me this baptism. I want it. I want your love. Please give it to me."

After just a moment, he felt a warmth enveloping him. At the same time he started to cry. He wasn't sure why. Was it because he was shocked that a prayer could be answered so fast? Or because he finally discovered that God was real and really cared about *him*? Whatever the reason, it felt good. And for the first time in years, he felt important. God, if it truly was he—God, the Creator of the cosmos, was touching *him!* This infinite being was stooping down to touch a tiny piece of protoplasm named Scott! He felt honored. He felt—could he say it?—loved.

During the next few weeks Scott attended as many prayer meetings and Bible studies as time would permit. He tried desperately to hold on to that delicious feeling of being valued and loved. For the most part he was successful. As he read the Bible and tried to pray, he felt closer to God.

In the next two years Scott gave more and more of his time to the fellowship on campus. He became a Bible study leader and member of the leadership team. He never again felt the passionate surge of emotion that had overwhelmed him in his sophomore year, but there were gentle reminders of God's love every now and then.

Then some of Scott's new Christian friends, who had personal experiences similar to Scott's, fell away from the group and, seemingly, the Christian life. Sarah, for instance, started dating a non-Christian and after a while regarded her time in the fellowship as an emotional delusion. Alan, who had come out of a riotous lifestyle, returned to it with gusto. He ignored the pleadings of Christian friends that he was cutting himself off from the Source of life. And Randy, who had been a small group leader, started attending meetings of the Reverend Moon's Unification Church. He was impressed by the love he found there, as well as Moon's earnest testimonies of having spoken to eminent figures from Bible times.

News of these defections left Scott reeling. Alan, Sarah and Randy were friends who had converted to Christ before Scott. Some of them had seemed to be very strong Christians. How could they turn their backs on their faith? Scott wondered if they knew something he didn't. Before long he was doubting the validity of his original conversion experience. Was it really the Spirit of God that had led him to faith? Or was it simply an emotional experience driven by his need for love?

How Can We Judge?

Like Scott, many of us are confused about the spiritual life. We want to know what is really true, both in the abstract and *for us*, but at the same time we feel hesitant to conclude, even tentatively, that some Christian or church is false or bad. We hesitate because there is another part of us that says we should be tolerant of religious diversity. As someone has put it, one man's devil is another man's god. Our own confusion reminds us that we don't know for sure what is spiritually true or false, so who are we to proclaim so dogmatically that someone's god is really the devil? That someone's spirituality is false and ours is true?

As Christians we are convinced that Jesus of Nazareth is to be our exemplar—that he represents both ideal humanity and holy divinity. But beyond that we are confused by the dizzying array of people and groups claiming to be Christian. We don't know with much certainty which one to prefer over the others. And maybe we are sometimes persuaded that no one *is* to be preferred over others. After all, didn't Jesus tell us not to judge? We don't want to make people feel guilty and condemned by discounting their spirituality.

Judgment Is Sometimes Necessary

We are embarrassed by the Jim Bakkers and Jimmy Swaggarts and appalled by the David Koreshes and Jim Joneses. They show us all too clearly that sincere spirituality can become destructive fanaticism—and that religious deception is more common than we used to imagine.

And what are we to make of conflicts—when one spokesperson for Christ recommends a path that leads in the opposite direction from the one recommended by another "Christian" group or leader? Karl and Laura, for example, are wonderful friends of mine. Years ago, when they had just become engaged, they asked their pastor what to do with the powerful sexual attraction they felt for each other. The pastor replied unabashedly that they should sleep together because they needed to learn if they were sexually compatible. My friends were confused, because another Christian friend whom they trusted warned them that sex outside marriage was condemned by Scripture and would damage their spirituality as well as their marriage.

Karl and Laura were faced with a genuine dilemma. Both advisers seemed to be Christians, but they disagreed with each other profoundly. Sex before marriage couldn't be both right and wrong at the same time. They realized that they had to make a judgment—that one way of being a Christian was right and the other wrong.

The situation is even more complicated for those of us whose trust has been betrayed by a spiritual leader or institution. Then we have additional questions. How can we overcome our past hurts and confusion in order to discern true religion from false? How can we have assurance that one group is closer to the truth than another? That our pastor is not leading us astray? That our own spirituality is sound? In other words, how can we know with assurance what it really means to be a Christian—a disciple of Jesus in a living and growing relationship with him? And more generally, how can we judge the spirituality of a religious group or leader? What is the difference between a good shepherd and a hired hand intent on fleecing the flock?

How This Book Can Help
In the following chapters I address these questions by charting a pattern of godliness that has been recommended by saints for two millennia. I will draw from Scripture, church history, the classics of Christian spirituality and my own experience to outline what I consider to be a genuinely Christian spirituality. I have borrowed my outline and most of my arguments from a book that I consider the greatest work ever written on spiritual discernment: Jonathan Edwards's *Religious Affections*. Edwards (1703-1758) was a theologian, pastor and leader of revivals. He is most famous for his leadership of the Great Awakening, a powerful revival that swept up and down the American colonies in the 1730s and 1740s, changing the religious and political landscape of America forever after.

In many respects the Awakening was a great success. Thousands were saved, and American Christianity was recharged and reformed in ways that still affect us today. But the Awakening was not an unmixed blessing. Some of its leaders seemed more concerned for their own reputations than for the gospel. Many of their followers boasted of visions and ecstasies but continued to live materialistic, self-absorbed lives. Churches fractured and split as leaders hurled mean-spirited accusations at one another.

To help protect future generations from similar problems, and to teach spiritual discernment to participants in future awakenings, Edwards wrote *Religious Affections* in 1746.[5] Harvard historian Perry Miller called it the greatest work of religious psychology ever written on American soil. Edwards's objective in this work was to draw the fine line between true and false religion. He aimed to so describe the nature of genuine spiritual experience that both insiders and outsiders to evangelical Christianity could distinguish between the Holy Spirit's work and its counterfeits.

This book uses Edwards's work as a skeleton. It puts flesh on the skeleton by drawing from the discoveries of such masters of spirituality as Teresa of Ávila, John of the Cross, Thomas à Kempis, Dietrich Bonhoeffer, C. S. Lewis, Thomas Merton and Richard Foster. It also draws on the experiences of individual Christians past and present. Its object is to provide a manual of discernment for the twenty-first century—a blueprint for spirituality in today's confusing world.

Before we start exploring this pattern of spirituality, let me offer some encouragement to persevere. The jumble of competing spiritualities "out there" seems so tangled that we may despair of ever finding a way through it. But let's not give up before we even begin. And let's not become discouraged and disillusioned by the presence of so much sin and corruption in the church of God.

We need not be surprised to find so much good mixed with so much bad in the church of God. It is no more surprising than the astonishing mixture of good and bad within each one of us. Think of it: each truly regenerate Christian has God's *Holy* Spirit—his divine nature, with all of its power and love and other graces, dwelling within (Rom 8:9-10; 1 Cor 1:30). But dwelling in the same heart are also corruption, hypocrisy and sin. Is this any less surprising than the mixture of grace and egoism in the church? Jeremiah reminds us that "the heart is devious above all else; it is perverse—who can understand it?" (Jer 17:9). Paul tells us that as a result of the Fall our minds were darkened (Rom 1:21). Even as saints, we see only "dimly" (1 Cor 13:12). Because we are finite and still disabled by sin, we should not be shocked to find a mixture of good and bad not only within ourselves but also in the church.

Not the First Time

The problem is not new. Such a mixture of true religion with false, deliverance with deception, has occurred in every revival in history. For example, there was a mixture of sincere and counterfeit conversion in the revival during the reign of King Josiah (seventh century B.C.; see Jer 3:6, 10). In the days of John the Baptist there was an outpouring of the Spirit of God that awakened many. But shortly thereafter most fell away: "you were willing to rejoice in his light for a time" (Jn 5:35). We see the same pattern in Jesus' ministry. Thousands were thrilled by his preaching; they admired him and rejoiced in his miracles. But few were true disciples; many were called but few were chosen. Most were like the stony or thorny ground mentioned in the sower and seed parable (Mt 13:20-22). They received the gospel with joy but fell away when touched by persecution or the lure of the world.

The revivals during the apostles' time were no different. There are indications that members of these first churches betrayed one another and departed from the faith. False teachers apparently led many astray (Mt 24:10-13). Paul complained that his Galatian church had been "bewitched" (Gal 3.1) and despaired that his work among them "may have been wasted" (Gal 4:11). He lamented to his Philippian friends that some church workers were "seeking their own interests, not those of Jesus Christ," (Phil 2.21) and that "many live as enemies of the cross of Christ" (Phil 3.18).

This trend was seen in the European Reformation of the sixteenth century as well as America's Great Awakening (eighteenth century). Luther often grumbled that his congregation failed to live out the implications of his Reformation preaching. In a 1528 sermon he scolded them: "You ungrateful beasts, you are not worthy of the treasure of the gospel. If you don't improve, I will stop preaching rather than cast pearls before swine."[6] Edwards's congregation seemed miraculously transformed as it enthusiastically welcomed his preaching in the 1730s and early 1740s. Yet this same congregation turned against much of what he stood for by the end of the 1740s and ejected him from the pulpit in 1750.

A Reason for Hope

Although it is disconcerting to learn that so much bad has always been mixed with the good things of God, we need not despair. We are not the first to confront confusion and betrayal. The church has been threatened with deception and treachery before. If Christians of ages past were able to distinguish the truth from its hosts of subtle counterfeits, so can we. If they remained faithful despite their cohorts' desertions, there is no reason that the grace of God cannot enable us to do the same.

So there is good reason to hope. Paying attention to the wisdom of past spiritual masters and trusting in the grace of God, we can begin our journey with confidence in our ability to learn the difference between true and false spirituality.

Part Two

· · · · ·

The Affections

2

· · · · ·

Feelings, Beliefs & the Affections

TRUE RELIGION, IN GREAT PART,
CONSISTS IN HOLY AFFECTIONS.
JONATHAN EDWARDS

T WENTY-THREE HUNDRED YEARS AGO THE AUTHOR OF ECCLESI-
astes wrote, "There is nothing new under the sun. Is there a thing of
which it is said, 'See, this is new'? It has already been, in the ages before
us" (Eccles 1:9-10).

Spiritual confusion is nothing new. As we saw in chapter one, people
from the biblical period to the present have been confused about what
is true religion. Christians in colonial America were no different. They
had difficulty deciding which of a variety of spiritualities was the closest
to true Christianity. There were generally two camps of opinion. One
proclaimed that religious feeling is the essence of true spirituality. It is
not so important what you believe or do, these folks said, as long as you
feel the love of God for your soul. Most of these people supported the
Great Awakening, a mighty revival that swept up and down the eastern
seaboard in the 1740s.

This camp has its counterpart in American religion today. Charismatics tend to emphasize experience at the expense of doctrine. Some charismatic groups (but certainly not all) think that what we believe doesn't matter so much as long as we have had the emotional experience of the baptism of the Holy Spirit with its manifestations of tongues or prophecy. Some (but certainly not all) fundamentalists seem to believe that Christians must check their minds at the door in order to believe. These folks discourage worshiping God with the mind or using the mind to try to understand what has happened in a spiritual experience. Of course it's not just conservative Christians who overemphasize feelings in spirituality. A large and important tradition in liberal Christianity, stemming from the influence of German theologian Friedrich Schleiermacher (1768-1834), discounts doctrine and theology as far less important (and for some, finally unimportant) than the "feeling of absolute dependence."

The other camp in the Great Awakening taught that the heart of true religion is right thinking. Proponents of this view held that feelings are far less important than doctrine and mental attitude. For while proper beliefs keep the soul anchored to a foundation of truth, feelings are fickle and often lead the unsuspecting to chase the wind. Since so many of those revived by the Great Awakening had emotional experiences, this camp reasoned, the revival must not have come from God.

The modern counterpart of this camp includes a number of those fundamentalist and evangelical churches whose Sunday services (and, for that matter, entire religious programs) revolve around the careful exposition of Scripture. In some of these churches, the spirituality is intellectualistic, lacking in feeling or real enthusiasm. "Worship" is the tired, passionless singing of hymns. People are "saved" if they give mental assent to the doctrine that Jesus died for their sins. The expression of emotion in worship is regarded with suspicion. Some mainline churches also bear similarities to this camp. In not a few of these churches true religion is considered to be simply adherence to the tradition, for whatever reason ("I believe my church is closer to the truth" or "I'm in this denomination because it's what I know and feel comfortable with"). Sometimes lip service is paid to tradition, but there is no heartfelt understanding of the truths to which it points. Or religion has become merely the profession that Jesus is the best role model Western culture has produced. In some of these churches there is little passion for Jesus; few are animated by wholehearted love for God. What is considered important is not warm piety but belief in doctrine, denomination or social program.

Jonathan Edwards, who both defended and criticized the Awakening, argued that both camps were taking a shallow view of spirituality. It is misleading, he charged, to think that true religion is centered in either feelings or beliefs. Neither the mind nor the heart is more important than the other. Both are essential to true spirituality. Because the human person is a unity, spirituality involves every dimension of being—feelings, thoughts and actions. To oppose thoughts and feelings, or mind and heart, is to partition a person into disconnected compartments—which is false to human psychology and experience.

Instead, Edwards insisted, religious experience is centered in what he called the "affections." These lie at a deeper level of the human person than either thoughts or feelings, and in fact are the source and motivating power of thoughts and feelings. Indeed, they are at the root of all spiritual experience, both true and false. *Holy* affections are the source of true spirituality, while other kinds of affections lie at the root of false spiritualities.

In this chapter we shall first explore what Edwards meant by "the affections" and then discover why he insisted that they are at the heart of true spirituality.

What Are the Affections?

Webster's dictionary defines *affection* as "fond attachment, devotion or love" and *affections* as "emotion, feeling, sentiment, [or] the emotional realm of love." Edwards meant something far stronger than the first definition and more encompassing than the second. For him the affections are the strongest motivations of the human self, ultimately determining everything the person is and does. "Fond attachment" is far too weak and limited to describe these powerful wellsprings of human behavior. The second definition restricts affections to *feelings* of love, but as we have already said, Edwards's affections motivate not just feelings but thoughts and actions as well. I define the "affections" as Edwards has described them as *strong inclinations of the soul that are manifested in thinking, feeling and acting.* I use the word "soul" for the deepest and most essential part of the human person—what the Bible calls the "heart."[1] By "inclination" I mean an attraction *toward* an object or a distaste that leads one *away from* an object. We might call it liking or disliking, approving or rejecting. For example, I have a strong attraction to the ocean. I love the smell of salt air, watching the tide come in and go out, body surfing on the waves and walking along the beach early in the morning. My strong inclination of the soul draws me *toward* the ocean—to think about it, visit it and enjoy it when I'm there. That strong inclination of my soul is an affection.

On the other hand, I dislike shopping malls. Sometimes I wonder if hell is a giant shopping mall with no exit. Wandering through a mall invariably gives me a headache and leaves me exhausted. I do my best to stay away. When I am forced to be there, I grit my teeth and look for every opportunity to leave. The inclination of my soul that steers me *away from* malls and inspires unpleasant thoughts and feelings when I'm at a mall is what I call an affection.

So the affections are of two kinds—those by which the soul is drawn to an object and those which cause the soul to oppose and draw away from an object. Of the first kind of affections are love, desire, joy and gratitude (and others); of the second kind are hatred, fear, anger and grief (and others).

Affections can be either good or bad. In religion, some affections lead us toward God, and others lead us away from God. The first are called holy affections; the second are unholy affections. See the tables at the end of the chapter for examples of both holy and unholy affections.

Not all inclinations are affections. Inclinations that are only mild preferences, that just barely move the soul beyond the point of indifference, are not affections. Affections are strong and vigorous inclinations of the soul. Because they are strong, they will affect not just the person's thinking but her feeling and acting as well.

Since the affections are frequently confused with emotions, and sometimes also confused with mild preferences, it will be helpful to discuss these distinctions at further length (you may want to refer to the tables at the end of the chapter as you read these pages).

The affections are not simply emotions. Emotions (feelings) are often involved in affections, but the affections are not *defined* by emotional feeling. Some emotions are disconnected from our strongest inclinations. For instance, a student who goes off to college for the first time may feel doubtful and fearful. She will probably miss her friends and family at home. A part of her may even try to convince her to go back home. But she will discount these fleeting emotions as simply that—feelings that are not produced by her basic conviction that now it is time to start a new chapter in life. The affections are something like that girl's basic conviction that she should go to college, *despite* fleeting emotions that would keep her at home. They are strong inclinations that may at times conflict with more fleeting and superficial emotions.

If affections are not to be equated with emotions because the latter are too shallow, can they be identified with the violent emotions we call "passions"? Not if the passions are sudden, violent emotions that overpower the mind. You may recall that the men accused of beating Reginald Denny in the Los Angeles riots of 1992 were exonerated of felony charges because, the jury decided, mob hysteria had incited them to act against their better judgment. This sort of fleeting passion that is sudden and strong but at war with the mind is not what we mean by affection. An affection is more permanent and is consistent with one's basic convictions.

The affections are not simply preferences of the mind. Preferences of the mind may or may not be reflected in action. I may prefer that my filing cabinet be better organized than it is, but I don't feel strongly enough about it to invest the time necessary to clean it up. On the other hand, my oldest son prefers climbing cliffs and mountains to any other activity, but his preference is so deeply rooted that it translates into action. Ryan spends most of his spare time either hiking and climbing or, when he can't get on the trail, reading about hiking and climbing. His preference for climbing is based on a powerful conviction, unlike my preference for a better-organized set of files. The affections, therefore, are strong enough to motivate to action.

Affections involve a coordinated interplay of mind, will and feeling. Because they are the strongest inclinations of the human soul, the affections are manifested in every part of the person: thoughts, feelings and behavior. Let me try to illustrate by describing two of my friends. One is a Christian, and the other is not.

Remy is a student from Haiti who became a Christian when he was a young boy. By Edwards's sense of things, Remy has true spirituality grounded in holy affections. One senses Remy's deepest inclinations (affections) shortly after meeting him. Despite losing his father to death several years ago, being separated from his mother and nine siblings for years at a time and living with very little money, Remy exudes a joyful love (feeling) for God and neighbor. If fellow students are hurting or needy, Remy is at their side to help or console. Because Remy wants to worship God and grow in his faith, he reads the Bible, prays and goes to church regularly (actions). One spring when Remy took my course on world religions, he was able to articulate his faith in ways that showed he had thought through the implications of faith for both learning and living (thinking). It is clear that Remy's spirituality is not simply a matter of having certain feelings or certain beliefs. Instead, Remy has warm and vigorous inclinations of the soul (affections) that produce a pattern of thinking, feeling and action.

The same could be said of my friend Ray, who is an industrial chemist. In his heart of hearts—at the level of deepest inclinations—he has rejected the notion of faith in a supernatural God. In its place he is committed to faith in himself and the light of reason. The result is a pattern of feeling distaste and sometimes disgust for active Christians, particularly fundamentalists (feelings), believing that there are good intellectual reasons for rejecting faith (thinking), and refusing to pray, go to church or promote the influence of religion in society (actions).

Both Remy and Ray have powerful affections that can be seen in what they think, feel and do. Because their affections are so radically different—one turns toward God in love and the other turns away from God in aversion—their thinking, feeling and acting are also very different. My point is that affections are the strongest inclinations of our souls and so lie at the heart of what we do and who we are.

Holy Affections Are at the Heart of True Spirituality

At this point I want to take a slightly different tack. So far I have tried to define the affections. But now I want to show that affections lie at the heart of true spirituality. That is, true religion is not a casual preference that one can put on and off like a hat. Neither is it simply an emotional experience that happens once or twice in life without noticeably changing one's lifestyle. Nor is it a matter of simply accepting certain beliefs, such as the doctrine that Jesus died for our sins. Rather, it is a passionate affair of the soul—one's innermost being—that is reflected in every part of one's life. As Edwards put it, true religion doesn't consist in weak desires that barely move us beyond the point of indifference, but fervency of spirit that vigorously engages the very center of our being.[2]

That true spirituality is a matter of the affections, and not simply a set of beliefs or an emotional experience, is clear from Scripture. The Old Testament calls us to love God with all of our heart, soul, mind and strength, and to walk in *all* of God's ways (Deut 6:4-5; 10:12; 30:6). Paul tells us we should be "boiling"[3] with the Spirit while we serve the Lord (Rom 12:11). True spirituality, he maintains, is not just a matter of outward lifestyle but of inner power (2 Tim 3:5), for God has given us a "spirit of power" (2 Tim 1:7).

There are many other indications in the New Testament that true spirituality is powerful and dynamic. Jesus said that his followers would be baptized with the Holy Spirit and fire. His apostles reported that their hearts "burned within" them when they talked with their Savior. Throughout the New Testament Christian discipleship is portrayed as a passionate pursuit. It is compared to running, wrestling, agonizing to win a race, going to war and using violence to capture a city or kingdom.

New Testament spirituality is also practical. It issues in action. Jesus said, "Everyone who hears these words of mine and does not act on them will be like a foolish man who built his house on sand" (Mt 7.26). Spirituality which is not manifested by a distinctive lifestyle cannot claim to be true spirituality by biblical standards. Again, Edwards is to the point: "He that has doctrinal knowledge and speculation only, without affections, never is engaged in the business of religion."[4]

But even more to the point than action are the inner affections that inspire action. The Bible is abundantly clear that true spirituality is a matter of the affections. The saints of the Bible (for the authors of Scripture, all true Christians, both dead and alive, are saints) have godly fear, for instance. They are said to tremble at God's word, fear in his presence and be afraid of his judgments. His glory makes them take fright, and his dread falls upon them. Godly fear is so characteristic of the saints that they are often referred to as simply "those who fear the Lord."

But the *most* characteristic affection of saints is love. Edwards asserted that true spirituality consists most essentially of this—when all is said and done, the single most distinctive characteristic of the truly spiritual person is love for God and neighbor. Not only is it the chief of all the affections, but it is also the fountain of all the others. From a "vigorous, affectionate, and fervent love to God, will *necessarily* arise other religious affections."[5] From love to God will come hatred for sin, fear of sin, gratitude to God for his goodness, joy in God when he is manifestly present, grief when he is manifestly absent, joyful hope when contemplating our future glory and fervent zeal for the glory of God. And from love for neighbor will arise all compassion, mercy, forgiveness and all the other virtuous affections for our neighbor.[6]

When I think of love, I call to mind Mary Lynn, a nurse who works in the cancer ward of a local hospital. After a long, exhausting day trying to relieve pain and fear amidst blood, spilled urine bottles and involuntary bowel movements, most of us would groan upon hearing that a new cancer patient was being admitted. When seriously ill cancer patients come to the hospital, they are often in very bad shape. At times they have uncontrollable bowel movements, and not uncommonly they have open wounds. Many health care workers fear—legitimately—that they could be infected with AIDS, hepatitis or some other infection. In addition, admitting a new patient often means lifting a heavy body from one cart or wheelchair to another, which strains Mary Lynn's sore back. But even though she may feel tired and frustrated, Mary Lynn jumps up enthusiastically to greet the new patient, anxious to share the love and joy of Jesus. Before long, a fearful and hurting patient feels that someone else—and maybe even Jesus—cares. The pain and fear are not so hard to bear.

Mary Lynn demonstrates the affection of true love. It is not simple friendliness, but a strong inclination to do good to another. It is not an emotion, but a powerful movement of the soul that is reflected in action, thinking and (often, but not always) feelings.

It is also clear in Scripture that these strong inclinations involve the mind. One who has experienced God is typically shown to have received knowledge. John says that "everyone who loves . . . knows God" (1 Jn 4:7). Paul prays that "your love may overflow more and more with knowledge and full insight" (Phil 1:9) and says that the new self of the Christian is "renewed in knowledge" (Col 3:10). He criticizes spiritual experience devoid of knowledge; the Jews, he tells the Roman church, rejected Jesus because they have a zeal for God, but not according to knowledge (Rom 10:2).[7] As Edwards put it, "Holy affections are not heat without light." They always arise from spiritual instruction which the mind receives.[8] Chapters ten and eleven describe more fully the role of the mind in the affections.

The Scriptures point to other affections demonstrated by saints. They hate sin, evil and false ways (Ps 97:10; 119:104; Prov 8:13). They hunger and thirst for God and his righteousness (Mt 5:6). The psalmists particularly illustrate this passionate desire for God's presence and righteousness. In Psalm 42 David wrote poetically, "As a deer longs for flowing streams, so my soul longs for you, O God. My soul thirsts for God, for the living God" (vv. 42:1-2). When in the wilderness he cried, "O God, you are my God, I seek you, my soul thirsts for you; my flesh faints for you, as in a dry and weary land where there is no water" (Ps 63:1). Another psalmist wrote, "My soul longs, indeed it faints for the courts of the Lord; my heart and my flesh sing for joy to the living God" (Ps 84:2). And the author of Psalm 119 exclaimed, "My soul is consumed with longing for your ordinances at all times" (v. 20).

Joy is another mark of true saints. Paul says that when the Spirit inhabits a person, there is joy (Gal 5:22). Both he and David exhort saints to rejoice in the Lord. David tells them to "take delight in the Lord" and promises that God will give them the desires of their hearts (Ps 37:4). Paul tells them repeatedly to rejoice in God (v. 3:1; 4:4) at all times (1 Thess 5:16).

Joy is not the same as pleasure. Pleasure can be superficial, something quite different from the strong inclination of the soul (affection) called joy. Jim, a cancer patient, is a good illustration of this difference. For months Jim had suffered from a tumor under his cheekbone that grew back into his brain and down into his jaw. You could hardly say that Jim knew pleasure in these months, but in the midst of real agony (not only the physical pain but the mental anguish of knowing that he was leaving his family after only fifty years on this planet) Jim knew joy. On the day before he died, he spent several hours with his doctor—a very close friend of mine—discussing the joy of life with Jesus. As the doctor turned to leave, Jim called out, "I love you, Doctor!"

One time Jim lay in terrible pain for forty-five minutes because a nurse had been slow to bring his pain medication. The physician was angry at the nurse, but Jim begged him not to discipline her. Jim could love because he knew a joy in God that was deeper and stronger than the pain and fear he felt in his body.

Paradoxically, saints are called to mourning even as they are called to rejoicing. Jesus said, "Blessed are those who mourn" (Mt 5:4). He was referring to the mourning that characteristically accompanies repentance from sin. This mourning, according to David, invites God to come to us: "The Lord is near to the brokenhearted, and saves the crushed in spirit" (Ps 34:18). It is particularly pleasing to God: "Thus says the high and lofty one who inhabits eternity, whose name is Holy: I dwell in the high and holy place, and also with those who are contrite and humble in spirit" (Is 57.15). "This is the one to whom I will look, to the humble and contrite in spirit, who trembles at my word" (Is 66:2).

The list of affections which the Scriptures describe goes on and on. There's heartfelt gratitude, which is portrayed so often in the Psalms, compassion and mercy (which both Testaments urge on the saints—for example, Mic 6:8; Mt 5:7; Col 3:12-13) and zeal, which was the missing factor in the Laodicean church. Jesus' words to those professing Christians reinforce the message of this chapter—that true spirituality is a dynamic, heartfelt commitment that transforms one's entire being: "I know your works; you are neither cold nor hot. I wish that you were either cold or hot. So, because you are lukewarm, and neither cold nor hot, I am about to spit you out of my mouth" (Rev 3:15-16).

Of course, the Scriptures do not simply encourage us to model these affections. They *illustrate* these affections by showing us that they are at the very heart of the spirituality possessed by the great saints in the Bible. David, for example, is shown to thirst and pant after God, delight and rejoice in God, feel sweet gratitude for God's goodness, dance in holy exultation, delight in God's Word, weep for his own sins and feel zealous outrage at threats to God's kingdom.

Paul's spirituality was no less illustrative of the affections. His letters reveal a man who was consumed by love for Jesus Christ. He considered everything worthless—like animal excrement, he said!—compared to the joy of knowing Christ. His affections for people were just as fervent.

To the Thessalonians he wrote, "We were gentle among you, like a nurse tenderly caring for her own children. So deeply do we care for you that we are determined to share with you not only the gospel of God but also our own selves, because you have become very dear to us" (1 Thess 2:7-8). Apparently he shed many tears for the people in his churches (Acts 20:19, 31; 2 Cor 2:4). And Paul's affections for his fellow Jews were so great that he said he was willing to be damned if only they could be saved (Rom 9:3).

If Jesus' life is a model for spirituality, as it certainly should be, then his death teaches the same lesson. In Edwards's words, "He was the greatest instance [example] of ardency, vigor and strength of love, to both God and man, that ever was. It was these affections which got the victory, in that mighty struggle and conflict of his affections, in his agonies, when he prayed more earnestly, and offered strong cryings and tears, and wrestled in tears and in blood."[9] It was Jesus' holy affections which gave him the strength to overcome his natural feelings of fear and grief when he was tempted in the Garden of Gethsemane to give up.

But it wasn't just in his death that Jesus illustrated powerful affections. His life was also full of holy affections. He showed such zeal for God that he was willing to risk the wrath of the religious authorities by smashing the concession stands at the temple (Jn 2:17). He grieved for the sins of men: "He looked around at them with anger; he was grieved at their hardness of heart" (Mk 3:5). He wept when he saw that his friend Lazarus was dead and when he contemplated the future miseries of Jerusalem (Jn 11:35; Lk 13:34). And he often felt compassion for people, such as when he was in Galilee: "When he saw the crowds, he had compassion for them, because they were harassed and helpless, like sheep without a shepherd" (Mt 9:36).

Preliminary Conclusions

What conclusions can we draw from this chapter? There is far more to say about the dimensions of genuine spirituality, but at this point we can draw some preliminary inferences. We can say, for instance, that although the affections are not equivalent to feelings, they usually involve feelings because they are strong inclinations. Those who refuse any place for feelings in true spirituality are making a mistake. Edwards said that the devil likes to persuade people that emotional spirituality is suspect because he knows that religion without any emotion is "a mere lifeless formality."[10] And once spirituality has been stripped of all feeling, it does not threaten his work. For where there is light (truth) without heat (fervor), the divine is absent.

We can also say that there are false affections and there are true. The presence of religious feeling does not prove that spirituality is true. As the next three chapters will show, there are plenty of affections that involve feeling but are nevertheless unholy. Yet the absence of religious feeling indicates that true spirituality may be absent as well.

This chapter also has something to say to those whose spirituality is all heat and no light. Holy affections are not feelings, but warm and fervent inclinations that involve the mind. They involve both heart conviction and intellectual understanding. If someone's spiritual experience is purely emotion without a shred of coherent reflection, the affections are not holy.

Most important, true spirituality is a matter of the affections—strong inclinations of the soul. People who are in the kingdom of God will be moved by spiritual conviction that affects everything they are and do: their feelings, their thinking and their actions.

Understanding that true spirituality is a matter of strong inclinations called affections—comprising thought, feeling and action—we are prepared to look more closely for particular signs of true spirituality. These will enable us to discern more clearly the differences between true affections and false affections. The first step, however, is to recognize false signs—misleading criteria that are often used to distinguish between true and false spirituality. The next three chapters will outline twelve of these false signs.

Table 1. Affections versus emotions

Affections	Emotions
1. Long-lasting	1. Fleeting
2. Deep	2. Superficial
3. Consistent with beliefs	3. Sometimes overpowering
4. Always result in action	4. Often fail to produce action
5. Involve mind, will, feelings	5. Feelings (often) disconnected from the mind and will

Table 2. Affections versus beliefs

Affections	Beliefs
1. Always influence behavior	1. Do not always influence behavior
2. Influence feelings	2. Often disconnected from feelings
3. Strong	3. Often weak

Table 3. Holy affections versus unholy affections

Holy Affections	Unholy Affections
1. Always inspire feeling, thinking and doing	1. All feeling with no thinking
	or
	2. All thinking with no feeling
	or
	3. Mere doing with no thinking or feeling

Table 4. Examples of affections

Holy Affections	Unholy Affections
1. Love for God and others	1. Hatred for God and others
2. Hatred of sin	2. Love of sin
3. Hunger for God and divine things	3. Disgust for, or indifference to, God and divine things
4. Joy	4. Cynicism
5. Gratitude to God	5. Bitterness toward God

Part Three

· · · · ·

Unreliable Signs
of True
Spirituality

3

. . . . .

Unreliable Signs Involving Religious Experience

MY FRIEND,
DO NOT TRUST THE WAY
YOU FEEL AT THE MOMENT,
FOR YOUR FEELINGS WILL SOON CHANGE.
THOMAS À KEMPIS

WE SAW IN CHAPTER TWO THAT RELIGIOUS AFFECTIONS ARE AT THE center of true spirituality. You may have concluded that because you have affections, your spirituality is true. Don't be so sure. Just as it is wrong to condemn all affections in spirituality, so too it is wrong to *approve* all affections, as if whoever has affections has true spirituality. Just as there is true and false spirituality, so there are good and bad affections. Holy affections make for true spirituality, while unholy affections inspire false spirituality. So we must distinguish *among* religious affections if we are to recognize true spirituality. We must determine which affections are holy and which are not.

The first step toward discernment is to understand unreliable signs. Some signs that people employ to distinguish between true and false spiritualities are misleading. They can't tell us whether or not a person is truly a Christian. Thus people who believe that these signs are reliable indicators of true or false religion commonly make bad judgments. Sometimes the results are tragic. In this chapter we will look at six unreliable signs that involve the affections.

Intense Religious Affections

Peter was the leader of my charismatic youth group in the days of the "Jesus Revolution." It was 1971, the year that Jesus was on the cover of *Time* magazine. Fifty to sixty longhaired ex-hippies, from thirteen to twenty-five, met every Sunday night to sing, pray and listen to Peter teach. Peter had little more experience in faith than the rest of us. But his rugged looks, warm manner and winsome "aw-shucks" speaking style made him a natural leader.

We all were convinced that Peter had a deep relationship with Jesus. Playing his guitar with closed eyes and an earnest voice, his stringy blond hair dangling around his shoulders, Peter seemed smitten by the love of his Savior. He spoke with passion of his gratitude for salvation and seemed genuinely excited by what he said God had in store for us. But in the next year Peter's faith began to falter. He began to show up at meetings only intermittently; then he stayed away altogether. We discovered soon after that he had returned to the sexual promiscuity and drugs from which he had come. As far as I know, Peter never did embrace serious discipleship and has nothing to do with church today.

For a number of months Peter did have intense religious affections. Clearly, then, intensity of spiritual feeling was no sure sign of saving grace. This is a familiar pattern in Scripture: intense religious affections do not guarantee that the person possessing them is truly saved. For example, the Galatians (Christians in Asia Minor to whom Paul wrote a letter) had intense religious affections. In a time when Paul was probably having trouble with his eyes, they swore that they would tear out their eyes for him (Gal 4:15). Despite this display of concern, Paul laments that his work among them "may have been wasted" (Gal 4:11). The Israelites at the Red Sea sang God's praises after he had miraculously delivered them from Pharaoh's army. But shortly thereafter, the Bible says, they "tested the Lord," forgot his works and cried to go back to Egypt (Ex 17:2-3; Num 14:3; Ps 106:14). At Mount Sinai, feeling the mountain shake and hearing the trumpet blow, they were deeply moved. With great feeling they pledged their loyalty to Yahweh: "All the words that the LORD has spoken we will do" (Ex 24:3). Yet a short time later, when they saw that Moses was delaying his return from the mountain, they prevailed on Aaron to mold a golden calf for them to worship. Then "the people sat down to eat and drink, and rose up to revel" (Ex 32:1-6).

Intense affections, then, are the first unreliable sign. They cannot be used to determine with certainty that a person is a citizen of the kingdom of God; the same crowds that shouted praises and hosannahs to Jesus as he rode into Jerusalem only days later cried for his crucifixion. Nor can it be said, as we saw in chapter two, that a person with intense affections is *not* in the kingdom of God. The affections are at the heart of true spirituality and are strong enough to affect every aspect of our being. My point is that intense affections, in and of themselves, are not reliable indicators either way. True spirituality cannot be determined by the presence or absence of very intense affections. As the devotional writer and monk Thomas à Kempis put it in the fifteenth century, "Don't think highly of yourself, or consider yourself to be especially loved if you have strong feelings of devotion or sweetness, for it is not by these feelings that a true lover of virtue is known. Nor does the spiritual progress and perfection of a man consist in these things."[1]

Many Religious Affections at the Same Time

That someone has many different kinds of spiritual inclinations is another unreliable sign that cannot be used to determine whether a person's spirituality is true or false. There are counterfeits of all true affections. Most of us know that love, for example, is easily counterfeited. Boyfriends and girlfriends who professed true love later showed that their "love" was only infatuation or raw self-interest. Perhaps we ourselves have told others that we loved them, only to realize later that we didn't know the first thing about love. The Bible is full of such shallow professions of love. For example, there was the lawyer who vowed to Jesus that he would follow him wherever he went. But when Jesus replied that he wasn't always sure that he even had a room at night, the man departed (Mt 8:20). Then there were the crowds who proclaimed their devotion to Jesus but abandoned him when he became politically incorrect.

Godly sorrow for sin can also be counterfeited. Pharaoh, for instance, seemed to have truly repented after the seventh plague (hail). To Moses Pharaoh wailed, "This time I have sinned: the LORD is in the right, and I and my people are in the wrong. Pray to the LORD! Enough of God's thunder and hail! I will let you go; you need stay no longer" (Ex 9:27-28). But once the hail stopped, "he sinned once more and hardened his heart" (Ex 9:34). He again refused to let the Israelites leave Egypt.

There are descriptions of counterfeit worship in the Bible. We read of the Samaritans in the eighth century B.C. who "worshiped the LORD but also served their own gods" (2 Kings 17:33). Gratitude and joy can also be counterfeit. Think of the rocky-ground hearers in Jesus' parable of the sower and the seed. These are people who hear the gospel and receive it with gratitude and joy but then fall away when trouble or persecution comes (Mt 13:20-21). We can say the same of zeal and hope. The Jews of Paul's time showed "a zeal for God, but it [was] not enlightened" and hence not the true zeal that God desires (Rom 10:2). The Pharisees had the earnest hope (the word *expectation* is closer to the meaning of the Greek word usually translated as "hope") that they were going to heaven, but according to Jesus were sadly deceived (Mt 23:13-15).

It is also important to recognize that false affections usually run together. One false affection almost always exists in a cluster of others. Consider the actions of the crowds after Jesus raised Lazarus from the dead. They were filled with a multitude of false affections. They showed desire for Jesus by traveling long distances to hear him, professed love for him by crying hosanna, displayed reverence by flinging off their outer clothes for him, sang songs of gratitude and praise, and demonstrated zeal for God's kingdom when they shouted, "Blessed is the one who comes in the name of the Lord" (Jn 12:13). The noise of their songs and cries filled the air with what passed for holy joy.

Why do false affections run in clusters? Because, just as true love inspires a host of other true affections, false love excites many other false affections. Edwards portrayed a counterfeit conversion as a constellation of false affections. First, he wrote, a man is in terror and despair because he has heard a message promising damnation to those who are not converted. Imagining the mental and physical torments of suffering forever in hell fills him with horror. Then the devil, Edwards suggested, sends him a vision or voice promising salvation. "You're one of God's favorites," the devil whispers. Immediately the man is filled with joy and gratitude. He is awestruck by his sudden reprieve and can't keep himself from telling others about God's mercy to him and urging them to praise God. He realizes he is unworthy of this amazing gift and talks openly of his sin.

But his newfound humility is no more genuine than that of King Saul. Upon hearing that he had been chosen as king, he protested, "I am only from the smallest tribe and humblest family of Israel. Why me?" (1 Sam 9:21). False humility bears an uncanny resemblance to the true humility shown by David when he was chosen for the throne: "Who am I . . . and what is my house, that you have brought me thus far?" (2 Sam 7:18).

The new "convert" desires to spend time with those who acknowledge his conversion and feels what he takes to be righteous indignation toward those who don't. He denies himself in order to promote his new cause and those who support him.

Unfortunately, says Edwards, this is conversion without genuine repentance. Therefore it is counterfeit conversion. Many religious affections are present, but they are false because they spring from self-love masquerading as love for God. Edwards says this pattern of spiritual experience can result from either demonic influence or human nature (the compulsion to assuage religious terror and enhance self-esteem). John of the Cross, the great mystical writer of the sixteenth century, said the same.[2] The devil often increases the fervor of the proud, John wrote, and turns their virtues into vices. At the same time, John advised, many strong desires fixed on God or spiritual things are simply the result of human and natural desires.

A Certain Sequence in the Affections

Many Christians believe that if a person's religious affections follow a certain sequence, they must be true. The pattern typically thought to be the sign of genuine conversion is the one that leads from terror to comfort, fear to peace. This is what theologians call the sequence of "terrors of the law" followed by the "comfort of the gospel." Indeed, this pattern is supported by Scripture. After Peter's speech at Pentecost, the crowd in Jerusalem was "cut to the heart" with fear of God's judgment. "Brothers, what should we do?" they cried. After repentance and baptism, the text implies, the Holy Spirit comforted them with assurance of forgiveness (Acts 2:37-42).

This sequence of affections seems to describe not only conversion but postconversion spiritual experience as well. Paul testified that in Asia he felt "so utterly, unbearably crushed that [he] despaired of life itself" (2 Cor 1:8). He thought he had received the death sentence. But he was delivered, he wrote, because God wanted to teach him not to rely on himself but "on God who raises the dead" (2 Cor 1:9). Paul felt fear and then relief, despair but later hope.

One problem with this sequence of affections is that some people follow this sequence but do not experience true affections. We saw this in the false conversion of the last sign. We have seen it also in King Saul, who confessed with tears, "I have done wrong. . . . I have been a fool, and have made a great mistake" (1 Sam 26:21), but never stopped committing the sin he was confessing (trying to kill the Lord's anointed). In the late 1980s TV evangelist Jimmy Swaggart displayed a similar pattern. He confessed tearfully on the TV screen that he had met with a prostitute and professed his repentance. But about a year later he was seen in a car with yet another prostitute.

Edwards knew of people in the Great Awakening who openly proclaimed their "terrible sinfulness" yet could not identify even one of their particular sins. Others announced that they had seen a vision of their sins standing in a circle around them. But interestingly enough, none of those sins included their most glaring faults. They had frightful visions of hell as a pit of flames ready to swallow them up and of demons standing around ready to seize them. Yet there was little or no true conviction of sin, convincing them of their actual transgressions.

How do we account for this? Edwards said the devil may be responsible for some of these delusions. He can terrify people just as well as the Spirit of God can. But while Satan can imitate the *sequence* of affections usually present in conversion, he cannot reproduce the *nature* of true affections. So we should never judge the truth or falsity of spiritual experience (that someone is or is not truly a Christian) by the sequence of the affections. "We are often in Scripture expressly directed to try ourselves by the *nature* of the fruits of the Spirit; but nowhere by the Spirit's *method* of producing them."[3] Edwards said that a sensitive (human) spirit can also produce these false affections. The imagination and the affections can reinforce each other so that the affections become extremely intense, and the person loses all awareness of the self. I remember a woman in a church I once attended who often gave prophecies of what she felt God wanted to say to the congregation. Sometimes, she told us, she saw visions. This woman was gifted with a delicate, extremely sensitive spirit, resulting in part (I think) from a childhood of great pain and rejection. She easily empathized with those who suffered and readily rejoiced with those who succeeded. After the church was disbanded because of internal conflicts, this woman stopped going to church entirely and took up with a New Age group that emphasized one's inner potential and discounted Christian orthodoxy. I am not sure about the source of this woman's visions and prophecies, but I can't help but think that they were at least partly inspired by her very sensitive *human* spirit.

Another reason we shouldn't use the sequence of affections to determine the truth of one's spirituality (whether the person is a true Christian) is that there are other orders of affections in both Scripture and Christian experience. Cornelius, for example, seemed to feel no (new) conviction of sin, fear of hell or despair before he came to Christ. He was already "a devout man who feared God." Apparently he was saved simply by hearing that Jesus was anointed with the Holy Spirit and power and would be the judge and source of forgiveness. The Holy Spirit then fell on him (Acts 10:1-48).[4]

Mel was a friend of mine from the hippie generation who came to Christ by gazing at a sunrise on the Gulf of Mexico. Mel was drawn by the beauty of God's creation, not by the terror of the law. Later he came to experience Christ as Savior and Lord, but initially it was the magnificent beauty of creation that drew him to God.

When I became a Christian at the age of eighteen, I had a momentary sense of my sin of indifference. But it was my overwhelming sense of Jesus' reality and love that led to my conversion, not fear that I wouldn't be forgiven. I was suddenly convinced that Jesus was the key to reality, that it made no sense to go on with life without this Truth and that I could no longer ignore his suffering love.

I don't mean to imply that true conversions are always dramatic experiences that occur on a specific date. Many wonderful Christians cannot remember a time when they didn't trust in Christ. Or they believe that saving grace was given them at baptism, to which they responded over time. As I shall discuss more fully in a later chapter, the important thing is that we now trust Christ and live by the power of the indwelling Spirit. There are many sequences in the affections. Some are drawn by sorrow for sin, some by beauty, some by truth, some by the sense that they are missing something. Others are led to Christ by the fear of hell. It was perhaps this diversity of orders in spiritual experience (among other things) to which Paul referred when he exclaimed, "How inscrutable are [God's] ways!" (Rom 11:33).

Affections Not Produced by the Self
In Edwards's day, affections thought to have been produced by an external agent were automatically regarded by most of the social and religious elite as fanatical. That is, a person who said, "My conversion clearly did not come from my own thoughts or feelings; I was feeling hopeless and empty when suddenly God zapped me," was suspect. Such an experience was considered fraudulent. Today there are many who also suspect sudden, dramatic conversions. They think that genuine conversion is always a gradual, silent, largely hidden movement of the soul that takes place over a period of years.

Is this a reasonable—or for that matter, biblical—position? Why would God always want to hide his power when it is his intention to teach us "that this extraordinary power belongs to God and does not come from us" (1 Cor 4:7)? And when he desires that none might say, "My own hand has delivered me" (Judg 7:2)? In biblical times God seemed to delight in showing that deliverance came from him alone. He reduced Gideon's army from thirty-two thousand to three hundred and "armed" them with trumpets and clay jars so that they could not claim credit for the victory (Judg 7). David was armed with a slingshot against a giant twice his size "so that all the earth may know . . . that the LORD does not save by sword and spear" (1 Sam 17:46-47). Paul was suddenly saved by a dramatic vision and voice, as if to remind him for the rest of his ministry that none other than Jesus himself had changed his life.

But there is also biblical evidence that dramatic experiences originating from outside the self are not a sure sign of saving grace. Paul warned his churches that Satan often disguises himself as an angel of light and that there are other dark spirits seeking to influence us (2 Cor 11:14; 1 Thess 5:21). John of the Cross said that when God wants to minister to the soul, Satan often intervenes by sending "a certain horror and perturbation of spirit."[5] Edwards was convinced that Satan sends not just terrors and "horrid suggestions" but counterfeit comforts and joys as well.[6]

Even the Holy Spirit can be the source of powerful spiritual experience in the absence of true conversion. The author of the letter to the Hebrews refers to those who had once been enlightened, "tasted the heavenly gift . . . shared in the Holy Spirit, and . . . tasted the goodness of the word of God and the powers of the age to come," and yet never experienced the "things that belong to salvation" (Heb 6:4-5, 9). The Old Testament tells of Balaam who was given true prophecies regarding the future of Israel by the Holy Spirit but later led Israel into immorality and idolatry (Num 23—24; Rev 2:14; see also 2 Pet 2:15 and Jude 11). There is evidence as well that Judas Iscariot, with the other apostles, was used by the Holy Spirit to perform miracles (Mt 10:8; Mk 6:13; Lk 9:6).

So we see that spiritual experience sometimes comes from outside the self in a dramatic, even sudden manner. God may act in this way to bring people to conversion and then later to remind them of his power. But a dramatic spiritual experience does not always and necessarily mean that God has brought salvation to a person. Dark forces of evil work on the soul from the outside, and the Spirit sometimes touches people who do not convert.

Scriptures Come Miraculously to Mind

Even having Scriptures arise remarkably in one's mind is no sure sign of saving grace. After all, Satan showed that his mind could be focused on Scripture when he used it to tempt Jesus in the wilderness. The rocky-ground hearers in the parable of the sower and the seed heard the Word and were delighted by it but never persevered to saving faith. Scripture also makes it clear that the human heart is deceitful (Jer 17:9) and can use the Bible for selfish and even demonic purposes. Adolf

Hitler helped himself get elected to power in Germany by proclaiming his devotion to the Bible.

Church history is full of false prophets who had remarkable knowledge of Scripture. Mormon church founder Joseph Smith, for example, was able to attract disciples in part because of his knowledge of the Bible. Many of the "revelations" of the Book of Mormon that he claimed God put into his mind were paraphrases of passages from the Bible.[7] David Koresh also claimed to have received revelations from God, and these sometimes included biblical texts which he said were put into his mind by the Holy Spirit.[8]

Having the Scriptures in one's mind, therefore, and feeling joy or even tears because of it, is no sure sign of saving grace.

Physical Manifestations of the Affections

It isn't difficult today to recognize that spiritual experience affects the body. We know from both psychology and medical research that there is a close connection between mind and body, and between the emotions and the body. Since the affections comprise both mind and emotion, it shouldn't surprise us that the affections, which are *strong* inclinations of the soul, affect the body. We would expect, in fact, that the stronger the affections, the greater their effect on the body.

But we also recognize that bodily effects are no sure sign that the Holy Spirit is at work. After all, think of all the effects on the body produced by secular affections—interests related to things such as sports or the lottery. We're not at all surprised when fans jump and shout at a ball game or when lottery winners scream and leap upon learning the good news. We know instinctively that these physical manifestations of strong affections are not particularly inspired by God.

Students of Scripture also know that physical responses to spiritual experience are no sure sign of true conversion. Saul, for instance, felt compelled to lie naked all day and all night during the period when he was trying to murder David. Saul's experience was from the Holy Spirit (Saul was prophesying), but this was no clear sign that Saul was in what the New Testament came to call the kingdom of God (1 Sam 19:23-24).

On the other hand, students of Scripture know that true spiritual affections often affect the body. How could we believe otherwise, if Paul was correct in saying that there's a power at work in believers that is greater than all we can ask or think (Eph 3:20)? If believers truly have infinite power within them, isn't it reasonable to think that such power will affect their bodies at times? This is especially true since the human person is not comprised of disconnected parts but is an interrelated unity of body, mind and spirit. Is it any wonder that catching a glimpse of God's glory would cause us to feel faint or cause our hearts to skip a beat, as the saints of old trembled in the presence of an angel?

Examples from Scripture are legion. Holy affections in people of the Bible produced trembling (Ezra 9:4; Is 66:2,5), groaning (Rom 8:26), crying out (Ps 84:2), panting (Ps 38:10; 42:1; 119:131), fainting (Ps 119:81; Song 2:5; 5:8) and a host of other physical effects.

We must conclude, therefore, that physical reactions to spiritual experience do not identify with certainty the source or nature of that experience. True spirituality often has physical manifestations. But the presence of physical manifestations does not guarantee that spiritual experience is from God.

This chapter has shown us that religious experience is no guarantee of saving grace. People may experience intense religious affections, many affections at the same time, the "proper" sequence of affections and affections that don't seem to be produced by the self but nevertheless are outside of the kingdom of God. Bible verses may come miraculously to mind, and their affections may produce physical manifestations, but these experiences are not necessarily signs of salvation. They may be signs of spiritual reality, but they are unreliable when interpreted as signs of true grace. In the next chapter we will look at unreliable signs involving religious behavior.

4

· · · · ·

Unreliable Signs
Involving Religious
Behavior

*IF I GIVE AWAY ALL MY POSSESSIONS AND GIVE UP MY
BODY TO BE BURNED, BUT HAVE NOT LOVE, I GAIN
NOTHING.*
P A U L

O NE EASTER SEVERAL YEARS AGO THE AMERICAN MEDIA REPORTED THAT
a Philippine man had persuaded friends to nail him to an improvised
cross. The crucified man, who somehow survived this self-imposed
torture, told reporters he was imitating the suffering of Jesus in order
to demonstrate his devotion.

Most Christians consider such actions to be nothing short of lunacy.
Jesus, we reason, would never call us to do something so bizarre to show
our love for him. This seems to be a clear example of behavior that is
religiously motivated but unrelated to true holiness.

In this chapter we will look at four other kinds of behavior (the next
four unreliable signs) that are religiously motivated but unrelated to
true holiness. They are not grotesque, as this self-directed crucifixion
was; in fact, they are commonly thought to be reliable signs of true

spirituality. My intent in this chapter is to show that they are precisely the opposite. Rather than being pointers to true faith, they are highly ambiguous. They tell us nothing with certainty about the faith of the person who manifests such behavior.

Much or Eloquent Talk About God and Religion

Many people, particularly the more sophisticated, are suspicious of those who speak openly about their faith. To discuss religion in public is thought to be awkward at best, fanatical at worst. The cultural elite often boast that they don't wear their religion on their sleeve. The open profession of faith, and worse, the attempt to persuade others to believe, are considered offensive and intolerant. Far better to let God remain a private hobby, or the opiate of the unenlightened.

Then there are those who try to shove their religion down everyone else's throat. A student of mine who doesn't know if God exists went to get a haircut recently. He discovered to his dismay that he couldn't get out of the chair until he had heard the barber's testimony and explained to him why he didn't want to "get saved." Many Christians believe that a person who talks a lot about God and faith must be genuinely saved. Particularly if the person, like this barber, is zealously confronting strangers with a gospel message. If someone gives a passionate testimony at church, many whisper or think, "God must have touched her!"

Scripture gives us signs to help us discern the validity of our own or others' spirituality. These signs will be outlined in chapters seven through nineteen. But talking a lot about God (even with great eloquence) is *not* one of these signs. Never does the Bible say that the ability to talk about God is a reliable indication of true conversion. It does say that "out of the abundance of the heart the mouth speaks" (Mt 12:34). But this cuts both ways. A wicked heart will produce words of death, while a good heart will produce words of life. But the words themselves do not infallibly indicate what kind of heart produced them.

In fact, it is natural for the affections to cause us to talk. As we saw in chapter two, the affections are *strong* inclinations of the soul. Since the human person is a unity of body and soul, it follows that strong inclinations of the soul will move the lips to speak.

The Scriptures make it clear that talking a lot about God is no sure sign of true spirituality. Some of the same people who said excitedly of Jesus, "Never has anyone spoken like this!" (Jn 7:46), probably urged the authorities to kill him. Peter and Jude warned their readers to beware of false teachers who are full of talk but empty of life (2 Pet 2:17-18; Jude 12). Paul taught that the kingdom of God does not consist of talk but of power (1 Cor 4:20).[1]

This is particularly true of doctrinal or theological debate. As Luther pointed out, theological disputation can hinder spiritual growth: "Disputations bring with them this evil, that men's souls are, as it were, profaned, and when they are occupied with quarrels they neglect what is most important."[2] And theological debate is sometimes a smoke screen for refusal to obey. Bonhoeffer tells us that the rich young man in Matthew 19 was more interested in discussion and self-justification than truth: "Eternal life is for him an academic problem which is worth discussing with a 'good master.' . . . [He is] trying to evade the revealed will of God, while all the time he knows that will already."[3]

I remember Mike, a headstrong young Christian who argued with his church elders that women should wear head coverings in obedience to 1 Corinthians 11:10. Although the elders showed Mike that loose, flowing hair was typically associated in that day with promiscuous women or priestesses of pagan cults, Mike refused to back down. He stubbornly insisted there was no other way to regard this text than with a straightforward, literal application. Shortly after this dispute Mike returned to the alcoholic lifestyle he had previously pursued, abandoning his wife and children for another woman. I don't know the condition of Mike's heart today, but it was clear then that his passionate talk about "staying true to the Bible" was *not* a sign of true devotion.

Jonathan Edwards commented acidly that people with false religion are more eager to talk than true saints. The early American Puritan Thomas Shepard (1605-49) said something very similar: "A Pharisee's trumpet shall be heard to the town's end, when simplicity [the true saint] walks through the town unseen."[4]

The bottom line is that true religious affections will move people to talk about their faith, and sometimes eloquently. But so will false affections. Religious talk, therefore, is an unreliable sign of true affections.

Frequent and Passionate Praise for God

It's one thing to talk a lot about God, or to discuss theology. But it seems far better to praise God. Praise might seem to indicate that the heart has humbled itself before God or at least submitted itself to God.

But in and of itself, the presence of praise is not a reliable sign of true grace. We cannot conclude that a person who praises God is truly submitted to God. The crowds that followed Jesus, *and later called for his execution,* showered him with praises. After Jesus healed the paralytic, "they were all amazed and glorified God, saying, 'We have never seen anything like this' " (Mk 2:12). On another occasion after Jesus had cured the lame, the maimed, the blind and the mute, "the crowd was amazed.... And they praised the God of Israel" (Mt 15:31). After Jesus raised the widow's son at Nain, "Fear seized all of them, and they glorified God, saying, 'A great prophet has risen among us!' and 'God has looked favorably on his people' " (Lk 7:16). When he taught in the synagogues of Galilee, "he . . . was praised by everyone" (Lk 4:15). Shortly before he was crucified, the crowds cried, "Hosanna to the Son of David! . . . Hosanna in the highest heaven!" (Mt 21:9).

Scripture also includes other examples of praise coming from unregenerate hearts (that is, hearts that have not been "generated anew," or "born again"). Luke tells us that after God healed the lame man through Peter and John, "all of them [the crowds] praised God for what had happened" (Acts 4:21). But it is clear from the text that many in the crowds did not become disciples. At the Red Sea the Israelites sang God's praises but soon forgot his works (Ps 106:12-13). And there is Yahweh's telling indictment of the Jews after the exile who praised God but persecuted the faithful remnant: "Your own people who hate you and reject you for my name's sake have said, 'Let the LORD be glorified' " (Is 66:5).

Bonhoeffer says that hypocritical praise is a problem in the modern church, particularly when it is no longer unfashionable to be a Christian.

> [When Paul says that "no man can say 'Jesus is Lord,' but by the Holy Spirit," he] is deliberately reckoning with the possibility that men may call Jesus Lord without the Holy Spirit, that is, without having received the call. It was harder to understand this in days when it brought no earthly gain to be a Christian and when Christianity was

a dangerous profession. "Not everyone that saith unto me 'Lord, Lord' shall enter the Kingdom of Heaven." "Lord, Lord" is the church's confession of faith. But not everyone who makes this confession will enter the Kingdom of Heaven. The dividing line will run right through the confessing church. Even if we make the confession of faith, it gives us no title to any special claim upon Jesus. We can never appeal to our confession or be saved simply on the ground that we have made it.[5]

Heeday was an undergraduate Japanese student whom I befriended when I was in graduate school. He was tall, bright and outgoing. When I shared with him some of the parables of Jesus in a series of one-on-one Bible studies, Heeday said he was convicted of his sinfulness and wanted to receive Jesus as his Savior. Soon Heeday was praising God in church and at student Bible studies. But when it came time for Heeday to go off to grad school, something inside him seemed to change. His spiritual interest disappeared suddenly. He dumped his Christian girlfriend and stopped going to church and Bible study. When I asked him why he had changed so suddenly and warned him of the dangers of this new direction, Heeday smiled, "Yes, I know, Gerry. I just want to do this." Since that time many years ago, I have wondered what was going on in Heeday's heart. He may have turned away from God temporarily, only to return later. Or his spiritual experience may have been, like those described in Hebrews 6:4-6, without genuine repentance and therefore not true conversion.

> For it is impossible to restore again to repentance those who have once been enlightened, and have tasted the heavenly gift, and have shared in the Holy Spirit, and have tasted the goodness of the word of God and the powers of the age to come, and then have fallen away, since on their own they are crucifying the Son of God and are holding him up to contempt.

In any event, Heeday was like the thorny-soil people of the sower and the seed parable (Mt 13:22), who were drawn away from the Word by the "lure of wealth." Like them, Heeday praised God for a while but then went off to seek fame and fortune. (The question whether true Christians can backslide indefinitely or even lose their salvation is a very difficult one; I explore this in some detail in chapter eighteen.)

The Appearance of Love

Love is the most important and most distinctive characteristic of the Christian. Jonathan Edwards called love "the life, essence and sum of all true religion." He said it is that which best prepares us for heaven and makes us worst suited for hell.[6]

Yet love is often counterfeited. This isn't surprising. Anything of value, and only things of value, is a target of the counterfeiter. Fake diamonds and funny money have fooled many. Counterfeit cures abound as well. Hundreds of products claim to cure cancer, but very few actually work.[7] Love and humility, Edwards wrote, are imitated more than any other Christian virtues because they are the two most distinctive attributes of the Christian. In them "the beauty of the true Christian does especially appear."[8]

In graduate school I did a paper on the Unification Church. Most Americans know the members of this church as the "Moonies." Before I started my research, I wondered why this bizarre group seemed to attract so many followers. Once I began investigating, I discovered that Moon's influence and the size of the church have been grossly exaggerated by the media. But I also discovered that those who are drawn to the church tend to be intelligent college graduates. How, I asked myself, could these sincere, educated people be led astray so easily?

It wasn't long before I found an answer to this question. When I visited a Unification Church prayer meeting one Friday night, I was met by men and women in their twenties who showered me with warmth and attention. They offered to take my coat and showed an interest in me. Where was I from? What was I studying? What were my career goals? They smiled and listened carefully to what I said, both before and after a well-organized lecture on world history and personal salvation. If such interest is love, I felt loved. It wasn't hard to imagine how this combination of personal warmth and philosophical confidence could attract lonely, insecure college students who were looking for answers.

I don't think these people were insincere. Quite the opposite: they had given their lives to the cause. And I think they were truly concerned for me, to the extent that they wanted me to join their struggle to change the world. But their love was not the love of Jesus—at least, not of the Jesus of the New Testament. The Jesus they preach failed to save humanity; his death on the cross, according to the Reverend Moon, was a victory for Satan, a shameful death that frustrated God.

The love of these Moonies was a human love, which, in Bonhoeffer's words, "is capable of prodigious sacrifices. . . . Often it surpasses genuine Christian love in fervent devotion and visible results."[9] The Moonies' devotion surpassed that of many Christians I know. They stood on cold, windy street corners for twelve hours every day selling flowers for their church. At the end of the day they returned to their spartan living quarters for several hours of lectures and group prayer. Bonhoeffer warns us that such heroic devotion that passes for spiritual love may in fact be demonic: "Jesus reveals to the disciples the possibility of a demonic faith which produces wonderful works quite indistinguishable from the works of the true disciples, works of charity, miracles, perhaps even of personal sanctification, but which is nevertheless a denial of Jesus and of the way of discipleship."[10]

Jesus, Paul and John spoke of counterfeit love that passes for true Christian devotion. Jesus said that in times of trial and persecution the "love of many will grow cold" (Mt 24:9-12). Paul referred indirectly to some whose love for Jesus dies (Eph 6:24); John wrote of the church in Ephesus that had left its first love (Rev 2:4).

How do we recognize this counterfeit love? First, by the way it serves. Richard Foster suggests that it serves capriciously. It "is affected by moods and whims. It can serve only when there is a 'feeling' to serve ('moved by the Spirit,' as we say). . . . True service ministers simply and faithfully because there is a need."[11]

Counterfeit love seeks attention for itself. Screwtape, the peevish archdemon whom C. S. Lewis so delightfully portrays in his *Screwtape Letters*, advises his nephew that many people surrender their rights in a showy demonstration of so-called love, "not that others may be happy but that they may be seen as unselfish."[12]

Counterfeit love selects only those who are easy to love. When instructing his nephew how to lead a Christian astray, Screwtape suggests that the demon direct the Christian's attention away from those who are nearby and difficult to love: "Thrust benevolence . . . out to the remote circumference, to people he does not know."[13] According to Bonhoeffer, counterfeit love never loves an enemy, a person who "seriously and stubbornly resists it."[14]

Finally, counterfeit love is absorbed with itself. It seeks to control, to bind others to itself, to rule over others and to make others an extension of itself. In reality, it is narcissism. Bonhoeffer writes:

[Counterfeit] love makes itself an end in itself. It creates of itself an end, an idol which it worships, to which it must subject everything. It nurses and cultivates an ideal, it loves itself, and nothing else in the world. Spiritual love, however, comes from Jesus Christ, it serves him alone; it knows that it has no immediate access to other persons.[15]

Zealous or Time-Consuming Devotion to Religious Activities

Some in our culture think that significant involvement in religion is a sign of intellectual or emotional immaturity. Fundamentalists are sometimes criticized by liberal Christians because they spend so much time reading the Bible, praying, evangelizing and going to church. So much time spent in religious activity, particularly when not balanced by participation in secular culture, is thought to be fanatical and neurotic.

Yet the Scriptures show that saving grace causes a person to delight in such activities. Anna the prophet "never left the temple but worshiped there with fasting and prayer night and day" (Lk 2:37). The early Christians seemed to use all their free time for spiritual pursuits: "Day by day, as they spent much time together in the temple, they broke bread at home and ate their food with glad and generous hearts, praising God and having the goodwill of all the people" (Acts 2:46). The Bible says that Daniel and David prayed three times each day. It suggests that saints love to worship God (Ps 26:8; 27:4; 84:1-2, 10) and sing praises to him (Ps 135:3; 147:1).

But the Bible also indicates that a love for religious activity is no sure sign of grace. The Jews in Isaiah's day brought offerings to God, held special meetings on holy days and stretched out their hands in many prayers. But God said their religiosity would do them no good: "When you stretch out your hands, I will hide my eyes from you; even though you make many prayers, I will not listen" (Is 1:15). At the end of his prophecy, Isaiah explains why God refused to listen to the Jews' prayers. They delighted to know God's ways but didn't walk in them (Is 58:2).

The spirituality of the Jews in Ezekiel's day was also hypocritical. But this time the problem was avarice; they were more concerned with how much money they could make than pleasing God. God told Ezekiel, "They [the Jews] come to you as people come, and they sit before you as my people, and they hear your words, but they will not obey them. For flattery is on their lips, but their heart is set on their gain" (Ezek 33:31).

The Jewish leaders of Jesus' time also prayed long prayers. They fasted two days every week and gave generously to the poor. Yet Jesus called them whitewashed tombs that look beautiful on the outside but are filthy on the inside.

Jesus warned that on Judgment Day many will remind him that they had been very religious. They will say they had prophesied, cast out demons and even performed miracles. Most of us in today's church, I think, would conclude with certainty that these people must surely have had saving grace. If the Holy Spirit has used them to do miracles, we conclude, they must surely be born again and citizens of the kingdom of God. Yet listen to Jesus' frightening reply: "I never knew you; get away from me, you evildoers" (Mt 7:22-23).

Notice that Jesus doesn't say, "Once I knew you. At that time you were in my good graces. You were members of my kingdom. But then you turned away. So now I must kick you out." Rather, he says that he *never* knew them. They were *never* regenerate; they were *never* members of the kingdom. All the time they were doing religious deeds—all the time they were considered good Christians by their fellow church members—they were not really in the kingdom at all. Religious activity is no sure sign of true spirituality.

Donna, a teacher, was a zealous church member known for her disciplined devotional life. After serving as a short-term missionary to Mexico one summer, she came to teach in the Christian school that I served as a principal. Donna was well organized and conscientious in her teaching duties, but I noticed a certain hardness about her. She was short and abrupt in conversation, and she rarely smiled. Toward Christmas, after several of her students complained to me that she wasn't very friendly, I started to have questions about the depth of her spirituality.

When she failed to return to school after the Christmas holidays, I called her home. Her mother answered the phone and refused to let me talk to Donna. When I reminded her mother that Donna was breaking her contract with the school, the mother simply replied that Donna did not want to return.

Several days later one of Donna's friends revealed to me that Donna had been sexually involved with several men in Mexico and that at least one of them had followed her back to the States. She had maintained this relationship throughout the fall term. By Christmas she apparently could not continue living a double life.

Perhaps Donna was among those described by Philipp Spener (1635-1705), founder of German Pietism. He insisted that true spirituality is a matter of inner renewal:

There are not a few who think that all Christianity requires of them (and that having done this, they have done quite enough in their service of God) is that they be baptized, hear the preaching of God's Word, confess and receive absolution, and go to the Lord's Supper, no matter how their hearts are disposed at the time, whether or not there are fruits which follow, provided that they at least live in such a way that the civil authorities do not find them liable to punishment.[16]

I do not mean to imply that sexual sin is a sure sign of false affections, or that it is the unforgivable sin. True Christians do sometimes fall into sexual sin. And sexual sin, like every other sin, can be forgiven. But Donna's affairs were symptomatic of what seemed to be a persistent inconsistency. Others who knew Donna told me that Donna's escapades that summer and fall were part of a pattern, and that her cold-blooded insensitivity was a tip-off that her heart may never have been warmed by the grace of Christ. I didn't know if that was the case. I hoped that her behavior represented a temporary departure from grace, to be followed by a return to Christian discipleship. But whatever the condition of Donna's relationship to Christ, she taught me that outward religiosity is no sure sign of true grace.

In the next chapter we will look at two more signs that are often thought to be sure signs of true spirituality: the sincere belief that I am saved and my certainty that someone else is saved.

5

· · · · ·

Unreliable Signs
Involving Assurance
of Salvation

IN NORTHERN PALESTINE DURING THE FIRST CENTURY THERE LIVED A magician named Simon. Simon performed miracles that amazed the people of his city. Because his magic seemed to be performed by divine power, the people of this city called Simon "the Great One from God." Few doubted that Simon was one of God's special chosen ones.

But then Philip came to the city preaching Jesus, curing the sick and casting out demons. The people of the city recognized that here was a power greater than Simon's. Simon himself "believed" and was baptized. When Simon offered to pay Philip for a dose of Philip's power, Philip sharply rebuked him, telling him that he had no part in God's kingdom. No doubt there were many in northern Palestine that day who shook their heads muttering, "We all thought Simon was God's special wonder worker. Little did we know!" (See Acts 8:4-25.)

The purpose of this chapter is to show that assurance of salvation is not a clear sign of grace. It cannot tell us with certainty if someone is or is not in the kingdom of God. Even if many are convinced that someone is among God's chosen—as the Samaritans were sure of Simon—it is not necessarily so. Just because a person is convinced about his own salvation, as Simon probably was before Philip came to town, we cannot be sure that he is right.

But before we explain why assurance of salvation is not a reliable sign of grace, we need to look at the possibility of assurance itself. Can we know for sure that *we* are on the road to heaven, even though others mistakenly think *they* are? Is there such a thing as true assurance—the reliable conviction that I am saved?

Being Convinced That One Is Saved

Many Christians believe that assurance of salvation is a sign of *false* spirituality. They think that a true Christian will never be sure of salvation. Lack of assurance, they say, is a sign of humility. To be convinced of one's salvation, on the other hand, is arrogant and boastful, certainly not befitting a true Christian. Only a tiny number of Christians will ever have assurance during this life—martyrs who need assurance to strengthen them during their painful ordeals. But the rest of us should never expect to have assurance. In fact, we should be suspicious of anyone claiming to have assurance of salvation.

This is the position of the Roman Catholic Church. It was officially decreed at the Council of Trent in the sixteenth century in order to refute the claims for assurance made by the Protestant reformers Luther and Calvin. Assurance is not impossible, the Trent theologians declared, but it is very rare and comes only by a special revelation from God.[1] Thomas Aquinas had written three centuries before that a Christian could lose his salvation by committing a mortal sin.[2] It seemed only reasonable that if you could lose your salvation by a very serious sin, then you could never have final assurance that you would be saved because you could never be sure of your future choices.

Yet the biblical authors were convinced otherwise. Abraham's faith in God's promise that his descendants would be multiplied is described by Paul as full assurance (Rom 4:13-25). Despite many struggles, the psalmist demonstrates the same confidence of salvation (Ps 22; 40—44; 46; 102; 130). The author of Hebrews defines faith as "the *assurance* of things hoped for" (Heb 11:1). Peter reminds his persecuted church to focus on the "inheritance . . . kept in heaven for you" (1 Pet 1:3-5). Peter does not doubt that his readers will enjoy that inheritance in heaven. In Romans 8 Paul tells us that we are assured of our salvation by the Spirit ("bearing witness with our spirit that we are children of God," Rom 8:16), by our sense of God's calling ("those whom he predestined he also called," Rom 8:30) and by Christ's love (nothing "will be able to separate us from the love of God in Christ Jesus our Lord," Rom 8:39). The first letter of John repeatedly tells its readers *how* they can know if they are saved and explains that the very purpose of the letter is to provide such assurance: "I write these things to you who believe in the name of the Son of God, so that you may *know* that you have eternal life" (1 Jn 5:13).

I therefore conclude that it is wrong to use assurance of salvation as a sign of deception. Assurance of salvation is not arrogant presumption but a wonderful gift God wants to give his children while they are still on earth. It is not a sign of pride but the joyful realization that God has saved me—an unworthy sinner—for eternity. When understood rightly, it brings humility rather than pride (1 Cor 4:7). And 1 John indicates that it is part of the normal Christian life, not a rare gift that God reserves for the superstars of the faith.

On the other hand, assurance is not a sure sign of regeneration. There is no guarantee that the person who claims to be going to heaven will actually get there. The Pharisees, for example, were convinced they were in God's kingdom. But Jesus told them that they were deceived (Mt 23:13). So there is always the possibility of deception. Experience teaches, and Jeremiah reminds us, that "the heart is devious above all else; it is perverse—who can understand it?" (Jer 17:9). Scripture indicates elsewhere that the human ego often flatters itself, exalts itself and is blindly self-confident.

Life provides many demonstrations of this truth. Gerald May is a psychiatrist who has worked for years in drug and alcohol treatment programs. May found that even those with a history of failure can be blinded by an exaggerated self-confidence. "It is not at all unusual to hear aged alcoholics, who have lost jobs, families, and homes, and who are now hospitalized with advanced cirrhosis of the liver, saying, 'Hell no. I've never had any trouble with booze. I can take it or leave it.' "[3]

Two kinds of people seem to be particularly susceptible to false assurance. The first kind are noted for outward morality or religiosity. These people are often well regarded in the community because of their charitable activities or church work. They go above and beyond the call of duty; they volunteer when others hesitate. They try their best to be good persons. They believe that being a nice person will get them to heaven, and they are doing their best. But they have never been inwardly renewed by the Spirit of God. All their good works are the strivings of the human self, not the natural outflow of a transformed heart.

Then there are those who have had visions, heard voices or had other kinds of remarkable spiritual experiences. Willis, for instance, is a lecherous, heavy-drinking old farmer who ignored his handicapped son for years because he was embarrassed by his inability to play baseball like other boys. But because he heard a voice many years ago promising him salvation, Willis resists the urgings of his relatives to repent and turn his heart to God. Willis insists that he is already saved and has no need for organized religion.

It is difficult to know whose voice spoke to Willis years ago. Perhaps it was his own desire to be free from spiritual terror. Or it may have been what Paul referred to when he said that Satan sometimes disguises himself as an angel of light. In any event, Willis's extraordinary experience keeps him from realizing that his assurance of salvation rests on a false foundation.

Why are people like Willis and the busy folks noted for their religiosity so easily deceived? Why are they so oblivious to signs that they are *not* in the kingdom of God? According to Edwards, it is because they lack four restraints on presumption; that is, four things are missing from their lives which true saints possess to prevent them from falling into deception about salvation.

First, they have no fear of deception. They don't realize that spiritual deception—particularly about one's assurance of salvation—is common and easy to fall into. So they lack the caution that saints possess. Saints are careful to check their experience against biblical norms to confirm their perception that they are saved. They know that they are finite and sinful and therefore liable to misunderstand the things of God. But people like Willis never do such checking. It never occurs to them that their thinking might be wrong.

Second, they don't question their own spiritual judgments because they don't know that their hearts are often blind and deceitful. Since they have neither spiritual experience nor spiritual sensitivity, they are not aware of their own tendency to be blinded by self-interest. But true Christians recognize this problem. The greatest saints bemoan the duplicity of their hearts.

Third, the devil doesn't attack the assurance of the unregenerate. Since their assurance hinders them from entering God's kingdom, Satan is happy to keep them complacent, rejoicing in a salvation that does not exist. True saints, on the other hand, find their assurance often attacked by the devil. Just as Jesus was challenged by Satan in the desert ("*if* you are the Son of God . . ."), many of Jesus' disciples find that Satan assaults their own assurance of salvation. Revelation 12:10 states that Satan accuses God's children day and night.

Luther said that the devil's attack on his assurance usually took the form of accusing him that he hadn't done enough good works. Luther resisted this challenge by a bold proclamation of faith.

When I awoke last night, the devil came and wanted to debate with me: he rebuked and reproached me, arguing that I was a sinner. To this I replied, "Tell me something new, devil! I already know that perfectly well; I have committed many a solid and real sin. Indeed there must be good honest sins—not fabricated and invented ones—for God to forgive for His beloved Son's sake, who took all my sins upon Him so that now the sins I have committed are no longer mine but belong to Christ."[4]

Fourth, sinners deceived about their salvation don't comprehend their own sinfulness. They think they are virtuous and even better than most.

When I was fifteen I spent a summer in Greece. For part of the summer I worked as a dishwasher on a ship in the Aegean Sea. During the rest of the summer I lived with the family of a Greek architect who boasted to me that he had never purposely hurt anyone. At the same time he openly courted other women, to the evident hurt and humiliation of his wife. And I discovered later that he had embezzled money from a company for which he worked. Yet this architect was firmly convinced that he was an upright, moral man.

True saints are dismayed by their sin. They are sometimes overwhelmed by the depth and breadth of their sinfulness and wonder how they could possibly be saved. The greatest saints in church history typically have believed that they were terrible sinners. Paul, for example, said that he was the "foremost" of sinners (1 Tim 1:15). Edwards wrote about himself,

> It has often appeared to me, that if God should mark iniquity against me, I should appear the very worst of all mankind; of all that have been, since the beginning of the world to this time; and that I should have by far the lowest place in hell. . . . My wickedness, as I am in myself, has long appeared to me perfectly ineffable, and swallowing up all thought and imagination; like an infinite deluge, or mountain over my head. I know not how to express better what my sins appear to me to be, than by heaping infinite upon infinite, and multiplying infinite by infinite.[5]

There is one more reason the unconverted can think they are saved. Sometimes they have misunderstood the gospel's promise of grace. They have thought that God's gift of salvation is license to sin. That is, they have believed that since Christ's death has brought forgiveness of sin, they need not concern themselves with sin in their lives. As Bonhoeffer put it so aptly in *The Cost of Discipleship*, they have turned God's "costly grace" into "cheap grace." Because Bonhoeffer's analysis penetrates an acutely significant problem in today's church, I quote him at length:

> Cheap grace is the preaching of forgiveness without requiring repentance, baptism without church discipline, Communion without confession, absolution without personal confession. Cheap grace is grace without discipleship, grace without the cross, grace without Jesus Christ, living and incarnate.
>
> Costly grace is the treasure hidden in the field; for the sake of it a man will gladly go and sell all that he has. It is the pearl of great price to buy which the merchant will sell all his goods. It is the kingly rule of Christ, for whose sake a man will pluck out the eye which causes him to stumble, it is the call of Jesus Christ at which the disciple leaves his nets and follows him.
>
> Costly grace is the gospel which must be *sought* again and again, the gift which must be *asked* for, the door at which a man must *knock*.
>
> Such grace is *costly* because it calls us to follow, and it is *grace*

because it calls us to follow *Jesus Christ*. It is costly because it costs a man his life, and it is grace because it gives a man the only true life. It is costly because it condemns sin, and grace because it justifies the sinner. Above all, it is *costly* because it cost God the life of his Son: "ye were bought at a price," and what has cost God much cannot be cheap for us. Above all, it is *grace* because God did not reckon his Son too dear a price to pay for our life, but delivered him up for us. Costly grace is the Incarnation of God. . . .

Luther had said that grace alone can save; his followers took up his doctrine and repeated it word for word. But they left out its invariable corollary, the obligation of discipleship. There was no need for Luther always to mention that corollary explicitly, for he always spoke as one who had been led by grace to the strictest following of Christ. Judged by the standard of Luther's doctrine, that of his followers was unassailable, and yet their orthodoxy spelt the end and destruction of the Reformation as the revelation on earth of the costly grace of God. The justification of the sinner in the world degenerated into the justification of sin and the world. Costly grace was turned into cheap grace without discipleship.[6]

Many have convinced themselves that because Jesus' death on the cross has won for them a berth in heaven, there is no need for a life of discipleship. These people have never appropriated the message of the cross for themselves; they have never truly repented and been born again. They have no love for following in Christ's footsteps. Yet they reassure themselves that they are children of the light.

Before I close this section I must add that sometimes lack of assurance *does* arise from unbelief. And this is to the good. That is, some of these folks whom Bonhoeffer describes finally realize one day that they may not be saved because there is no evidence of grace in their lives. They realize there is no evidence because they have never truly exercised trust in God. They have never believed sufficiently to allow their head knowledge about Jesus to actually affect their hearts and actions. So they have never exercised *saving* faith in Christ. It's no wonder they have not seen evidence of grace in their lives.

For these people, lack of assurance is just what they need. It causes fear, but it is a proper fear of God that provokes them to true repentance and faith. Their true repentance and faith bring them to an experience of Christ's love, which "drives out fear" (1 Jn 4:18). This lack of fear is based not on false presumption but on true assurance of salvation. They understand that they are sinners deserving hell, but sinners nevertheless redeemed by the love of Christ, whose Spirit is transforming them day by day.

Others' Being Convinced That Someone Is Saved

So far we have seen that there is both true and false assurance of salvation. Scripture makes clear that true saints can have assurance of salvation. But it also indicates that people can think they are saved when they really aren't. So the mere fact that someone has assurance is not a reliable sign of true grace.

Now let's shift our attention to the assurance that *others* may have about a person. Here too there can be no certainty. That is, nothing can be concluded with certainty about the nature of religious affections from this: that the outward manifestations, and the testimony of those who possess them, greatly impress true saints. To put it another way, even those with true spirituality cannot have certain knowledge of who is in the kingdom of God—at least not by any special inner revelation.

True saints cannot get inside the mind or heart of another. They can see the outward appearance only. And Scripture tells us that judging by outward appearances is uncertain at best and liable to deception. "The LORD does not see as mortals see; they look on the outward appearance, but the LORD looks on the heart" (1 Sam 16:7). Isaiah prophesied that the Messiah would not "judge by what his eyes see, or decide by what his ears hear" (Is 11:3).

Finding indications of true spirituality in others obliges us as Christians to receive them in love and to rejoice in them as brothers and sisters in Christ. But we must realize that the most discerning of us can be deceived. The church has extended an enthusiastic welcome to many a person loudly proclaiming Christ, who then fell away and came to nothing. This has been a pattern throughout church history, and it is common today. Think of Jim Bakker, Jimmy Swaggart, Eldridge Cleaver and even Bob Dylan, all of whom were thought to be examples of true conversion. Now it is clear that Cleaver's and Dylan's "conversions" never lasted, and that much of what passed for true spirituality in Bakker and Swaggart was a disguise for inner corruption.

If you've come this far in the book, you shouldn't be surprised that so many can be so mistaken. You know from the previous chapters that a person can have many intense religious affections, fear hell and then feel relief because of a promise of salvation, experience spiritual influences—even Scripture verses—coming from outside the self and with physical manifestations, talk a lot about God and even praise him, appear to be loving, be zealously engaged in time-consuming church activity, be assured of salvation and yet not be saved. These spiritual experiences and affections can come from natural or deceitful workings of the human heart, the delusions of Satan or even the Holy Spirit's "common influences" (those working on the unregenerate).

A true saint and a hypocrite (someone who appears to others to be saved but really isn't) may be similar in outward appearance. Only God, the great searcher of hearts who separates the sheep and the goats, knows with certainty the condition of a person's heart. We are presumptuous to think that we can have God's *certain* knowledge of who is and who isn't in his kingdom. As a friend recently told me, "You can tell who is a Christian and who is not every time—if you are God!"[7]

Many believe that someone is saved if that person's testimony touches their heart. They are particularly convinced when the testimony is similar to their own, uses some of the same words they use, recounts an order of experience similar to theirs, or is expressed with great assurance and deep feeling. A true saint will easily believe the testimony because he loves God and his glory and is delighted when he hears of God saving another sinner. This is why David believed Ahithophel's testimony. He was sorely disappointed when he discovered Ahithophel's hypocrisy.

It is not enemies who taunt me—
     I could bear that;
it is not adversaries who deal insolently with me—
     I could hide from them.
But it is you, my equal,
     my companion, my familiar friend,
with whom I kept pleasant company;
     we walked in the house of God with the throng. (Ps 55:12-14)

Bill is an engineer who was my best friend during a period earlier in my life. He was also a committed member of our church. Bill served as church treasurer and usher, and sometimes he preached when the pastor was away. He was also devoted to personal Bible study. Besides attending a weekly home Bible study for couples, he got up in the dark every Tuesday morning to study Genesis with a group of men. Bill was loyal to me when I needed help, and he was a devoted husband and father. Or so it seemed.

One autumn morning Sally, Bill's wife, discovered that he was having an affair. When she confronted him, he refused to break it off. The pastor and several elders who met with Bill experienced the same resistance. Bill said that he felt overwhelmed by the responsibilities of caring for a family of five and that Sally was not meeting his needs. His new girlfriend, a wealthy divorced woman, showered him with affection and made no demands.

By this time I had moved to another state. Sally called me to ask for help. She told me that Bill had moved out, leaving their three children hurt and confused. So I called Bill and asked why he had done this. He said that he and Sally weren't getting along. "Why don't you move back home?" I asked. "You and Sally can go for counseling and try to work things out. It would be good for your kids to see you at home, trying to get things back together with Sally."

"I can't, Gerry. I just can't." Bill sounded like a little lost puppy.

"Why not?" I implored.

"I don't know. I just don't know."

I got the same answer when I asked Bill why he was willing to risk the destruction of his marriage and great hurt to his children. Bill was confused and bewildered. The affair seemed to be entirely out of his control.

I told him that I loved him and Sally and pleaded with him to call me if there was any way I could help. Then I hung up. I couldn't figure out why this Christian man was willing to risk losing his family and integrity for a relationship that would probably go nowhere. No doubt Bill was right when he confessed that he didn't understand what he was doing. Sure, he'd had problems with Sally, but they were nothing that good counseling and concerted effort couldn't fix.

After some months Bill still had not broken off the affair and kept lying about it. I began to wonder if Bill had ever had the spiritual transformation called Christian conversion.[8] If not, it was no wonder that he couldn't understand his own actions and felt himself drifting further and further away from his own ideals.

After several years of estrangement, Bill eventually returned to his family. As far as I know, he has repented of what he did, and his marriage to Sally is in the process of being restored. I'm still not sure what to make of it all. I think it was presumptuous of me to conclude that he was never converted because he had the affair. Perhaps it was a tragic lapse in an otherwise admirable life of faith—like David's adultery with Bathsheba (and subsequent murder of her husband!).[9]

My friendship with Bill reminds me that judging another's status with God is dangerous. Outward devotion to God is no guarantee of inner spirituality. And no one pattern of sin, at least over a relatively short time period, is a reliable indication that the sinner is not saved. After all, we're all sinners who struggle and are often discouraged by persistent patterns of sin in our own lives.

Jesus told us that wheat and weeds look exactly alike until harvest time, when the blade of wheat bears its own recognizable fruit (Mt 13). Only then, when the fruit is manifest, will we have any degree of certainty that someone has true spirituality.

We cannot know the state of a person's soul by inner revelation or mystical voice. Scripture never says a word about judging the spiritual state of a person by these methods. It says only that we are to "judge them by their fruits." Jesus tells us that we will know false prophets by their fruits (Mt 7:16). And we are to receive brothers and sisters in love as members of the body of Christ if they demonstrate some growth in the fruit of the Spirit: love, joy, peace, patience, kindness, generosity, faithfulness, gentleness and self-control (Gal 5:22-23).

But Scripture also warns us that we can never know with certainty the state of another's soul before God. Jesus told the church at Pergamum that he gives to "everyone who conquers . . . a new name that *no one knows* except the one who receives it" (Rev 2:17). Paul wrote the Romans that a true Jew's circumcision is a matter of the heart, and that he receives "praise *not from others but from God*" (Rom 2:29). He rebuked those who were confident of their own discernment, sure that they were guides to the blind, instructors of the ignorant, a light to those in darkness and teachers of babes. It was only by presumption, Paul suggested, that they took it upon themselves to judge others (Rom 2:1, 17-20).

To the Corinthians Paul said that he regarded human judgment of his spiritual state as inconclusive: "With me it is a very small thing that I should be judged by you or by any human court. . . . It is the Lord who judges me. Therefore do not pronounce judgment before the time, before the Lord comes, who will bring to light the things now hidden in darkness and will disclose the purposes of the heart. *Then* each one will receive commendation from God" (1 Cor 4:3-5). Paul taught that the more godly members of the church are to rebuke and sometimes discipline the fallen (1 Cor 5:3-5; see also Mt 18:15-18). But he was skeptical of judging the final destiny of others. As the author of 1 Kings put it, "Only you [O God] know what is in every human heart" (8:39). Therefore the mere fact that others *believe* Jane is a saint is no guarantee of Jane's spirituality.

This completes our study of the *unreliable* signs of true spirituality. The next chapter will begin the longest section of the book, where we will look at the twelve *reliable* signs of grace. These are twelve manifestations of affections that appear in the life of a true saint—a person with true spirituality.

Part Four

· · · · ·

Reliable Signs
of True Spirituality

6

· · · · ·

Let the
Reader Beware

IN MY MOST CLEARSIGHTED MOMENTS
NOT ONLY DO I NOT THINK MYSELF A NICE MAN,
BUT I KNOW THAT I AM A VERY NASTY ONE.
I CAN LOOK AT SOME OF THE THINGS I HAVE DONE
WITH HORROR AND LOATHING.
C. S. LEWIS

BEFORE WE BEGIN TO LOOK AT THE RELIABLE SIGNS OF SAVING GRACE, some cautions are in order. First, we shouldn't get the impression that knowing the twelve reliable signs that follow will enable us to identify with certainty the spiritual state of others. As we saw at the end of chapter five, this kind of certainty is impossible.

At the same time, however, we must recognize that the Scriptures do give us signs for detecting false prophets and teachers. Jesus said, for example, that we will know false prophets "by their fruits" (Mt 7:16). We are given these instructions to protect us against false teaching and abusive leadership.

The corrupt spiritual state of some people is obvious from their words and actions. But our knowledge of others stops there. We have not been given a list of criteria that allow us to clearly evaluate the spiritual condition of the vast majority of our neighbors. It was never God's intention to give us rules by which we can separate with certainty the sheep from the goats. To search hearts and know their eternal destiny is the prerogative of God alone.

Knowledge of these twelve reliable signs will not give us certainty about the spiritual state of most people. Neither will it enable negligent Christians—who are not pressing on into God's grace—to know with certainty their own spiritual condition. Lazy Christians will have no assurance of salvation until they repent of their laziness and commit themselves unconditionally to God. As Bonhoeffer put it, "The only man who has a right to say that he is justified by grace alone is the man who has left all to follow Christ." Assurance of salvation comes primarily from the evident work of grace in one's life; so a person who fails to appropriate grace has little or no evidence that saving grace is present.

Jonathan Edwards said that there are two reasons lax saints have a difficult time finding assurance. First, there is little grace in such a person's life, and whatever grace is present is mixed with abundant corruption. It is hard to detect—just as it is difficult to tell the difference between a star (which, like a true saint, gives sustained light) and a comet (which, like a pseudosaint, shines only for a time) when looking at them through a cloud. It is no wonder that a negligent saint will be plagued with guilt and fear, unable to find the peace and joy that come with assurance of salvation.

A second reason negligent saints have trouble gaining assurance is that sin clouds vision, just as disease can dull our sense of taste. Lax saints cannot see clearly, because sin blurs their vision; they don't have the spiritual acuity that fully committed saints possess.

What negligent saints need to do, in order to gain assurance, is *not* to pray for discernment or look harder at these signs. Figuratively speaking, they need to slay Achan, the Israelite whose theft of gold and silver turned God's anger against all Israel until he was executed (Josh 7). Negligent saints will never receive clear assurance until they clean the unrepented sin out of their lives. As Edwards remarked, it would be silly to try to tell a man how to distinguish colors while he is in the dark. Only when backslidden saints repent of their listlessness and compromise will the scales fall from their eyes. Then they will be able to see their hearts for what they are.

Assurance comes not through self-examination but through action. Paul said that he made a practice of forgetting what lay behind and pressing forward to gain the prize of the high calling of God in Christ Jesus (Phil 3:13). Peter told his churches to gain their assurance by supporting their faith "with goodness, and goodness with knowledge, and knowledge with self-control, and self-control with endurance, and endurance with godliness, and godliness with mutual affection, and mutual affection with love" (2 Pet 1:5-7, 10). The remedy for doubt about one's salvation, in other words, is to press on in faith and obedience.

If these rules and signs cannot give us certainty about the spiritual state of others and are of little help to backslidden saints trying to gain assurance, they are nevertheless of great help to saints who want to deepen and purify their faith. By them true saints will be able to detect false affections within themselves when true spirituality has been mixed with deceptive imitations. Genuine disciples of Jesus will better know the goals toward which they should aim. Knowing the map and signposts on the trail of true spirituality, they won't miss the delights and treasures the trail has to offer. Finally, walking the trail—this narrow way—will purify their faith. Like gold purified by fire, their spirituality will emerge from the journey gleaming with integrity and beauty.

A final word of caution is needed before we look at the twelve reliable signs: don't get discouraged. Don't think that your life must perfectly match each of these twelve reliable signs. If you are a true saint—that is, if you have been regenerated or "born again" and are now walking with the Lord—your life will have something of each sign. But there will be days when you'll wonder if you have *any* of these signs. On those days you may feel condemned; you may think that you're the sorriest excuse for a Christian there ever was.

On those days remember this: every true Christian has this experience from time to time. The normal Christian life contains the *principle* of victory over sin (by the power of the Holy Spirit), but no Christian lives in continuous victory over sin. As we have already seen, the greatest saints in church history have always proclaimed that they were heinous sinners and could not understand why God would save them. Their lives testify to the fact that the normal Christian life is a struggle between good and evil, God and the devil, the spirit and the flesh. The apostle Paul himself bemoaned, "I do not do the good I want, but the evil I do not want is what I do" (Rom 7:19). And he pointed out that "we have this treasure in clay jars" (2 Cor 4:7). That is, the *Holy* Spirit dwells within *unholy* vessels that break easily.

The mere fact that we worry about our spirituality, hating the sin within us, is a good sign. It is the unregenerate who tend to think that sin is not a problem for them. So the next time you feel that you have failed God so miserably that you doubt your salvation, remember to wait awhile. Wait a few days or weeks before you do inventory. After your despair or depression has lifted, look again at these twelve reliable signs. If they *roughly* portray your life, rest assured. And be thankful that the heavenly treasure is at work in your clay jar.

7

. . . . .

The First Reliable Sign
A Divine &
Supernatural
Source

H AROLD PAYNE WAS BORN IN 1929 IN ADA, OKLAHOMA. HIS PARENTS SENT him to church, but because they couldn't get along, they got a divorce and sent young Harold to live with his grandparents.

Harold's father remarried and worked in a California shipyard during the war. When Harold was fifteen, he went to live with his dad and his new stepmother. Harold was glad for a change of scenery, but after several months on the West Coast he decided that he wanted to return to his grandparents in Oklahoma. When he reached his grandparents, he told them that his father and stepmother didn't love him. Harold's grandparents assured him that they did and urged Harold to stay with them. Instead Harold hit the road.

That began six years of living on the road. Harold hitchhiked from state to state, visiting every one of the forty-eight and staying in every capital. Sometimes he slept along the road, scared to death. Other nights he stayed at missions or at the Salvation Army. Along the way he picked up odd jobs to pay for food and lodging. "I remember standing out on the road," Harold told me not long ago, "feeling so lonely for my family. I wanted to go home. But I was afraid of how I would be received if I went home. I was sure I'd be whipped. Or, even if I wasn't, at least I'd be lectured." Even a lecture would hurt, so he swallowed his loneliness and kept heading down the road.

Pretty soon Harold started drinking. He spent the nights in bars, frequently with women, in the hope of easing his loneliness. One day when he was twenty-two years old, he ran out of money. He had no job and was dying for a drink. So he looked in a phone book, picked out a name at random and forged a check for $228. With that check he bought a bottle of liquor and an orchid for a barmaid. He saved the change for rent and food.

Not too many days later, there was a knock on his door. "Harold Payne?" a man's voice called out.

"No, he's not here," Harold said. Somehow he knew it was a detective. So he headed for the back door. When he opened it, he found several other policemen waiting for him.

The judge gave Harold one to twenty years for forgery and sent him to the Ohio State Penitentiary. After the sentencing Harold was very quiet. He knew he was guilty. When they took him back to his cell, he was shaking with fear. For the first time in his life, he was called not by a name but a number: 107873.

That night Harold tried to pluck up a little courage. He told himself he'd be out in a year. *A year is not very long,* he thought. *And besides, I'll get my meals free.* After years of scavenging for the next meal, that didn't sound too bad.

But there was a problem. Harold was not a model prisoner. Several times he was caught with contraband (cigarettes and cash) and thrown for three days at a time into the hole, where there was just a cot and a dirt floor. When he came before the parole board at the end of that year, they told him he wasn't ready for freedom.

Harold still hadn't learned his lesson. Not much later he was caught making potato whiskey and sentenced to another five years. By the time he was released he had done sixteen years at the Ohio State Penitentiary. During that period he had survived two riots and witnessed many stabbings. "I saw hundreds of men die. And I learned that a screwdriver can be a dangerous weapon."

When Harold left prison, he went to Roanoke, Virginia, and got a job making Texas-style chili at a little restaurant. There he met Mary, a wonderful woman who told him that he had to go to church if he wanted to date her.

"As soon as I got to church," Harold explains, "I felt the Spirit of God drawing me." At the end of the service there was an altar call. Harold went forward. He felt like a nervous wreck. He was embarrassed by the people looking at him, but the strong sense of guilt before God prevented him from returning to his seat.

"I knew from my church upbringing that I had shut God out of my life from the time my parents divorced. So I cried out to God in my heart: *Please forgive me, Lord. I've dragged you through bars and through the mud of my sinful life. I ran away from you on the highways and in the flophouses all these years.*"

Then God's voice spoke clearly to Harold's heart: *I know, Harold. I was with you the whole time, protecting you.*

When he realized that he had been forgiven, Harold nearly jumped with joy. He'd never felt so good. Now he knew that God was a forgiving God who wouldn't hold things against him. It was a great feeling to have his record wiped clean.

Several nights later he called Mary on the phone. "Will you marry me?" he asked.

There was a long silence. "What time is it?" she finally asked.

"Four-thirty a.m.," Harold replied.

"Couldn't this have waited till the morning?"

"No," he insisted.

After a minute, Mary said yes. Harold said OK and hung up the phone.

The next day Mary told Harold she would marry him on the condition that he call his father and stepmother and tell them where he'd been for the last twenty years. He told her he couldn't. She said he'd have to.

Harold did, and his parents shocked him. There was no screaming lecture. Instead they rejoiced. They said they'd loved him the whole time. Harold was stunned and cried like a baby.

The next seventeen years were happy for Harold and Mary. Harold was a new man. He was able to talk to God as he had never talked to anyone. He sensed God listening to his prayers and saw many of them answered in remarkable ways. He was no longer so afraid of what people thought of him but was eager to tell others about the Jesus who had saved him.

"But most important, Jesus gave Mary and me a wonderful marriage. Before Christ came into my life, I chased women. But after Christ forgave me and his Spirit came into my heart, I didn't want anyone else. Because of him, we never argued. Every night between eight and nine we had devotions together. It was a marriage made in heaven."

Mary died seven years ago, and Harold longs for the day when he will see her again. In the meantime he sings beautiful gospel ballads for our church and shares Christ with his neighbors and fellow workers at his factory job. He is a joy and inspiration to all who know him.

The Permanent Indwelling of the Holy Spirit

The first reliable sign of true spirituality is the indwelling of the Holy Spirit. True saints have the Holy Spirit living inside them on a permanent basis. From within, the Spirit imparts his holiness and a new spiritual sense to the saint. This is the only explanation for the change in Harold's life. Harold still has blind spots and problem areas that he struggles with, but there is a marked difference in his soul and character from the time when he first met Christ. He would be the first to say that he has changed because of the work of the Holy Spirit within him, not because of his own natural abilities and efforts. This is why I say that the first reliable sign is a divine and *supernatural* source of spirituality. And the source is the Holy Spirit, who dwells permanently in the true believer.

As I have pointed out in previous chapters, many people are touched and influenced by the Holy Spirit but without the Spirit's permanent indwelling. Balaam, we have seen, prophesied by inspiration of the Spirit about the future of Israel and the Christ. Yet he led Israel into immorality and idolatry and was not in the kingdom of God. The Spirit led Saul to defeat the Ammonites and twice threw him into a prophetic trance, but Saul is portrayed as a wicked man. As I have also noted,

Judas was probably used by the Spirit to perform miracles. Yet the Scriptures tell us that he was not in the kingdom.

Paul tells us in his famous chapter on love that people can speak in tongues, prophesy, have religious knowledge and faith to move mountains, and yet be nothing because they are without love. We know from elsewhere in Paul's writings that these people are not of Christ and therefore do not have the indwelling Spirit (Rom 8:9). Yet they have been used by the Spirit! We also know from the author of Hebrews that it is possible to "share in the Holy Spirit" and taste the goodness of the Word of God but not have the indwelling Spirit that saves (Heb 6:4-6). It is evident, then, that what matters eternally is that we have the permanent presence of the Spirit, not just his gifts.

If the work of the Spirit is this ambiguous, how can we tell the difference between his "saving" work in true saints and his "common" work with the unregenerate? Here again Edwards is helpful. He suggests two points of difference.

A New Principle and Nature

The first point of difference is that the indwelling Spirit produces a new principle of life, or a new nature, in the saint. It only stands to reason that people who have received the very Spirit of God within themselves will have a new principle or nature animating their being. This is just what Scripture describes as happening to the believer. The believer is said to be "God's temple" (1 Cor 3:16), "the temple of the living God" (2 Cor 6:16), in whom abides the "Spirit of truth" (Jn 14:17). This Spirit within is a "spring of water gushing up to eternal life" (Jn 4:14). Paul writes as if the Spirit of Christ now dominates his being: "It is no longer I who live, but it is Christ who lives in me" (Gal 2:20). The result is a new creation. "Everything old has passed away; see, everything has become new!" (2 Cor 5:17).

The life of St. Augustine provides powerful testimony to the new nature that the indwelling Spirit imparts. Before his conversion Augustine was tormented by sexual lust. He knew that the Christian faith was true but couldn't muster the strength to tear himself away from the pleasures of the flesh. But then the power of the indwelling Spirit supernaturally enabled him to make the change.

What I once feared to lose was now a delight to dismiss. You [God] turned them out and entered to take their place, pleasanter than any pleasure but not to flesh and blood, brighter than all light yet more inward than any secret recess, higher than any honour but not to those who think themselves sublime. Already my mind was free of "the biting cares" of place seeking, of desire for gain, of wallowing in self-indulgence, of scratching the itch of lust. And I was now talking with you, Lord my God, my radiance, my wealth, and my salvation.[1]

In his magnificent *Confessions*, a classic of Christian literature, Augustine explains that he continued to be plagued with lust and pride after his conversion. But the power of those temptations was broken. The power of the Spirit ended his slavery to those vices.

Another way to understand the difference between having this new principle and simply being influenced by the Spirit is to think about the difference between a planet and a star. An unregenerate person, whom Paul calls a "natural man," is like a planet that reflects the light of the sun but does not have light of its own. If the sun does not shine on it, the planet is dark, because light is not part of its nature. But a star is light by nature. It generates light. So too, the regenerate produce light and life because they have a light generator within them—the indwelling Holy Spirit. One could say that the Holy Spirit works from *within* a true Christian, but the Spirit acts on a non-Christian from the *outside*.

The Spirit Communicates Holiness to the Christian

A second distinction that Edwards points out between the saving and common works of the Spirit has to do with holiness. Because the peculiar characteristic of the Spirit is holiness (hence *Holy* Spirit), the person inhabited by the Spirit will gradually become holy. This is the chief reason that saints have a sweetness and beauty about them—their inner nature is (gradually) being transformed by a principle of holiness. But in the common work of the Spirit, whereby the Spirit influences or uses an unregenerate person for only a time, there is no communication of holiness.

The authors of Scripture made it abundantly clear that the indwelling Spirit conveys his holiness to the believer. Peter wrote that believers are "participants of the divine nature" (2 Pet 1:4). According to the author of Hebrews, that means sharing in God's very holiness (Heb 12:10). As we will see in chapter nine, the essence of holiness is love. Sharing in God's holiness means that the saint receives and is filled by God's love. John wrote that "God lives in us, and his love is perfected in us. . . . God is love, and those who abide in love abide in God, and God abides in them" (1 Jn 4:12, 16). John's Gospel says that Christ's love dwells in the saints (Jn 17:26). Paul prayed that Christ's love would fill the saints in Ephesus (Eph 3:17).

Alice, a friend of mine, was a wild and rebellious teenager who got her kicks by breaking into suburban garages and stealing tires and beer. She was proud and hard, not a friendly person. When she was nineteen, she was saved through the Jesus People in Milwaukee. Over the years since then, by the power of the indwelling Spirit, she has become soft in heart and strong in spirit. Where she once sought to take, now she seeks to give. Friends and acquaintances sense a holy sweetness about her—which is the love of Christ that the indwelling Spirit has produced in her.

The Spirit may touch or influence the "natural man," but he never communicates his holy indwelling presence to the natural man on a permanent basis. Just as the Spirit "swept over the face of the waters" during creation without imparting his nature or presence to them (Gen 1:2), so too he touches unregenerate persons for a time and then moves on. Paul said that the unregenerate "do not receive the gifts of God's Spirit, for they are foolishness to them, and they are unable to understand them [the things of God] because they are spiritually discerned" (1 Cor 2:14).[2]

I remember when I was an unregenerate freshman in college. I concluded my study of Western civilization with the thought that since Christianity was so important to that civilization, I should read the New Testament. I got no further than the Gospel of Matthew. I read the entire Gospel, but only one verse seemed meaningful, and that was for a perversely self-centered reason. The verse was a quote from Jesus: "He who humbles himself will be exalted." At that point in my life I was very interested in being exalted, and this verse seemed to provide the key to future success. So I determined to "humble" myself with the purpose of being exalted.

In retrospect I realize that I didn't have the foggiest notion of true humility and that my attempt to humble myself was actually a form of pride. So I understood this verse no more than the rest of the Gospel—which made no sense to me at all. I could not understand because I did not have the indwelling Spirit. The things of God were foolishness to me because I had no spiritual discernment.

I was like the rest of unregenerate humanity, who, according to Scripture, have no true love or holiness (1 Cor 13), no true spiritual life or light. This is why conversion is described by the Bible as such a radical change—opening the eyes of the blind, raising the dead, being born again, creating anew. Nothing that is purely of nature is capable of such miraculous events. Only something *above* nature can produce such unearthly effects.

When I became a Christian at the end of my freshman year, I found things happening to me that seemed to come from a power outside me. Before Christ found me, I had a foul mouth. Swearing and cursing—even creating my own filthy expressions—came as easily as breathing. But a few weeks after my experience with Jesus I realized, to my surprise, that my mouth was no longer in the gutter. Without my even thinking about it, without any effort on my part, the crude language had disappeared. I was convinced that the source of the new power in my life was beyond mere nature (my natural abilities)—hence supernatural.

A New Spiritual Sense

So far we have focused on the source of true religious affections. I have said that they originate in a divine and supernatural work of the indwelling Holy Spirit. Now I want to look more closely at one result of this work: its effect on the perception of the saint. The indwelling Spirit gives the saint a new perception that makes all of life and experience look different.

Several years ago a young student of mine was converted by reading Paul's epistles. After class one day he stopped at my lectern with a gleam in his eyes. "Dr. McDermott, everything looks different now." When I asked him what he meant, he continued, "Since I've been reading Galatians, it's as if a light has gone on. Now nothing is the same. Everything I see looks different from what it looked like just a week ago. I can't describe it precisely, but it's as if I've got a new pair of glasses or a strip of colored paper in front of my eyes that makes everything take on a different color."

Edwards compared this new perception to getting a new (spiritual) sense. It makes human experience entirely different from anything that was experienced before. Take the taste of honey, Edwards suggested. A man who has never tasted honey can look at it and feel it and think that he has a pretty good idea of how it tastes. But once he actually tastes it, he realizes that there is an enormous difference between what he imagined and what he tasted. The difference in perception and taste between pre- and postconversion experience is even greater.

Because of this enormous difference in perception, an unregenerate person can never really get close to comprehending this new spiritual sense. It would be like a woman going into a flower garden at night to try to distinguish the different colors. She can feel the flowers and measure their sizes and even smell them. But she can no more distinguish their colors than a person born blind can imagine the beauty of a rainbow, or a person born deaf can conceive of a melody.

Regeneration (the theological term for the new birth or receiving the indwelling Spirit) is like the sun shining on the garden. Then the woman can see the colors of the flowers in all their splendor. The Scriptures compare this event to giving eyes to see, opening the eyes of those born blind and turning a person from the darkness to the light. Edwards said that this is the point at which faith is transformed from mere rational belief to a *sense* in the heart (the meaning here has an experiential implication—something akin to the five senses of sight, hearing, smell, taste and touch) of God's beauty and glory. Listen to him describe how his perception changed after his own experience of regeneration:

The appearance of every thing was altered; there seemed to be, as it were, a calm, sweet cast, or appearance of divine glory, in almost every thing. God's excellency, his wisdom, his purity and love, seemed to appear in every thing; in the sun, moon and stars; in the clouds and blue sky; in the grass, flowers, trees; in the water and all nature; which used greatly to fix my mind. I often used to sit and view the moon for a long time; and in the day, spent much time in viewing the clouds and sky, to behold the sweet glory of God in these things: in the meantime, singing forth, with a low voice, my contemplations of the Creator and Redeemer.[3]

I should add that this new sense or perception is not a new power of understanding. It uses the same reasoning faculty as before, but now it is inspired and empowered by a new principle. One's reason and vision operate on a new basis, from a new and different foundation. It may be easier to understand this by comparing it to the Spirit's common work in the unregenerate. In that work the Spirit improves or assists natural principles but does not give a new spiritual principle or basis for operation. For example, the Spirit assisted Balaam's natural mind and vision to see Israel's future but did not give Balaam a new principle or nature in his heart. The Spirit improved Bezalel and Oholiab's natural skills as craftsmen (Ex 31), but there is no indication that it imparted an entirely new spiritual principle within them that remained as a lasting habit. The Spirit will sometimes increase the courage of a soldier on the battlefield or the practical reasoning of a head of state. But that is very different from infusing a new spiritual habit that enables one to see all of life differently. In the former cases, the Spirit is strengthening or assisting natural abilities for a short time but not imparting a supernatural principle that will remain forever. In short, the Spirit acts *upon* the mind of a natural person but *in* the mind of the saint as an indwelling principle.

Practically speaking, this means that the loves of a natural person will differ in quality from the loves of a saint. The natural man may love his wife and children, but the saint's love for his family will be different. The first will love his family for personal and other earthly reasons. The saint will share these reasons but add others—his love for God and desire to advance God's glory.

Edwards compared the two kinds of love to the loves of two persons for a certain fruit. One person was born without the sense of taste, while the other very much enjoys that sense. The first person loves, let's say, the mango because of its beautiful coloring and elegant fragrance. The other person loves the mango because of its color and smell but primarily because of its fabulous taste (I'm describing myself here). Both of them love the mango, but their loves are different loves. Their loves are *qualitatively* different. It is not just that the second person loves the mango more than the first, but that this love is of a different kind from the first person's.

So too, the loves of a regenerate person are different in kind from the loves of the unregenerate. They both love their family, but the rationale and, yes, even the taste of their loves will be different.

Voices and Visions

It is easy to mistake the regeneration that I have been describing in this chapter for hearing a voice or seeing a vision. But these experiences alone do not guarantee regeneration. Nor are they anything like the new perception and sense that I have been describing.

As we know from the previous chapters, there are people who hear voices or see visions but are not regenerate. Some claim to have seen Christ hanging on the cross, blood running from his wounds. Others say they have seen Jesus with his arms outstretched toward them, ready to embrace them. Still others swear they have had visions of heaven, with Christ on his throne amidst shining crowds of saints and angels. Then there are those who testify that they have seen God smiling on them and have heard God speaking to their heart that they are among his beloved.

What many don't realize, however, is that all of these experiences are possible for the natural, unregenerate person without the indwelling Spirit. It is clear from Scripture that God sometimes speaks and gives visions to his saints. But psychiatrists tell us that physical and mental instability can cause people to hear voices and see visions. Some of us know from personal experience that a high fever or a period of emotional depression can open us up to these kinds of experiences.

The Bible refers to many unregenerate persons in ancient times who heard and saw such things. The people of Jesus' day saw Jesus hanging from the cross, but most of them never came to saving faith. The Israelites saw God's glory at Mount Sinai but died in the wilderness because of their stubborn hardness of heart. Balaam saw Jesus Christ as a star rising out of Judah, but the Daystar never rose in his heart (2 Pet 1:19). On the day of judgment many will see the glory of Christ but be unwilling to rejoice in that glory.

The Bible also indicates that history is full of false visions, inspired by either demonic power or human fancy. The false prophets in biblical times led people astray with their deceptive visions (Deut 13:1; 1 Kings 22:22; Is 28:7; Ezek 13:7; Zech 13:4), and Satan himself gave Jesus a vision of the kingdoms of the world in all their glory (Mt 4:8). None of these visions and voices impart true spiritual perception. No holiness is shared. There is no indwelling of the Holy Spirit.

Tragically, the entire spiritual experience of some people is limited to these voices or visions. They have built their assurance on the very shaky foundation of these sudden experiences. They are joyful not because the divine realities of Scripture are evidenced in their lives, but because of the sudden and explosive manner in which certain words or visions once came to them.

True spirituality is very different. It imparts a new vision, a new perspective on reality and a new taste. It gives the soul a joyful sense of God's goodness and holiness, an appreciation for his grace and gratitude for his faithfulness. Edwards's experience is a good illustration of this:

> The first instance, that I remember, of that sort of inward, sweet delight in God and divine things, that I have lived much in since, was on reading those words, 1 Tim. 1:17: *Now unto the King eternal, immortal, invisible, the only wise God, be honour and glory for ever and ever, Amen.* As I read the words, there came into my soul, and was as it were diffused through it, a sense of the glory of the Divine Being; a new sense, quite different from any thing I ever experienced before. Never any words of Scripture seemed to me as these words did. I thought with myself, how excellent a Being that was, and how happy I should be, if I might enjoy that God, and be rapt up to him in heaven, and be as it were swallowed up in him for ever! I kept saying, and as it were singing, over these words of scripture to myself; and went to pray to God that I might enjoy him, and prayed in a manner quite different from what I used to do; with a new sort of affection.[4]

Edwards's experience shows us the difference between the sudden and shallow experience of voices and visions, on the one hand, and true spirituality, on the other. True spirituality imparts a new perception of the world and particularly of God. The soul sees the beauty and holiness of God, and some of that holiness begins to be shared with the soul. It is especially manifested in a new love for God and others. In fact, it has been a nearly universal experience of saints that, as Paul put it, "hope does not disappoint us, because *God's love has been poured into our hearts through the Holy Spirit that has been given to us*" (Rom 5:5). Charles

Finney, the great American revivalist of the early nineteenth century, recalled, "Instead of feeling that I was sinning all the time, my heart was so full of love that it overflowed. My cup ran over with blessing and with love."[5] Nathan Cole, a carpenter and farmer from Connecticut who was born again after hearing George Whitefield preach in 1740, said that the experience melted his hatreds: "Now I had for some years a bitter prejudice against three scornfull men that had wronged me, but now all that was gone away Clear, and my Soul longed for them and loved them; there was nothing that was sinfull that could anywise abide the presence of God; And all the Air was love."[6]

In summary, then, the first reliable sign of true grace is the indwelling Spirit of God, who lives in the saint on a permanent basis. By a supernatural power the Spirit imparts to the saint a new nature that begins a gradual process of making that person holy. The Spirit also gives the saint a new spiritual sense that makes all of reality look and taste different.

8

· · · · ·

The Second
Reliable Sign
Attraction to God
& His Ways
for Their Own Sake

NATURE DOES EVERYTHING FOR ITS OWN GAIN
AND INTEREST. IT CAN DO NOTHING WITHOUT PAY.
[BUT GRACE] ASKS FOR NO REWARD
OTHER THAN GOD ALONE.
THOMAS À KEMPIS

JOB WAS THE RICHEST MAN IN THE EAST. HE WAS ALSO A RIGHTEOUS MAN.
In fact, God boasted to Satan one day that Job was the most righteous
man on earth. Satan replied cynically that Job was good only because
God bribed him. In other words, Job's spirituality was rooted in self-
interest: love for self rather than love for God. If God took away Job's
wealth and family, Satan charged, Job's spirituality would disintegrate:

> Does Job fear God for nothing? Have you not put a fence around
> him and his house and all that he has, on every side? You have
> blessed the work of his hands, and his possessions have increased in
> the land. But stretch out your hand now, and touch all that he has,
> and he will curse you to your face. (Job 1:9-11)

Amazingly, God took up Satan's challenge. He agreed to let Satan take away all that Job had, in the hope of proving that Job's faith was *not* based simply on self-interest. Notice the intriguing implication: God conceded Satan's assumption that spirituality based only on self-interest is worthless. This is why God allowed Job to be put to the test. God knew that Job's faith was rooted in more than just self-interest and allowed Satan to attack him in order to prove that point. As the story shows, Job argued with God and at times was angry with God, but he never gave up on God. Job never cursed God, as Satan had predicted and his wife had suggested (Job 2:9). Job's faith held, seemingly against his self-interest.

The Love of Pagans
The point here is not the outcome of Job's faith but the suggestion (clearly made by the author of Job) that true spirituality is not rooted in self-interest. Jesus made a similar point when he commented on the nature of pagans' love:

If you love those who love you, what credit is that to you? For even sinners love those who love them. (Lk 6:32)

For if you love those who love you, what reward do you have? Do not even the tax collectors do the same? (Mt 5:46)

Jesus' point is that love based on self-interest does not qualify as true spiritual affection. Love based on self-interest is very common in the world, something that even the most notorious sinners are capable of. Edwards suggested that corrupt judges who return favors for a bribe and pet dogs who show love for their kind masters display the same sort of love. This is "natural" love, or love of this world, which requires nothing supernatural to inspire it.

Saul showed this kind of loving gratitude to David after David spared his life. Yet Saul continued his murderous quest to hunt David down. Naaman the Syrian showed the same sort of loving gratitude to the God of the Hebrews after this God healed him of leprosy. Naaman worshiped God only as long as it didn't interfere with his worldly interests. Nebuchadnezzar was grateful to God for restoring him to sanity after a period of madness and living as an animal in the wilderness. But Nebuchadnezzar showed no other signs of truly submitting his heart to the Lord of the universe. All of these biblical characters illustrate the same pattern—a love rooted in self-interest that falls far short of truly spiritual affection.

The Saint's Love for God

The love of saints is different. Their love for God is grounded not primarily in self-interest but in the beauty and excellence of God and his glories. That is, the *primary* reason they love God is the shining magnificence, beauty and glories of God, not how God will benefit them. They are attracted to God's Son, God's works and God's ways, particularly God's plan of salvation for sinful human beings.

Several years ago I was doing research at the Beinecke Rare Book and Manuscript Library at Yale University. On my first Saturday there I decided to visit Yale's art museum because the Beinecke was closed that day. I'll never forget the wonder and rapture I experienced. The museum was exhibiting seventeenth- and eighteenth-century Baroque paintings from Holland, Italy and Spain. These paintings were of the holy family (Mary, Joseph and the baby Jesus) and saints of the early church. Many of them were examples of chiaroscuro, the artistic technique that creates a radiance of light on the canvas for dramatic effect. I found several of the paintings so captivating that I lost track of where and who I was. That is, I stood in front of them so enthralled by their brilliance and so enamored by their details that I was completely caught up in their little worlds. I lost all sense of myself.

In a similar way, true saints are caught up in the beauty, glory and goodness of God. They are drawn to God by the radiance of his magnificence as he is in himself and in his works for humanity, completely apart from how God will serve their interests. They have lost track of themselves, as I lost sense of myself in that art museum at Yale. Listen to what happened to Sarah Edwards, Jonathan's wife:

> [She experienced] a very frequent dwelling, for some considerable time together, in such views of the glory of the divine perfections, and Christ's excellencies, *that the soul in the meantime has been as it were perfectly overwhelmed, and swallowed up with light and love and a sweet solace, rest and joy of soul, that was altogether unspeakable;* and more than once continuing for five or six hours together, without any interruption, in that clear and lively view or sense of the infinite beauty and amiableness of Christ's person, and the heavenly sweetness of his excellent and transcendent love; so that (to use the person's own

expressions) the soul remained in a kind of heavenly Elysium [a mythological term for a state of perfect happiness], and did as it were swim in the rays of Christ's love, coming down from Christ's heart in heaven, as a constant stream of sweet light, at the same time the soul all flowing out in love to him; so that there seemed to be a constant flowing and reflowing from heart to heart.[1]

Enjoying the Benefits

This description of Sarah Edwards's experiences with God may appear to contradict my point. I have been trying to argue that true spirituality is rooted primarily in an attraction to God and his works in and of themselves and not because of the benefits he brings. Sarah was filled with joy and even ecstasy by her experiences with God. Wasn't her faith therefore based on self-interest?

I don't think so. Sarah was drawn first and primarily by "the glory of the divine perfections, and Christ's excellencies." It was only after she had been dazzled by those excellencies and had committed herself to serving the God who was so excellent that she experienced the bliss that comes from experiencing God. *So benefits come to saints from God, but only after and as a fruit of their first being drawn to God by a vision and taste of God and his ways as they are in and of themselves.*

Lovers are drawn to each other in a similar fashion. They are attracted to each other not because of the benefits that they expect from a relationship but because of something they see in the beloved. Benefits then follow, but they are not the primary reason the relationship was formed in the first place.

So too for true spirituality. Self-interest is not excluded. After all, the psalmist cried, "I love the LORD, because he has heard my voice and my supplications" (Ps 116:1). But something else has prepared the way and laid the foundation for relationship with God. Saints are typically moved by God's goodness and free grace. The God to whom all the nations of the earth are like a drop in the bucket or the dust on a balance, who created and continues to sustain moment-to-pulsating-moment the farthest galaxies of space, who is so wise that he charges his angels with folly and so holy that the heavens are unclean in his sight—they are dumbfounded that this same God permitted himself on their behalf to be born in a cave, to be spat upon and mocked and then to be executed as a common criminal.

It is a vision of the glory and goodness of God, in other words, that is at the foundation of the saints' love for him. Saints may know that this God will bring them good, but this knowledge is not the primary reason why saints are drawn to him. That is, saints enjoy God and realize that their perfect happiness can be found only in God, as Sarah Edwards discovered. But they also know that their *primary* reason for loving God has to do with the magnificence of God and his ways rather than what God will do for them.

A Willingness to Suffer

True love for God means a willingness to suffer for God's glory. This willingness in particular shows that love is not rooted primarily in self-interest. Jonathan Edwards said of Sarah that she was willing "to suffer the hidings of God's face, and to live and die in darkness and horror if God's honor should require it, and to have no other reward for it but that God's name should be glorified, although so much of the sweetness of the light of God's countenance had been experienced."[2]

This is one of the differences between true and false spirituality. False spirituality will suffer only in its own interest, and only with a reward in view. But true saints will suffer even if there is no earthly reward in view, because their love for God is primarily rooted in their vision of God and his ways as they are in themselves, not because of the benefits God will give them.

Bill Fintel, my oncologist friend, tells me that the difference between true and false spirituality is often apparent on the cancer ward. There are patients who understand even in their worst moments that God's love is still real and present. And then there are those who seem to pursue God only for his benefits. For them it is impossible to find God unless things are going well. Bill assures me that in the valley of the shadow of death it isn't hard to recognize the difference between true grace and its imitations.

A Difference in Focus

This points up an important difference between saints and merely religious persons (people who have had a counterfeit conversion). The saints' focus is primarily on God, but merely religious people focus primarily on themselves and their spiritual experiences. C. S. Lewis suggests that this is one of Satan's designs. In *The Screwtape Letters* Screwtape tells Wormwood to try to get the man in his "care" to look at himself: "In all activities favourable to the Enemy [God] bend his mind back on itself."[3] Merely religious people, then, are obsessed with themselves and their own spiritual experiences.

I came to faith during the "Jesus Revolution" of the early seventies, when thousands of long-haired "Jesus freaks" experienced genuine conversion. The validity of their experience has been proven by their Christian testimony and lifestyle in the years since. Many of them are leaders in the church today. But I remember some in my first prayer group who seemed obsessed with hearing a personal word of prophecy for themselves (that would make them feel important) or giving one in order to show others that they were "spiritual." They were far more focused on their own spiritual experiences than on God. Not surprisingly, these same people departed from anything resembling a Christian life shortly thereafter. Thomas à Kempis could have been describing these people when he asked, "Do they, who are forever thinking of their own comfort and gain, not prove that they love themselves more than they love Christ?"[4]

Spirituality Based on Idolatry
The joy of the merely religious is a natural gratitude that is based on false views of God. In one of his marvelous insights, John Calvin said that the human mind is a factory of idols. That is, the human mind is forever imagining new ideas about God in order to serve its own interests. If we fall into sin, for example, our minds will naturally try to convince us that God really doesn't mind because everyone else is doing it. Or that God is a God of love and so would never condemn us. But Calvin's point is that these views of God, insofar as they are unbiblical, are really attempts to create new and different gods. These new and false gods are every bit as silly and destructive as the idols of the ancient Near East which the biblical prophets condemned.

And this, Calvin implies, is what the merely religious do. They have concocted in their minds a God who loves them and thinks they are very special people. This is not necessarily untrue. But then they tell themselves that this God is not angry with them for their sins. Quite the contrary, they think. God is delighted and honored to have them in his kingdom. After all, they can make great contributions to his kingdom. They have not repented, as some Christians have insisted they do, but God would never send them to hell because they have done so many nice things for people. And more important, they have had some spiritual experiences. They have even been active in their churches. Because of all this virtuous behavior, God must be delighted with them.

Unfortunately for them, however, this is not the God of Jesus Christ but a god of their own imagination—an idol. Why can't they see this? Why are they so convinced of their virtue, despite the absence of real holiness in their lives? Previous chapters have given some answers to this question. But for the sake of illustrating this chapter's central points, we need to look at the foundation of their false assurance: their spiritual experiences.

A Familiar Pattern

Typically such people have seen a vision or heard a voice which they take to be from God and to be proof of his love for them. So they get excited. Their excitement produces intense religious feelings. They think God must be pleased with these religious feelings. This makes them even more excited, which in turn produces even more intense religious feeling. The feelings get stronger, and there is great religious emotion. But it is all a castle built in the air. Its foundation is only self-love and pride. John of the Cross said of these people that they serve God for the reward of pleasure. When their service is no longer pleasurable, they give up because they are more devoted to their own will than to God's.[5]

Lives That Show the Difference

Tim was a member of a Christian community I lived in for seven years. He was outgoing and friendly, an active member of the community. But it was never clear where Tim's heart was. He was excited and on fire when things were going well, but he became depressed and listless when things didn't go his way. When God seemed to manifest his presence to him, Tim was all smiles. "Cool, man!" he'd proclaim to anyone listening. After they married, Tim and his young wife left the community for a job in the Southwest. The last I heard, he was spending many long nights barhopping and seeing other women. Evidently Tim had been focused not on God but on spiritual feelings and what they could do for him.

Mike, on the other hand, is a different story. His father died when he was a boy. By the time he was a junior in high school, he had concluded that life was absurd and begun to experiment with drugs. But then he had a dramatic conversion experience in which he was awestruck by the beauty and love of Christ. Since then he has weathered many trials, including prolonged unemployment, misunderstanding by his family and opposition from professors who did not appreciate his evangelical faith. Now he is a determined and principled Christian professor who teaches graduate school. He has been able to persevere because his heart is fired by a love for God that reigns first and foremost in his life, despite the negative circumstances that came his way.

Mike is an example of a true saint who loves God because of who God is in himself—in all his beauty and glory. If Mike had been motivated primarily by self-interest, he would have given up his faith long ago. Of course, this is particularly true of Christians in countries where faith is persecuted. Millions of Christians in Eastern Europe and China in this century have suffered terribly for their faith. Their faith has survived, and indeed prospered, only because they are drawn by a vision of God's grandeur, not primarily by what God will do for them.

An Objection

It might be objected that the thesis of this chapter—that true spirituality is motivated more by the majesty of God's nature and ways and less by God's benefits to the self—is contradicted by 1 John 4:19: "We love because he first loved us." But this objection ignores the context of that verse. Earlier in the passage John makes it clear that our love is only an outgrowth of God's prior love for us; so our love will come only by first focusing on God's magnificent love: "God's love was revealed among us in this way: God sent his only Son into the world so that we might live through him. In this is love, not that we loved God but that he loved us and sent his Son to be the atoning sacrifice for our sins" (1 Jn 4:9-10).

John means that realizing God's love for us as particular persons causes us to be overwhelmed by God's incredible love for sinful humanity. Our later love for God arises primarily from being attracted to the beauty and greatness of God himself. Listen to Edwards describe this:

> True saints have their minds, in the first place, inexpressibly pleased and delighted with the sweet ideas of the glorious and amiable nature of the things of God. And this is the spring of all their delights, and the cream of all their pleasures; 'tis the joy of their joy. This sweet and ravishing entertainment [that] they have in the view of the beautiful and delightful nature of divine things, is the foundation of the joy that they have afterwards.[6]

In this chapter we have seen that true spirituality loves God because of who he is and what he does. In the next chapter we will look at what it is in God that the true saint sees and embraces.

9

. . . . .

The Third
Reliable Sign
*Seeing the Beauty
of Holiness*

*GOD HAS APPEARED TO ME
A GLORIOUS AND LOVELY BEING,
CHIEFLY ON ACCOUNT OF HIS HOLINESS.*
JONATHAN EDWARDS

D AVID KORESH WAS ONE OF THE GREATEST MYSTERIES TO APPEAR ON the American scene in the 1990s. Who would ever have guessed that a scruffy, dyslexic ninth-grade dropout who butchered the English language could earn the trust of scores of educated adults? Or that they would follow to the death a man who abused their children, slept with their wives and raped his own disciples?

Marc Breault was Koresh's right-hand man until he defected in 1989. He offers a number of explanations for this mystery.[1] First, he says, most of the Branch Davidians came from abusive homes and were looking for a better life. So they were people who would tolerate a level of emotional and physical violence that most of us would not because they believed that the situation offered the promise of a better future. Second, they were convinced that David Koresh had a pipeline to God, so whatever he said had divine sanction. If something he said didn't make sense, they believed it was because God's ways are not our ways, and Koresh was closer to God.

Third, although Koresh's followers believed in the Bible, they didn't know it very well. Koresh, on the other hand, could recite Bible passages from memory for hours on end. They were impressed by his command of Scripture and by his absolute certainty that he alone knew how to interpret it. So when he told them that he was the personal embodiment of Jesus, and that anyone who resisted his claim was going to hell, they were too frightened to resist.

"If you don't follow the truth [that Koresh is the Messiah]," he screamed at them, "you're going to Hell! Psalms 90! You'd better start fearing God, 'cause he's going to burn you in the lowest Hell. . . . Listen to the Lord! You don't know his fear now! You don't know his terror yet! You haven't seen His anger! But you go ahead and dare Him!"[2]

Why Koresh Knew So Much and Yet So Little

Koresh used threats like these to instill fear and guilt in his disciples. If they didn't follow his every command (which could be as trivial as not to eat hot dogs), they risked eternal damnation. He warned them of Korah, who disobeyed Moses and was swallowed alive, and of Elijah, who called down fire from heaven on one hundred men who mocked him.

Perhaps his most terrifying accusations were the insinuations that even his most loyal followers were on the verge of hell—implying that unless they had done miracles, they did not have the Holy Spirit (there is no biblical basis for this absurd claim):

Are you really a Christian? Do you have the fruits of the Spirit? The apostles of old used to heal the sick and raise the dead. They were Spirit-filled men. What about you? Do you do these things today? How can these stupid churches talk about the gifts of the Spirit when they don't even do what the apostles did 2000 years ago? How dare you, or anyone, claim to be led of the Spirit! . . . Nobody is perfect like Christ said to be perfect. So they sin against the Holy Spirit. They commit the unpardonable sin because they claim to be led by the Spirit, when they are actually led by the devil.[3]

David Koresh apparently knew something of God's power. And perhaps, in his own perverted way, he knew something about God's justice. But he knew nothing of God's true holiness and certainly nothing of what the King James Version of the Bible calls the "beauty of holiness" (Ps 29:2; 96:9). In a negative way, Koresh illustrates the main point of this chapter: the unregenerate can know something of God's power and justice, but they do not see what only the regenerate can see—the beauty of God's holiness.

Holy affections come from a vision of the moral beauty of God and his ways. They come from loving God for the beauty and sweetness of his moral greatness. I will explain this by first telling the stories of several people who were drawn to God by the beauty of his holiness. Then I will try to describe in more detail what all of this means.

The "Incomparable Beauty"

Lin Yutang (1895-1976) was born in China to Christian parents and educated in Christian schools. Shortly thereafter, however, he renounced his Christian faith and became an ardent disciple of Confucius. He studied at Harvard and at German universities, taught English at Beijing National University and served as a leader of UNESCO. In 1937 he published *The Importance of Living*, which became a runaway bestseller. In this book Lin explained, among other things, "why I am a pagan." He rejected Christian theology, he wrote, because of its "presumptuous arrogance" that it could know and define God. Confucius, on the other hand, showed how reason and human power are better used to improve the lot of humankind. In the next several decades Lin became a symbol of the sophisticated, cosmopolitan Asian scholar.

Lin spent his last decade in New York City. One Sunday his wife persuaded him to accompany her to the Madison Avenue Presbyterian Church. Lin agreed to go, perhaps because he had begun to lose confidence in Confucianism. Confucius and his disciple Mencius had enormous faith in the goodness of human nature. But the holocausts of the twentieth century convinced Yutang that there was something fundamentally wrong with human nature. The other religions of China didn't seem much better. Buddhism turned its back on earthly existence as simply an illusion, and Taoism's rejection of modernity seemed impractical.

That Sunday morning Lin was confronted by, in his words, "the incomparable beauty and soul-changing power of the teachings of Christ." Overwhelmed by the moral beauty of Jesus and his teachings, Lin gave his mind and heart to Christ. Here is a part of his description of that experience:

God, as Jesus revealed him, is so different from what men thought him to be. There is a totally new order of love and compassion in Jesus' prayer from the cross, "Father, forgive them; for they know not what they do." That voice, unknown in history before, reveals God as forgiving, not in theory, but visibly forgiving as revealed in Christ. No other teacher said with such meaning, "Inasmuch as ye have done it unto one of the least of these my brethren, ye have done it unto me." The "me" in this context is God sitting on the Day of Judgment with a first concern for the downtrodden poor, the humble widow, the crippled orphan. There, I said to myself, Jesus speaks as the Teacher who is Master over both life and death. In him, this message of love and gentleness and compassion becomes incarnate. That, I saw, is why men have turned to him, not merely in respect but in adoration. That is why the light which blinded St. Paul on the road to Damascus with such a sudden impact continues to shine unobscured and unobscurably through the centuries.[4]

A Lovely Friend
Sojourner Truth (1797?-1883) is another believer who was drawn to God by the beauty of the holiness of Jesus. Born a slave in New York, she was the property of a wealthy Dutch landowner until her emancipation in 1827. Then she traveled America as a powerful preacher for Christ and against slavery. In her autobiography she wrote that when she first drew near to God, a sense of her own sinfulness kept her at a distance. She felt that she needed someone to stand between her and God and plead on her behalf. Suddenly, she said, she saw "a friend" standing between her and God.

"Who are you?" the woman asked.

The figure then "brightened into a form distinct, *beaming with the beauty of holiness,* and radiant with love." She strained body and soul to see who it was. An answer came, "saying distinctly, 'It is Jesus.' "

Until this time, Sojourner explained, she had thought of Jesus as simply an eminent man, like Washington or Lafayette. But now it was different. He appeared to be "so mild, so good, and so every way lovely." She was overjoyed that God was not an avenging judge and that her friend was Jesus, who was "altogether lovely." Now that she could see the beauty of Jesus' holiness, all the world looked different. "The world was clad in new beauty, the very air sparkled as with diamonds, and was redolent of heaven."[5]

Marie of the Incarnation (b. 1599), the first French woman missionary to the New World, was also stirred by the beauty of Jesus' holiness. Her letters back to France reveal that she was enraptured by the person of Christ, especially his moral beauty. In 1647, for example, she shared with her son one of the prayers she had written to Jesus: "You are the most beautiful of all the children of man, O my Beloved! You are beautiful, my dear love, in both your divine and human beauty."[6]

Not Just the Superstars

Not just the superstars of the faith have been drawn to God by the beauty of his holiness. Lin Yutang, Sojourner Truth and Marie of the Incarnation are merely illustrations of an experience common to true saints: they were attracted and continue to be drawn by the moral beauty of God in Christ. Their holy affections arose primarily from a vision of and love for the beauty of God's holiness.

Harold Payne, the ex-con whose story was told at the beginning of chapter seven, is an ordinary saint who was drawn to Christ because of his beauty. The beauty of Christ's love won Harold's heart. After twenty years of "doing things my way" Harold was dumbfounded to discover that Jesus was willing to wipe his slate clean. "I couldn't believe it that this Jesus, who had suffered so horribly for me, was also willing to forgive me in an instant for all those years when I was stubborn and hardhearted," Harold told me. "All I can say is that he is a God so beautiful that I can never praise him enough."

Let's try to understand what this moral beauty means. We are *not* talking about mere outward behavior. Through the ages many have led lives that were outwardly moral but, like the Pharisees, have not known the inward sanctifying power of the Holy Spirit. It is one thing to follow the letter of the law, but quite another to love God for the beauty of his moral excellence.

Moral Goodness Versus Natural Goodness

To fully understand the beauty of holiness, which is God's moral goodness, we must see the difference between moral and natural goodness. Moral goodness encompasses character traits that have moral significance, such as telling the truth and remaining faithful to your spouse. Natural goodness, on the other hand, is not related to morality. Pleasure, strength and knowledge, for example, are all natural goods. It is easy to see that they are not moral goods. Knowledge of how to build a house is neither moral nor immoral. It is amoral; that is, it has nothing to do with morals (unless, of course, one purposely builds the house in such a way that it collapses after the owners move in!). We consider it "good" that a person knows how to build a house, but that knowledge does not make him a morally good person.

Just as natural goodness is distinguished from moral goodness in human beings, theologians distinguish between the moral and natural perfections of God. God's "natural perfections" are attributes that, when considered by themselves, have no moral significance: omnipotence, omniscience, omnipresence and eternity. These perfections represent various kinds of power (the power to do all things, know all things, be everywhere and be outside of time). Until they are used in specific ways, they have no moral significance. God's moral perfections, on the other hand, are moral in and of themselves. By their very definition they involve moral considerations. I refer here to God's righteousness, truthfulness, goodness, kindness, mercy, longsuffering, compassion, justice and faithfulness. Each attribute points to a moral quality: righteousness means adherence to what is morally right, truthfulness is refusal to tell a lie, goodness is the determination to do what is morally right and loving, and so on.

I have distinguished natural from moral goodness because God's holiness has to do with the latter, not the former. In short, holiness is moral goodness. The beauty of God's holiness is the splendor and excellence of his moral character. So when we talk about holiness, we are not talking about power or infinite greatness. Neither are we talking about a goodness that is only external or a matter of appearance. We refer instead to an intrinsic moral goodness. In God it is *absolute* moral perfection, the shining radiance of perfect love. It is moral goodness that is absolutely perfect, shining with absolute purity. God *never* acts in any way that is inconsistent with perfect love and justice. He *always* does the right thing, the loving thing, the just thing—even when it brings him infinite pain, as we saw on Calvary. This is the beauty of God's holiness.

A Cut Above—Infinitely So

So far we have only scratched the surface of what the beauty of holiness means. To dig a little deeper, we need to look at the word *holy*. Its root goes back to a Hebrew word meaning "to cut or separate." It refers to things that are "a cut above" or "a cut apart" from the ordinary. Because this holiness is *God's,* and God is infinite, these things are *infinitely* above or separate from everything else. As Søren Kierkegaard expressed it, there is "an infinite qualitative difference" between God and everything human. In Rudolf Otto's words, God is "Wholly Other."

God's moral goodness, then, is infinitely superior to any moral goodness we can imagine. It is an infinite purity that is absolutely distinct from all creaturely purity, infinitely exalted above human goodness. Drawing on biblical metaphors, Calvin said that our goodness is so pathetic in comparison to God's that we are rottenness itself (Job 13:28), worms and dirt (Job 7:5; Ps 22:6). Because of God's infinite purity the cherubim must veil their faces in fear (Is 6:2), the sun has to blush, and the moon is confounded (Is 24:23).[7]

The beauty of God's holiness is particularly demonstrated in his love. Unlike human compassion, God's compassion never fails (Lam 3:22). The infinitely intelligent Being who created galaxies and sustains them moment by moment allows himself to hurt when we hurt (Is 63:9). This is the spectacular love in the heavens that reduces the angels to a reverent awe.

Edwards saw the beauty of God's holiness most clearly in Jesus Christ, especially in the ways that Jesus combines divine infinity with care for finite humanity. For instance, Jesus combines infinite greatness with infinite care. He has perfect wisdom, infinite power, infinite terrifying majesty and infinite knowledge, yet he graciously stoops to love unworthy sinful human beings. He goes even further, to become their friend and companion—and further still, to expose himself to their contempt and spitting!

Second, Jesus combines infinite justice and infinite mercy. He hates sin and yet forgives the greatest of sinners. And he did the latter by suffering a shameful and horrifyingly painful death.

Finally, he combines infinite majesty with unparalleled meekness. Think of it! Scripture says that he is the one at whose presence the earth quakes and hills melt, before whom all the inhabitants of the earth are less than grasshoppers, who rebukes the seas and makes them dry, whose eyes are as a flame of fire. Yet he is meek and lowly of heart. He is strong enough to be meek. When insulted, he did not respond in kind. He forgave those who tortured and murdered him. With meekness he stood in a circle of soldiers who mocked and beat him. Silent, he opened not his mouth but went as a lamb to the slaughter.[8] This is the holiness that dazzles the saints with its beauty and creates in their hearts a holy love for God.

What Makes Divine Things Beautiful

During my years of teaching college students, I have found that students who do not have a living faith usually have a false view of what motivates Christians. They typically think that Christians do what they do (go to church, read the Bible and pray, do good deeds) because they are trying to earn a place in heaven. Generally they (particularly those who have never known a joyous Christian) have no idea that true saints do what they do because they are drawn by love. True Christians find that the love of God in Christ is so attractive, so beautiful, that they cannot help *wanting* to serve him. There is a splendor, a beauty, about God and his ways that *lures* human beings to him.

The Bible says that this splendor is found principally in God's holiness. In other words, it is the excellence of God's moral character— the infinitely pure, self-giving love so vividly seen in Jesus—that makes him beautiful and elicits the worship of his creatures. It was God's holiness that overwhelmed the seraphim in Isaiah 6: "And one called to another and said: 'Holy, holy, holy is the LORD of hosts; the whole earth is full of his glory' " (v. 3).

The four living creatures in John's vision (Rev 4) worshiped God for the same reason. Day and night they sang before God's throne, entranced by the beauty of God's holiness: "Holy, holy, holy, the Lord God the Almighty, who was and is and is to come" (v. 8). John also saw the martyrs who conquered the beast standing beside the sea of glass mixed with fire (Rev 15). With harps of God in their hands, they sang the song of Moses. More than anything else, they were struck by the holiness of God: "Lord, who will not fear and glorify your name? For you alone are holy" (v. 4). Centuries before, Hannah had been bedazzled by the same. "There is no Holy One like the LORD," she prayed, "no one beside you; there is no Rock like our God" (1 Sam 2:2).

The Bible indicates that what first and foremost impressed the New Testament saints about Jesus was his holiness. They called him the "Holy and Righteous One" (Acts 3:14), "your holy servant Jesus" (Acts 4:27) and "the holy one, the true one" (Rev 3:7). Its holiness is what makes God's word so precious. The psalmist writes, in lyrical language that exudes awe and reverence:

The law of the LORD is perfect,
    reviving the soul;
the decrees of the LORD are sure,
    making wise the simple;
the precepts of the LORD are right,
    rejoicing the heart;
the commandment of the LORD is clear,
    enlightening the eyes;
the fear of the LORD is pure,
    enduring forever;
the ordinances of the LORD are true
    and righteous altogether.
More to be desired are they than gold,
    even much fine gold;
sweeter also than honey,
    and drippings of the honeycomb. (Ps 19:7-10)

The same can be said for heaven: it is beautiful and wonderful because it is a place of holiness. Isaiah refers to it as God's "holy and glorious habitation" (Is 63:15). In John's Revelation heaven's holiness is its beauty, represented by precious stones and light: "It has the glory of God and a radiance like a very rare jewel, like jasper, clear as crystal. . . . Each of the gates is a single pearl, and the street of the city is pure gold, transparent as glass. . . . The river of the water of life [is as] bright as crystal, flowing from the throne of God and of the Lamb" (Rev 21:11, 21; 22:1).

The saints of Scripture frequently praise God because of his holiness. Listen to the psalmist, for example, in Psalm 99: "Let them praise your great and awesome name. Holy is he! . . . Extol the LORD our God; worship at his footstool. Holy is he! . . . Extol the LORD our God and worship at his holy mountain; for the LORD our God is holy" (Ps 99:3, 5, 9).

When we think of why we love the gospel, isn't it because (at least in part) of its holiness? Think of it! This is good news (the literal meaning of *gospel*) because by it a holy God joins an unholy people to himself at their regeneration, confers on them Jesus' own holiness so that in the Father's eyes they are holy, and then gradually makes them *actually* holy by the power of his *Holy* Spirit. This is mind-boggling, incredibly happy news!

The Beautiful People

Why do we think of saints as beautiful people? Isn't it because of their holiness? In *The Great Divorce,* C. S. Lewis's wonderfully suggestive description of heaven and hell, there is a woman in heaven who had not been known on earth for her physical beauty but who in heaven bore an "unbearable beauty" because of her holy love: "Few men looked on her without becoming, in a certain fashion, her lovers. But it was the kind of love that made them not less true, but truer, to their own wives."[9] The beauty of this woman's soul was so stunning that her physical appearance was nearly forgotten. In fact, the narrator of the story couldn't remember whether she was naked or clothed: "If she were naked, then it must have been the almost visible penumbra [shadow] of her courtesy and joy which produces in my memory the illusion of a great and shining train, that followed her across the happy grass."[10]

As I write this chapter, I am thinking of a dear friend who died just two days ago of complications related to his diabetes. Grady was one of the holiest men I have ever known. But he was no pious prude who worried, as H. L. Mencken scornfully put it, that someone somewhere might be having a good time. Grady loved to talk and laugh and eat and have fun. He was full of joy and love and faith. Though often in pain, he never complained but thought instead of the needs of others. He loved God, his church, his family and the lost, and worked with joy to serve them all. It shocks me that this young man of fifty-four, whose eyes and voice were so full of life and enthusiasm just three weeks ago, is now gone from this earth. And it hurts, because I miss him. But I can say—and everyone else who knew him would agree—that Grady shone with the beauty of holiness. Though no Tom Cruise, Grady was one of the most beautiful people I have ever known. Because the holiness of Jesus shone from his face and person, people were attracted to him and considered themselves blessed to have him for a friend.

What the Saints Sense and Taste

In chapter seven we saw that the saints have a new sense and taste. They perceive divine things that the unregenerate miss because they do not have this special sense and taste. What the saints perceive with their new sense is the beauty of holiness. This is the sweetness that their new taste enjoys. This is why the psalmist could say that the Word is "sweeter also than honey, and drippings of the honeycomb" (Ps 19:10). This is why Jesus could say after a long journey to Samaria (his starving disciples had gone to town to look for food) that he was satisfied without food: "I have food to eat that you do not know about. . . . My food is to do the will of him who sent me and to complete his work" (Jn 4:32, 34).

To the saint, the holiness of God and his works is beautiful. Contemplating it provides both food and enjoyment to the soul. For Edwards it was a source of spiritual ecstasy.

Holiness . . . appeared to me to be of a sweet, pleasant, charming, serene, calm nature; which brought an inexpressible purity, brightness, peacefulness and ravishment to the soul. . . . Once, as I rode out into the woods for my health, in 1737, having alighted from my horse in a retired place, as my manner commonly has been, to walk for divine contemplation and prayer, I had a view [something between a new understanding and a mental impression], that for me was extraordinary, of the glory of the Son of God, as Mediator between God and man, and his wonderful, great, full, pure and sweet grace and love, and meek and gentle condescension [compassion]. This grace that appeared so calm and sweet, appeared also great above the heavens. The person of Christ appeared ineffably excellent, with an excellency great enough to swallow up all thought and conception—which continued, as near as I can judge, about an hour; which kept me the greater part of the time, in a flood of tears, and weeping aloud.[11]

Don't Be Intimidated!

At this point a warning is needed. Don't be intimidated by the experiences of God's holiness described in this chapter. Don't think that the typical saint experiences them frequently. Even the great saints like Edwards had these passionate encounters only sporadically during their lives.

Don't think that your encounter must be emotional in order to be valid. Most perceptions of God's holiness are not emotional, but they do change one's view of God and life. Only rarely do they involve a mystical vision. Usually it is a seeing with the mind's eye or a new understanding that involves both mind and heart. *Typically, it is an understanding of what God's holiness means that cannot fail to move the heart.* The "seeing" may come only once a year or once a decade, but it leaves a residue of perception that changes one's view and taste of God in the following years.

Power to Change the Heart

In chapters three through five we saw that the unregenerate can have spiritual experiences in the absence of true spirituality. If I had to summarize in one statement what distinguishes true from false spirituality, it would be this: the unregenerate never see the beauty of holiness. They may see and have some understanding of God's holiness, but they never see that it is beautiful. They do not, indeed they *cannot,* love it. In theological terms, they never appreciate the aesthetic dimension of divine holiness.

For Edwards this, more than anything else, is what separates true from false spirituality. This is what prevents the unregenerate from ever producing on a permanent basis the fruit of the Spirit—love, joy, peace, patience, kindness, generosity, faithfulness, gentleness and self-control—which Paul said is the chief sign of the Spirit's indwelling a person (Gal 5:22-23). They cannot produce it, says Edwards, because only an appreciation of the beauty of God's holiness is powerful enough to change the heart. Only that vision (and here I don't mean a mystical vision but the kind of spiritual understanding I described above) can melt and humble the heart, weaning it away from attachment to this world and its values. This may help us understand some puzzling parts of the Bible. It helps explain, for example, why Paul wrote that "at the name of Jesus every knee [will] bend, in heaven and on earth and under the earth, and every tongue [will] confess that Jesus Christ is Lord, to the glory of God the Father" (Phil 2:10-11). If what I have been saying is correct, the demons and the damned on Judgment Day will acknowledge the natural perfections of God, but they will not love his moral perfections. They may recognize God's sovereignty and control by bending the knee, but like vanquished captives after a battle, they will not do so with any love for him in their hearts. They may see God's holiness, but they will not see its beauty. To recognize its beauty would be to love it. But instead they hate it.

10

· · · · ·

The Fourth
Reliable Sign
A New Knowing

*THIS IS ETERNAL LIFE,
THAT THEY MAY KNOW YOU,
THE ONLY TRUE GOD, AND JESUS CHRIST
WHOM YOU HAVE SENT.*

J E S U S

───────────

HOMER SHOWMAN IS A TALL YOUNG (THIRTY-FIVE-YEAR-OLD) IOWA farmer whose lifelong dream was to own the family farm. After graduating in agronomy from Iowa State University, he and his wife, Gail, worked as hired hands on several farms before they were able to take over the farm that Homer's family had worked for more than a century. It was a wonderful feeling to finally own the title to seven hundred acres. But Homer and Gail's joy turned to alarm when they discovered that inheritance taxes would plunge them into deep debt for many years.

It has never been easy to keep a small family farm in Iowa profitable, and the last decade has been more difficult than most. Low crop prices, drought and flooding plagued the Showmans from day one, bringing chronic financial insecurity.

But while Homer and Gail have battled dry skies, icy winds and unruly hogs, they've also experienced a spiritual revolution in their lives. When they first bought the farm, Homer was something of an atheist. He wasn't at all sure that God even existed. At a neighbor's funeral he told Gail he'd concluded that death is the end of everything. There was nothing to look forward to, he decided.

When I took over the pastorate of their little country church, the Spirit of God had started planting little seeds of faith in Homer's heart. He had begun to question his earlier atheism. There may be a God after all, he reasoned. It would be prudent to live a good life so that he would be admitted into heaven when he died.

Several months after I arrived, Homer came alive spiritually. The scales fell off his eyes. For the first time in his life, he realized that the living God is a God of grace. He saw that God saves human beings not because of the good lives they try to lead, but because of the perfect life his Son led. So salvation is a free gift that we don't deserve. It is by grace (the free, unmerited favor of God), not by good works. This new understanding set Homer free from doubt and fear.

Several years before, Homer had pulled his aunt's bleeding body from a car wreck. Since then Homer had lived in fear of death. He often woke up in the middle of the night gasping for breath, dripping with his own cold sweat. The thought of dying and meeting a God who judged human beings by their good works terrified Homer. He knew he wasn't ready for that kind of judgment.

When Homer realized that the true and living God is a God of grace, his fear of death disappeared. Homer was thrilled. When he stood up before the church at Easter to testify to his salvation and his newfound God of grace, Homer wept tears of joy.

A New Kind of Knowing

Homer is an illustration of the fourth reliable sign of true spirituality: true grace brings a new knowing. The mind is enlightened with new thoughts, or new light is shed on old thoughts. Holy affections are not heat without light. They always arise from new information—spiritual instruction that was previously unknown or is now seen in a new light. In Homer's case it was the knowledge that God saves by grace and not by good works. This revelation caused Homer to see God in an entirely new light. It showed God to be an entirely different God from the one

Homer had previously imagined. It was a seeing that enabled Homer to *know* God as his personal Savior.

The New Testament makes it clear that true spirituality involves a new knowing, a new understanding. There is a cognitive element in a work of grace. John proclaims that "everyone who loves... *knows* God" (1 Jn 4:7). Paul prays for the Philippians that "your love may overflow more and more with *knowledge* and full insight" (Phil 1:9). To the Colossians he speaks of the new self in Christ that "is being renewed in *knowledge*" (Col 3:10). We are told that the Jews who reject Christ are not enlightened (Rom 10:2), but true saints are taught by God and learn from the Father (Jn 6:45).

So there is a cognitive or intellectual dimension in a work of grace. Regeneration by the Holy Spirit involves the mind. The mind is given new thoughts that enable the heart to change. This only stands to reason: if regeneration is the radical change that the previous chapters have described, every part of the person must be affected—body, emotions, will and mind. When we meet God for salvation, not only do we feel and choose differently, but we see and know differently as well.

The Key That Opens the Heart

It has been said that "knowledge is the key that first opens the hard heart and enlarges the affections, and so opens the way for men into the kingdom of heaven."[1] It is a new vision or knowing of God and his ways that opens the heart to change. This new knowing can be compared to sunlight that shines on ice and causes it to melt. Saving knowledge of God is a supernatural light that shines on icy hearts and causes them to melt. When I was saved, it was knowledge of Jesus' patient love shown in his crucifixion that melted my heart and filled it with love for him. Without that knowledge—that image of Jesus from a scene in his life—I would not have known his love.

Perhaps this is why Jesus so sharply rebuked the lawyers: "Woe to you lawyers! For you have taken away the key of knowledge" (Lk 11:52). By withholding true knowledge of God from people, the lawyers prevented the transformation of their affections by the Spirit of God. For the Spirit works through knowledge. Therefore we have to say (and we know this from experience and biblical testimony) that intense religious affections without knowledge are not holy affections. When people claim to be saved but have no new understanding of God's nature and perfections, the beauty and virtues of Jesus, or the glorious grace of salvation, their claim is questionable.

I remember Jean, a young song leader in the first prayer group I joined after I became a Christian. Jean spoke in tongues, enjoyed the "Jesus jollies" and longed to hear the prophecies at the meetings. But if you asked her to describe God or Jesus or the way of salvation, her eyes would cloud over. She had no new knowledge of God to go with her spiritual experiences. I was not surprised to hear a year later that she had gone back to the ways of the world, and that she had been sleeping with a male song leader while serving our prayer group.

What This Knowing Is Not

It would be very easy to misunderstand or misinterpret what I am trying to say. One possible misunderstanding is that we come to know these new things by visions and voices. It is true that visions and voices often communicate new knowledge, but this is not the kind of knowing I am referring to. After all, most cults were started by people who (claim that they) saw visions and heard voices.

The Reverend Moon, for instance, traces his spiritual calling back to visions and voices he heard on a Korean mountainside when he was sixteen years old. Jesus appeared to him, Moon claims, and begged him to finish the work he (Jesus) had begun. Jesus explained that his work was not supposed to end with the cross, which (according to Moon) was a shameful, godless death. In later visions (involving Abraham, Moses, the Buddha and God himself) Moon learned that Jesus plays little or no role in our salvation but is merely an example for us to follow. Instead, we are to atone for our own sins by sacrificing (fasting and fundraising) for his movement.

New knowledge was imparted to Moon through these visions and voices, but it was false knowledge, not given by the living God. The knowledge that is given in orthodox Christian experience is not usually given through visions and voices. (I do not discount the possibility of Christians ever receiving a vision or hearing a voice, but this is very rare and is not the source of the supernatural knowledge I am describing.)

A more common misunderstanding is to think that Christian knowing is simply a matter of acquiring intellectual information or doctrine, like the knowledge that a circle is different from a square, or even that Jesus died for our sins. We have seen from the unreliable signs in chapters three through five that merely having this kind of knowledge does not mean that one has true grace. Even the devils in hell, James tells us, believe much true doctrine. And some theologians have true knowledge without knowing the living God.

A friend from grad school now writes articles and books on theology, but he's not sure if God exists. This man is a wonderful person, but there is no evidence that he possesses the indwelling Spirit. He knows many true principles of theology and what he should believe if he does become convinced that God exists. But until that day comes, if it ever does, his knowledge is sheerly speculative, not the supernatural seeing of which I speak.

Neither is this knowing an understanding of the mystical meaning of Scripture. Beginning with Origen, the first great theologian (c. 185-254), there developed in the church an elaborate science that assumed that much of Scripture is allegorical. Medieval practitioners of this science taught that the true meaning of many passages is hidden, revealed only to the devout or to faithful students of this science. For instance, this tradition held that the story of Israel's leaving Egypt and seeking the Promised Land is really the story of the soul leaving the sensual world for the promised land of blessedness. The Song of Solomon is not an erotic love poem celebrating marital bliss, this tradition taught, but a portrait of the love between Christ and his bride, the church. Today's practitioners of this tradition often find contemporary political meaning in the book of Revelation. In its symbols they claim to see a blueprint for the end of the world.

I do not mean to disparage all of this tradition, for it seems incontestable that some of the meaning of Scripture lies beneath the surface (literal) meaning of its language. Yet the knowledge that comes with true grace is not knowledge of the hidden meaning of a passage in Scripture, but a knowledge of God and his ways that opens up a new way of seeing the world.

Finally, this knowing is not a revelation of a Bible verse for one's personal situation. Some Christians open up the Bible at random ("led by the Spirit," they say) and assume that whatever verse their finger rests on speaks directly to their situation, regardless of the verse's literary and historical context. You've probably heard of the person who, using this method, opened up to the following three verses: "Judas went out and hanged himself"; "Go thou and do likewise"; "Whatever you do, do it quickly." This is patently absurd, but an astonishing number of Christians use a similar method.

Perhaps it is not surprising that the cults do something very much like this; they typically impose on Bible passages meanings wholly unrelated to original context. Maria Frances Ackley was the wife of Charles Taze Russell, founder of the Jehovah's Witnesses. At the beginning of their marriage she told Witnesses that Russell was the faithful and wise servant whom his master had put in charge of his household (Mt 24:45). But when Russell requested a legal separation after eleven years of marriage (because she wielded too much influence in the organization and wanted to change his writings), she turned on him. Now, she told all who would listen, God had revealed to her that Russell was the wicked servant (Mt 24:48-49) who beat his fellow servants and was cut in pieces when the master returned.[2]

I think it is clear from biblical and church history that the Holy Spirit can make a biblical story or passage come alive for us in ways that illumine a personal situation. I don't want to say that God does not use Bible verses to speak to our hearts. He has done this in the past, and he continues to do so today. But if this is to be helpful and truly from the Lord, it does not ignore the context of the biblical passage. Let the examples in the preceding paragraph serve as a warning to be very careful about taking a verse out of its context when applying it to our lives. This practice has done much damage to the church.

I am not referring here to knowledge about personal situations at all. I am referring rather to light that opens up a new vision of God and his ways.

What This Knowing Is
The knowing that true grace brings is a spiritual and supernatural understanding of divine things. Because it is spiritual, those who don't have the Spirit cannot participate in this knowing. In Paul's words, "Those who are unspiritual do not receive the gifts of God's Spirit, for they are foolishness to them, and they are unable to understand them because they are spiritually discerned" (1 Cor 2:14).

How are we to understand a knowing that can be experienced by some but not by others? It may be helpful to compare this knowing of divine things to knowing artistic beauty. (Some of what follows repeats the emphases of the last chapter, but there is an important reason for this. I want to show that this new knowing is not only cognitive in nature but aesthetic as well. That is, the regenerate get not just new facts but a new way of seeing.)

Beauty can be known only by those who enjoy it. When I was a high-school student, an aesthetically inclined teacher took me to the Whitney Museum of Modern Art in New York City. While he gazed with love and delight at one painting after another, I impatiently looked at my watch, wondering how long I was going to have to suffer through this boring ordeal. I saw the same paintings my teacher saw, but I did not see their beauty. I could not "see" because my heart and my mind didn't have the aesthetic capacity to enjoy the art.

Knowledge of the beauty of divine things is remarkably similar. People without the Spirit don't see the glory of God and Christ because they are not *able* to. Their eyes have not been opened to divine beauty, so they cannot enjoy it, much less see it. The beauty of divine things can be seen only by those who enjoy it, just as the beauty of art can be seen only by those who have the capacity to enjoy it.

A Seeing
The Scriptures often describe the knowing of the regenerate as a kind of seeing. John writes, "No one who sins has either *seen* him or known him" (1 Jn 3:6), and "Whoever does evil has not *seen* God" (3 Jn 11). He says that "all who *see* the Son and believe in him have eternal life" (Jn 6:40). John also records Jesus' suggestive statement "I came into this world for judgment so that those who do not see may see" (Jn 9:39).

I remember that when I first came to a saving knowledge of Christ as a freshman in college, it was "seeing" Christ hanging crucified on the cross that stopped me dead in my tracks. Since I had been raised Catholic, I had seen crucifixes before and had even heard homilies on the love of God shown in the cross. But this knowledge had never been "quickened" to me; it had never become real for me. For some reason on that spring night in 1971, the mental image of Jesus hanging on the cross, offering his body for my salvation, blew me away. What had been simply an intellectual notion suddenly became new supernatural knowledge. I became convinced that this Jesus was real and true and was overwhelmed by his patient love for me. It amazed me that Jesus had not coerced me into submission but had waited patiently—and painfully—for me during the years when I was ignoring him. This was a knowledge that was also a seeing—but a new kind of seeing that made real what had previously been only a lifeless concept. Christ and his way of salvation became real and beautiful to me, and knowledge of this reality melted my heart.

According to the Scriptures, I was given *light* that showed me the glory of Christ. In the beautiful words of 2 Corinthians 4:6, "It is the God who said, 'Let light shine out of the darkness,' who has shone in our hearts to give the light of the knowledge of the glory of God in the face of Jesus Christ." It is this very light that unbelievers do not have; the absence of this light keeps them from seeing the living God. "And even if our gospel is veiled, it is veiled to those who are perishing. In their case the god of this world has blinded the minds of the unbelievers, *to keep them from seeing the light of the gospel of the glory of Christ*, who is the image of God" (2 Cor 4:3-4).

Gail Showman, Homer's wife, was converted when her husband was. She too received this light. For Gail the light revealed the holiness of God, which appeared beautiful and overwhelmingly glorious. In comparison her life and heart seemed filthy. "The more I saw of God," she told me, "the dirtier and dirtier I felt."

I told Gail that saints throughout the ages have had a similar experience. The closer they drew to the light of God's holiness, the more they saw of their own sinfulness. But for them, as for Gail, seeing their own filth did not discourage them. They knew that God had forgiven their sins through the cross and were grateful that they were able to enjoy the beauty of God's light.

An Experience

If supernatural knowledge of the things of God is a seeing, it is also an experience. The Scriptures represent it as a knowing that one can relish, taste and feel. To illustrate the difference between mere intellectual knowing and this experiential knowing, I will again use the mango illustration. Someone who has tasted a mango knows far more about it than someone who has just looked at it or felt it. Similarly, knowing God is experiential. Paul likens it to smelling an aroma: "But thanks be to God, who in Christ always leads us in triumphal procession, and through us spreads in every place the *fragrance* that comes from knowing him" (2 Cor 2:14). Peter and the psalmist compare it to tasting food: "Like newborn infants, long for the pure, spiritual milk, so that by it you may grow into salvation—if indeed you have *tasted* that the Lord is good" (1 Pet 2:2-3); "O *taste* and *see* that the LORD is good" (Ps 34:8). To know the beauty of Christ is to smell his aroma and to taste his love.

That knowing the living God is far more than just knowing things *about* him was made real to me by my friend Sandy shortly after my conversion. During church services she was often moved to tears of joy. When I asked her about the tears, she smiled. "He's just so good and so beautiful!" Sandy was experiencing deep feelings of joy and delight from knowing God. She was tasting the glory of God.

I don't mean to imply that faith is not genuine unless it is accompanied by feelings. After all, Paul warned us that "we walk by faith, not by sight" (2 Cor 5:7). Even the greatest saints in the history of the church found that most of the time God's presence is *not* made tangibly evident. Nevertheless, they have testified that knowing God is also, at times, enjoying God. True grace gives one knowledge of God that is experienced as well as received by faith.

The Content of This Knowledge

I have been talking throughout this chapter about the new knowing a saint has, which is a kind of seeing and tasting. But we have not yet focused on the *object* of this knowledge and vision. *What* does the saint see? *What* does the saint know that is new? Again, some of what follows repeats the theme of the previous chapter. But it is important to understand the intimate connection in true spirituality between the cognitive and the aesthetic—that what we come to know in the experience of grace is a *beauty* we have never seen before.

The answer is the glory or beauty of divine things. This is what sets the saint apart from all others. Others may also see divine things, but they don't see their beauty or glory. Just as I saw the paintings at the Whitney Museum but didn't see their beauty, the unregenerate may see or know divine things (some don't ever see divine things at all), but they never see their beauty—which, as I said in the last chapter, is the beauty of holiness. This is the glory that the Bible says makes God and his ways attractive and lures human beings to him in love. This is the light that makes the person of Jesus so ravishingly beautiful, that has drawn the hearts of millions to him for two millennia. This glory is what Gail Showman saw that made her feel dirty by comparison; it is the brightness that all saints see, in comparison to which their own hearts appear filthy.

But it is not just the beauty of God himself that the saint knows and sees. Once we have caught a glimpse of the beauty of the Godhead, everything else in life—all the world and all of existence—takes on a new color. Everywhere we look there is beauty.

When I came home from college one warm spring night, my brother met me at the door. John had been a cynical intellectual for years. But as soon as I opened the door and looked into his eyes, I knew something was different. There was a light in John's eyes that had never been there before. He had seen something that now *changed his vision of everything.* "Gerry, it's hard to explain," he told me, "but this changes everything. I can't see anything now the way I used to."

Over the next few weeks he told me of the new love he had experienced in Christ. Since that evening more than twenty years ago, his life has been transformed; his approach to life and the way the world looks to him have been changed by this new vision.

C. S. Lewis had a similar experience. During the months when he was being drawn to Christ, he read a book by George MacDonald that for the first time in his life gave him a glimpse of holiness. This glimpse made everything else in his world look different.

Up till now each visitation of Joy had left the common world momentarily a desert—"The first touch of the earth went nigh to kill." Even when real clouds or trees had been the material of the vision, they had been so only by reminding me of another world; and I did not like the return to ours. But now I saw the bright shadow [of holiness] coming out of the book into the real world and resting there, transforming all common things and yet itself unchanged. Or, more accurately, I saw the common things drawn into the bright shadow.[3]

Because saints have seen the beauty of God, they see a certain beauty or attractiveness in the ways and acts of God. The Word of God becomes sweet and at times even beautiful; the way of salvation through the life, death and resurrection of Christ appears incomparably wondrous; the evil of sin seems deeper and darker than ever imagined before conversion. The world of nature takes on a new beauty.

Last year I was challenged by one of Richard Foster's books to meditate on the creation. I chose a leaf from a tree in my front yard. I spent a full ten minutes studying the intricate design and delicate coloring of this leaf. What I had previously ignored appeared beautiful after I considered its intricate design against its simplicity of form. Considering the Mind that created the nearly infinite number of leaves like this one, and the obvious physical beauty of nature, filled me with awe. This wasn't a leaf formed like trillions of others by the random forces of nature, but one of the innumerable creations of an infinite Being full of luminous love. The beauty of most leaves is never appreciated by anyone, and yet the God of love created an unthinkable number of similar leaves—every one beautiful and equally complex. I was dazzled by the beauty of it all, as well as the vast dimension of that beauty. But I would never have been dazzled by this leaf if I had not first known the beauty of God in his holy love for sinful humanity. Knowing that the same God created this beautiful world makes it even more spectacular.

Is This for the Spiritual Elite Only?

My description of true spirituality as a new "seeing" may lead you to think that I have limited this experience to super-spiritual mystics or experts in theology. The spirituality that this book describes may seem beyond the reach of the ordinary Christian.

Nothing could be further from the truth. This experience is for every saint—that is, every true Christian. No special education is needed. In fact, Jesus thanked God that he had "hidden these things from the wise and intelligent and . . . revealed them to infants" (Mt 11:25). Paul told the Corinthians, "Not many of you were wise by human standards" (1 Cor 1:26). It doesn't take a college degree to see the beauty of God's glory.

Nathan Cole, whom I mentioned a few chapters ago, was a simple carpenter and farmer. He too was overwhelmed by the beauty of Jesus, and this seeing made all the world look different: "I could say O my

God, and then I could think of no expression good enough to speak to Him, *he was altogether—lovely* and then I wou'd fall down into a muse [rapt wonder]. . . . Now every thing praised God; the trees, the stone, the walls of the house and every thing I could set my eyes on, they all praised God."[4]

If true spirituality required training in mysticism or theology, it would indeed be limited to a chosen few. But God in his goodness has made it available to both factory workers and university professors. It is a knowing that does not require a long process of thinking. Since it is something like a taste or disposition—we could also call it a spirit or habit of the mind—it guides one's behavior easily and intuitively, without requiring elaborate reasoning. The simple Christian can therefore come to a wise decision about behavior (how to act with Christian humility and love) far more readily and precisely than someone without the Spirit who diligently investigates what might be a "Christian response."

George Gwynn was the janitor who cleaned a school that I served as principal. George had never gone beyond high school, but he was one of the wisest men I ever knew. He walked closely with God for many years, spending hours daily in Bible study and prayer. His life radiated joy and love. On many occasions when I faced a difficult decision concerning a rebellious student, angry parent or cantankerous board member, I asked George for advice. George would usually say that he wanted to pray about the situation. Soon thereafter he would return with a word that was typically simple but incisive. He had a way of seeing clearly, indeed effortlessly, Christian principles that applied to complex situations. Following his advice almost invariably brought peaceful resolution to difficult problems.

George didn't need hours or days to figure out a Christian perspective on a problem. He had a holy disposition that gave him what might be called holy intuition. Like George, every regenerate person has been given a spiritual understanding of divine things. This understanding doesn't come from months of study and analysis. It may follow months of seeking God through the study of Scripture and Christian literature. That study, however, prepares the soul and mind to receive a knowledge that is not formed by study. This new knowing is a seeing of God and his ways that changes the way everything else in life looks. This holy intuition is a source of guidance for living one's life.

11

· · · · ·

The Fifth
Reliable Sign
Deep-Seated
Conviction

*NOW FAITH IS THE ASSURANCE
OF THINGS HOPED FOR,
THE CONVICTION OF THINGS NOT SEEN.*
LETTER TO THE HEBREWS

———————

ALAN WAS A POTHEAD IN THE EARLY SEVENTIES. A PLACE KICKER ON THE football team of a large Midwestern university, he lived up to the stereotype of the college student who is more interested in having fun than reading books. But a rap session about God at a party led Alan to find out for himself what Christianity was all about. He found a New Testament and started reading at Matthew 1:1: "An account of the genealogy of Jesus the Messiah, the son of David, the son of Abraham. Abraham was the father of Isaac, and Isaac the father of Jacob, and Jacob the father of Judah and his brothers."

As he read, Alan was struck by the realization that Christianity is based on historical facts. It is not simply a philosophy disconnected from the lives of real people. The New Testament describes real people who had real spiritual experiences, not heady theories composed by people who never experienced them personally. For reasons that Alan today can explain only by referring to the enlightenment of the Holy Spirit, he was immediately convinced that Christianity is true and real. It was more than just an intellectual realization. He had a deep-seated conviction, in ways that went beyond mere mental assent, that the claims of Christianity are true.

Today, two decades later, Alan teaches theology to Brazilians in São Paulo. The intellectual and spiritual conviction he was given that night at the party has deepened and solidified over the years to the point that now he can say, "I know that I know that these things are true."

Strong Confidence

This is the fifth reliable sign of true spirituality: a deep-seated conviction that the divine truths claimed by the Christian faith are true. Both mind and heart are convinced that divine things are real. Occasional crises of faith may bring on battles with doubt, and there may be times of spiritual dryness. But one can never forget seeing divine realities. No longer does the mind teeter on the fence between skepticism and faith, hoping that Christ is real but lacking heartfelt assurance. Now that the eyes of the soul have seen the glory and beauty of Christ, there is an inner knowing that goes beyond mere hoping. It is a conviction grounded not just in new thoughts but also in the experience of the heart.

This is the confidence out of which the authors of Scripture spoke. Peter told Jesus at Caesarea Philippi, "We have come to believe and *know* that you are the Holy One of God" (Jn 6:69). In his high-priestly prayer in John 17 Jesus told the Father that his disciples had heartfelt assurance that he was the Christ: "Now they know that everything you have given me is from you; for the words that you gave to me I have given to them, and they have received them and *know in truth* that I came from you" (vv. 7-8). Paul showed similar assurance: "I *know* the one in whom I have put my trust, and I am sure that he is able to guard until that day what I have entrusted to him" (2 Tim 1:12). John wrote, "By this we *know* that we abide in him and he in us, because he has given us of his Spirit" (1 Jn 4:13). And the author of Hebrews told his readers that "faith is the *assurance* of things hoped for, the *conviction* of things not seen" (Heb 11:1).

What Can You Know for Sure?

It never ceases to amaze me how many of my students think it is impossible to have strong convictions about things that really count. They think they can know with some assurance about less important things (for example, that Toyotas are better than Fords), but they are certain that they can never be certain about the Big Questions of life (such as, Does God exist? Are some moral beliefs better than others?). Matters of religion and philosophy, they think, can never be known with deep conviction or assurance.

My students are convinced, however, that the hard sciences provide certainty. We may not know if there is a God, or what kind of moral life we should lead. But we can know without any doubt that $F = MA$ (force equals mass times acceleration).

Is There Certainty in the Hard Sciences?

They are surprised when I tell them that philosophers of science are not so sure that the hard sciences can give us certainty. Oxford University Press, for example, recently published Nancy Cartwright's *How the Laws of Physics Lie.*[1] Cartwright and others have been telling us for decades that the laws of nature are descriptive, not prescriptive. That is, they aren't live forces out there causing things to happen or preventing things from happening. They are merely statistical observations of the way we think nature generally works.

I'll never forget my surprise to hear a physicist at the University of Chicago tell our philosophy of science class, "We really don't know for sure if $F = MA$. We have approximations of this theory, but we have never seen it demonstrated exactly. Until that happens, $F = MA$ is at best a guess about what happens."

If we can't have certainty about the laws of physics, neither can we know with absolute certainty something upon which nearly all science rests—the notion that the workings of nature are uniform, that nature possesses regularity.[2] Recent philosophers have concluded that the uniformity of nature is unproved dogma, not the result of empirical inquiry.[3] As molecular biologist (and theologian) Alister McGrath has put it, belief in the uniformity of nature comes remarkably close to being an article of religious faith.[4]

My more astute students will then point to sensory experience.

Surely this, they argue, provides certainty. But then I ask them if sensory experience can be proved. We may think that we have proved it many times. After all, we think we have walked along roads often and have seen a stone lying on the road ahead. When we come to that spot, we stop, bend down and pick it up. We look at it closely and feel it and tell ourselves that yes, we were right to have thought earlier that what we were looking at was a stone. Does this prove the reliability of our sensory experience? Not really. Think about what we did—we fell into the trap of circular reasoning. We tried to prove the reliability of sensory experience by an appeal to sensory experience. We proved nothing.

Philosophers have long recognized that it is impossible to prove the certain reliability of sensory experience. Descartes asked, "How can I know that I am not dreaming?" He concluded that reason cannot know with certainty. Bertrand Russell asked how it can be known that this hypothesis is false: the entire universe sprang into existence five minutes ago, exactly the way it then was, with all the appearance of age. He and others have concluded that reason cannot prove with certainty that this hypothesis is false.[5]

What about history? Don't we know many historical facts with absolute certainty? For example, don't we know without any doubt that Caesar crossed the Rubicon in 49 B.C. and that the Declaration of Independence was signed in 1776? Perhaps. But we also know that nearly all of our historical knowledge is based on testimony, which could have resulted from confusion, misunderstanding or even deception. How can we verify its accuracy with one hundred percent certainty? We may be able to determine that an event has occurred in the way we describe with something close to certainty, but not with *absolute* certainty.

Probability Versus Certainty

Do the scientist and historian therefore despair of ever knowing anything because they cannot have certainty? Do they abandon the enterprise of truth seeking because they have discovered that we can never know anything for sure? Of course not. Like all who try to make sense of human experience, they use the principle of probability. They come to what they think is the most probable explanation of experience and continue to work with that explanation until proven wrong.

It is no different in courts of law. To convict a person in a criminal case, a jury needs enough evidence to prove the defendant guilty "beyond reasonable doubt," not beyond any *possible* doubt.

This Conviction Involves the Mind

I have taken this little detour into science and history in order to make two important points about the conviction that comes with true faith. It is sometimes ridiculed because it cannot be proven with so-called scientific certainty (popularly thought to be absolute certainty). But we have just seen that even the most basic beliefs of science and history cannot be proven with this sort of "scientific certainty."

Religious conviction is criticized by some for being a blind leap in the dark. Mark Twain joked that faith is "believing what you know ain't so." More pertinent to our point is H. L. Mencken's claim that faith is an illogical belief in the occurrence of the improbable.

But the deep-seated conviction that this chapter describes is nothing of the sort. While not limited to the mind, it is based on knowledge of the mind. It starts with conclusions drawn from evidence.

C. S. Lewis's Trilemma

Let me give just two examples of the sort of evidence that is used to support Christian faith claims. The first is a demonstration of how reason can point to faith. It is an old argument that C. S. Lewis made famous in the twentieth century. He had often heard his Oxford professor friends concede that Jesus was a great moral teacher but contemptuously dismiss the church's claim that Jesus was God. Lewis got tired of hearing their summary dismissal of this most basic of all Christian claims. Here is how he handled it.

It is clear, he wrote, that Jesus presented himself as divine. Although he never flatly proclaimed, "I am God," he said he had the authority to forgive sins (which Jews knew only God has the authority to do), he referred to himself as "I am" (a designation that God claimed for himself in the Old Testament), and he made a host of other dramatic claims: "I and the Father are one," "He who has seen me has seen the Father," "I am the resurrection and the life," "He who believes in me, though he die, yet shall he live, and whoever lives and believes in me shall never die," "I am the bread of life," "I am the way, the truth, and the life," "No one comes to the Father except by me."

Lewis reasoned that either Jesus knew who he was or he didn't. If he knew who he was (an ordinary human being) but claimed to be God, then he was a liar. But this is not consistent with his being a great moral teacher. If he didn't know who he was but truly thought he was divine despite being quite mortal, then he was a lunatic. But it was no lunatic who gave us the Sermon on the Mount, who served his own disciples, reached out to the downtrodden and taught deep truths. Lunatics are not truly concerned about others, don't teach profound truths that inspire others and don't live exemplary lives. This is too difficult to believe.

For Lewis, the only other reasonable alternative is that Jesus was who he said he was—Lord of the universe, God incarnate. This is the least rationally objectionable option. This exercise in reasoning from what we know about Jesus to a deduction about his nature has been called Lewis's trilemma—liar, lunatic or Lord.[6]

Evidence for the Resurrection

Another example of the evidence that supports Christian conviction—and shows that faith is not a blind, irrational leap in the dark—is the historical evidence for Jesus' resurrection. There are three lines of evidence here.[7]

First, there is the empty tomb itself. We know that it was guarded by Roman soldiers who knew they would be executed if they failed to protect their charge. It is unlikely that Jesus' disciples, already discouraged by his death, would have had the courage or ability to resist these armed soldiers. Yet the disciples insisted that the tomb was empty. If the tomb was *not* empty, it would have been easy for the Roman or Jewish authorities to produce the body and thereby refute the claims of this troublesome sect. But the authorities never produced the body.

Second, there's the testimony of those who claimed to have seen the risen Christ. There is testimony from both individuals and groups. People who already believed and those who were skeptical, such as Thomas, claimed to have seen him. He even appeared to some who were actively opposed to him, like Paul. Many of these witnesses claimed to have experienced more than just seeing him. Thomas said he put his fingers into the holes in his wrists and feet. John said he

touched him with his hands. Peter and six others said they had break-
fast with him.

Third, there's the transformation of the disciples. During and immediately following the crucifixion, they were cowardly and disillusioned. But shortly thereafter they were boldly preaching this Jesus
whom they had abandoned. They went on to suffer and risk death for
their Lord. Some gave their lives for their testimony. This makes the
second line of evidence, their testimony, more believable. People aren't
willing to die for a story they know they have made up. The fact that
they were willing to lay their lives on the line for their claim that Jesus
rose from the dead is powerful evidence of the truth of their claim. As
Pascal put it, "I prefer those witnesses that get their throats cut."[8]

A Reasonable Conviction

The point of all this has been to show that the deep-seated conviction
that this chapter addresses is a *reasonable* conviction. It is not a mystical
sense divorced from the mind. It may not have sophisticated answers
like the ones just advanced. But it will have *reasons* for its confidence.
Most of those reasons will have something to do with the fact that God
came into history publicly in the person of Jesus two thousand years
ago. He taught, did miracles, died and arose in the most important city
in the Middle East; his followers proclaimed throughout the Roman
Empire that their gospel was based on historical events that they
themselves had witnessed. They had confidence and conviction because of their own historical experience. John said, "We declare to you
what was from the beginning, what we have heard, what we have seen
with our eyes, what we have looked at and touched with our hands,
concerning the word of life" (1 Jn 1:1).

Not Just an Intellectual Conclusion

While this conviction of the truth of the gospel is based on reasons of
the mind, it is more than an intellectual conclusion. It is also a
supernatural enlightening. Many are convinced intellectually of various aspects of the gospel but never see the vivid reality of those truths.
They are not solidly convinced that this is the life they should embrace.

Lewis told of an atheist he had known who told him, to his great
surprise, that the evidence for the historicity of the Gospels "was really

surprisingly good. . . . It almost looks as if it had really happened once."[9] This man had drawn a conclusion, but it was shallow. It never turned into heartfelt conviction. He never allowed himself to receive the supernatural revealing of which the New Testament speaks.

The Gospels indicate that when the disciples finally saw Jesus for who he really was, it was far more than a rational conclusion drawn from evidence. It was a supernatural revelation. When Peter told Jesus he believed he was the Messiah, Jesus replied that flesh and blood had not shown Peter this, "but my Father in heaven" (Mt 16:17). At another time Jesus said that the truths of the gospel are often hidden from the "wise and the intelligent" but are "revealed" to infants. No one knows who the Father is, he went on, except the Son and anyone to whom the Son chooses to *reveal* him (Lk 10:21-22). Paul told the Galatians that God "was pleased to *reveal* his Son" to him (Gal 1:15-16).

A supernatural revealing, then, transforms an intellectual conclusion into a heartfelt conviction. It provides the power to dispense with internal debate and commit one's life. Once more I will turn to Lewis to illustrate. By the time this Oxford don was ready to commit his life, he had already spent months and years thinking his way along the path to faith. Through books (mostly) and a few relationships, he finally concluded that the Christian faith was true. But it took more than intellectual reasoning. It took a supernatural revealing to finally cement his conversion and provide the heartfelt conviction.

I know very well when, but hardly how, the final step was taken. I was driven to Whipsnade one sunny morning. When we set out I did not believe that Jesus Christ is the Son of God, and when we reached the zoo I did. *Yet I had not exactly spent the journey in thought.* Nor in great emotion. "Emotional" is perhaps the last word we can apply to some of the most important events. It was more like when a man, after long sleep, still lying motionless in bed, becomes aware that he is now awake.[10]

A Word of Caution

Don't get the idea that you can't have doubts and still be a true Christian. All faith is mixed with doubt at one time or another. Lewis himself was tortured by doubt when his wife died of cancer. Times of crisis like the death of a loved one or financial disaster will often cause

Christians to lose their familiar assurance of God's presence and love. But they should not judge either God or their own faith during these times. As poet Luci Shaw wrote after she lost her husband to cancer, "I find [God] in the light but lose him in the dark."[12] It is difficult to see things clearly when we are going through a time of emotional darkness.

True faith will have heartfelt conviction that the teachings of the gospel are true. Its vision of God's glory and beauty will make these truths vividly real. There will be a waxing and waning of confidence, especially during times of trauma, but eventually the old assurance will return. For it was based not simply on reasoning of the mind but a supernatural revealing of the beauty of divine things.

12

· · · · ·

The Sixth
Reliable Sign
Humility

*THIS IS THE GREATEST AND MOST USEFUL LESSON
WE CAN LEARN: TO KNOW OURSELVES FOR WHAT WE
TRULY ARE, TO ADMIT FREELY OUR
WEAKNESSES AND FAILINGS, AND TO HOLD A
HUMBLE OPINION OF OURSELVES BECAUSE OF THEM.
NOT TO DWELL ON OURSELVES AND ALWAYS TO
THINK WELL AND HIGHLY OF OTHERS IS GREAT
WISDOM AND PERFECTION.*
THOMAS À KEMPIS

REMEMBER GEORGE GWYNN? HE WAS THE GODLY JANITOR I DESCRIBED
in chapter ten. When I recall why I and so many others liked George
so much, I think of his humility. Not that he didn't have other endear-
ing qualities. George was kind and wise and considerate, but it was his
humility that made those qualities all the more attractive. Without
humility his kindness would have been showy, his wisdom cocky and
his consideration of others self-serving. It was his humility that added
a luster—a holy glow—to all his other virtues.

George never promoted himself or boasted of his accomplishments.
It was not his way to insist that he alone knew what God's will was in a
certain situation, even if he felt that way. Instead, George quietly prayed
that God's will would be done and cheerfully trusted that it would. He

was quick to praise others when they did well and rejoiced with them when they were successful. He often pointed out to me the skills and virtues of our teachers and board members. In the years since I left that school, the word *humility* has called to my mind the kind, smiling face of George Gwynn.

A Confession

It is difficult for me to write about humility, the sixth reliable sign of true spirituality. I feel as if I am describing a beautiful foreign country that I have never visited. I have seen it in pictures and even in the faces of people from that land, and I long to go there. But it remains foreign, essentially unknown to me. As I have prepared this chapter, it has become painfully clear how far I am from ever seeing this wonderful country. I am reminded how natural it is for me to promote myself. There is something inside me that wants others to know of the books I have written or something else I have accomplished. When I am given a flattering introduction before a speech, a part of me winces at the attention, but another part of me secretly revels in it. When I discover that a colleague thinks my teaching or writing is deficient, I feel indignant and rush to defend myself. The colleague must be unaware of what I am really doing, I think; or perhaps the professor has a sinister motive. It is usually some time before I remember my real weaknesses as a teacher and writer, and consider how this criticism could help.

God Prizes Humility

Reflecting on the importance of humility is a bit disconcerting to those of us who have so far to go in this virtue. According to the greatest saints of the church, it is absolutely essential to true spirituality. Without it there is no genuine spiritual life, regardless of the intensity of religious feeling. Thomas à Kempis asked, "What good does it do, then, to debate about the Trinity, if by a lack of humility you are displeasing to the Trinity?"[1] Teresa of Ávila, the sixteenth-century Spanish Carmelite nun and mystic, wrote, "There is more value in a little study of humility and in a single act of it than in all the knowledge in the world."[2] Calvin's word on humility is equally powerful:

A saying of Chrysostom's has always pleased me very much, that the

foundation of our philosophy is humility. But that of Augustine pleases me even more: "When a certain rhetorician was asked what was the chief rule in eloquence, he replied, 'Delivery'; what was the second rule, 'Delivery'; what was the third rule, 'Delivery'; so if you ask me concerning the precepts of the Christian religion, first, second, third, and always I would answer, 'Humility.' "[3]
The Scriptures are even more pointed than the saints of the church. They indicate that God comes only to the humble. The psalmists, for example, write that "the LORD is near to the brokenhearted, and saves the crushed in spirit" (Ps 34:18); that "the sacrifice acceptable to God is a broken spirit; a broken and contrite heart, O God, you will not despise" (Ps 51:17); "for though the LORD is high, he regards the lowly; but the haughty he perceives from far away" (Ps 138:6).

The teacher in Proverbs tells us that God scorns the scorner, but "to the humble he shows favor" (Prov 3:34). In his typically majestic style, the God of Isaiah proclaims, "For thus says the high and lofty one who inhabits eternity, whose name is Holy: I dwell in the high and holy place, and also with those who are contrite and humble in spirit, to revive the spirit of the humble, and to revive the heart of the contrite" (Is 57:15). Several chapters later he again affirms the humble: "Thus says the LORD: Heaven is my throne and the earth is my footstool. . . . But this is the one to whom I will look, to the humble and contrite in spirit, who trembles at my word" (Is 66:1-2).

When Micah summarizes the duties of true religion, humility is a key: "He has told you, O mortal, what is good; and what does the LORD require of you but to do justice, and to love kindness, and to walk humbly with your God" (Mic 6:8). Jesus says that the kingdom of heaven belongs to the "poor in spirit" (Mt 5:3) and illustrates by saying that all who would enter must humble themselves "like little children" (Mt 18:3-4; Mk 10:15).

We can best understand what the Bible means by humility by looking at the people of its stories. The Roman centurion at Capernaum is a marvelous illustration of how humility acts. You may remember that the centurion's slave was close to death. His Jewish friends were sure that the centurion, who had been good to the Jewish community, was worthy of Jesus' attention. But the centurion didn't think of himself as worthy at all. In words memorialized by the Roman Catholic liturgy, the centurion told Jesus, "I am not worthy to have you come under my roof. But only say the word, and my soul shall be healed" (Lk 7:6 as liturgically adapted). This is the humility that recognizes the enormous difference between one's own sinfulness and Jesus' holiness.

Then there was the "woman in the city, who was a sinner" (Lk 7:37). She was probably a prostitute. Ashamed of herself but filled with love for this One who forgave her, she stood behind Jesus, bathing his feet with her tears. Then she bent down to dry his feet with her hair and anoint them with expensive ointment. Jesus, touched by this act of humble love, told her, "Your faith has saved you. Go in peace."

The story of the prodigal son is another demonstration of humility. You probably remember this young man's desperate confession to his father after returning from months of riotous living: "Father, I have sinned against heaven and before you; I am no longer worthy to be called your son; treat me like one of your hired hands" (Lk 15:18-19). This shows us that humility openly confesses its sin.

Jesus' fascinating parable of the Pharisee and the tax collector (Lk 18) gives us another example of humility confessing its sin. Jesus criticized the Pharisee (considered holy by his fellow Jews because he was religious and outwardly moral) who was thankful that he wasn't as bad as others, but praised the tax collector (despised by fellow Jews because of his compromise with Roman authorities) who was so grieved for his sin that he didn't dare look up to heaven. Instead he beat his breast and cried, "God, be merciful to me, a sinner!" Jesus said this tax collector, not the Pharisee, went home that day justified before God.

God Hates Pride

If God prizes humility and considers it indispensable to the spiritual life, he hates its opposite, pride. The church's greatest saints and theologians have usually regarded pride as the greatest of all sins. For Augustine it was "the beginning of all sin."[4] Thomas Aquinas and Dante characterized it as the ultimate sin; John Milton and Johann Wolfgang von Goethe dramatized it as the essence of sin. In the twentieth century, Russian novelist (and Orthodox believer) Aleksandr Solzhenitsyn has portrayed pride as endemic to the human condition; in his memorable words, pride grows on the human heart as lard grows on a pig.

The authors of Scripture are no less direct. The writer of Proverbs says God hates pride: "There are six things that the LORD hates, seven that are an abomination to him" (Prov 6:16). Pride is the first abomination on his list. "Haughty eyes and a proud heart—the lamp of the wicked—are sin" (Prov 21:4). The Spirit of God tells the psalmist, "A haughty look and an arrogant heart I will not tolerate" (Ps 101:5). Jeremiah proclaims that God is so incensed by Judah's pride that he is going to "ruin" Jerusalem (Jer 13:9). The psalmist suggests that pride is the root cause of atheism (Ps 10:4), and Daniel explains that pride was Nebuchadnezzar's downfall (Dan 4). The New Testament declares that God "scatters" and "resists" the proud but exalts the humble (Lk 1:51; Jas 4:6; 1 Pet 5:5). According to Paul, it was pride that kept the Jews of his day from accepting Christ's righteousness (Rom 9:30—10:4). For pride is absolutely opposed to the gospel: "Then what becomes of boasting? It is excluded" (Rom 3:27).

Is All Humility True Humility?

So pride is detestable to God, and humility is the beginning of true religion. But is everything that passes for humility in this world the sort of humility the Bible requires? Jonathan Edwards didn't think so. He said one often sees in this world, and particularly in our churches, a humility that recognizes its sin but still falls short of the true humility to which the Scriptures point. This "common" humility comes from seeing what God demands in the Ten Commandments and realizing that we fall short. It may be aware of God's infinite power and greatness (that is, God's natural perfections, which I described in chapter nine) and feel guilty and fearful because it knows that God punishes sin.[5]

But this feeling of sin and guilt is not the humility God demands. It is merely the work of the natural conscience, which is present in the unregenerate as well as the regenerate. As Edwards pointed out, the damned on the Day of Judgment will have similar feelings. They will feel sinful and guilty, knowing that they can do nothing to make themselves righteous. But they will still be proud and unbroken. Their submission to God will be forced. They will have no desire to throw themselves before God in worship, freely confessing and mourning their sins.[6]

Many today have similar feelings. They know that God is righteous and that they are not, but their proud will has not been broken. They don't mourn their sins, and they have no desire to throw themselves at God's feet in worship. St. Teresa said that the humility of such people "is the work of the devil." They think of God simply as One who "is always wielding fire and sword," because they have never seen the beauty of his holiness.[7]

The truly humble, on the other hand, feel conviction of sin not simply as a work of the natural conscience but as a result of seeing the beauty of God's love. They mourn their sins not because they fear punishment but because they know they have dishonored the One whose love is so great and beautiful. They prostrate themselves before God in worship and submission, not because they have to but because this is their delight.

Seeing Things for What They Are
Humility is a many-splendored thing. It arises from love rather than fear. And it acts in particular ways. So that we can see more clearly what it is and how it is distinguished from its counterfeits, I will first define it precisely and then describe how it acts.

First, a definition. *Humility is seeing things for what they really are.* It is seeing God for who he is, in all the glory and beauty of his holy love. When we see that—God!—we can't help but see ourselves for who we really are: sinful worms by comparison. Once we get a glimpse of God's pure, self-giving love for us, we will be overwhelmed by our own uncleanness and self-obsession. And when we see that God has created everything and continues to sustain everything moment by moment, we will realize that apart from him we can do nothing. This is reality. This is seeing things as they really are. This is humility.

Confessing our sinfulness and dependence on God is different from self-deprecation. It is not pleasing to God when we deny our gifts and talents. For an Olympic skater to deny that she can skate well is not humility. It is seeing things as they are not. She practices humility not by denying her skill but by acknowledging that God gave her athletic skill, training, caring parents and friends to support her, and the grace to take advantage of these gifts. C. S. Lewis said that God wants the Christian to "be so free from any bias in his own favour that he can rejoice in his own talents as frankly and gratefully as in his neighbour's talents—or in a sunrise, an elephant, or a waterfall."[8]

Humility Is Self-Denying

Now let's take a more careful look at how humility acts. Once it sees things for what they are, it tends to practice self-denial. It does so not because it feels coerced or because it is the Christian thing to do, but because self-denial is the logical and natural consequence of seeing things as they really are.

For instance, humility denies its worldly inclinations because it realizes that they lead away from true happiness. That is, it wants to ignore or redirect its undisciplined urges for money, sex and power when it sees that fulfilling those urges will bring conflict and unhappiness in the long run. Denying these urges is never easy, but it makes sense to the soul that has seen only God's natural perfection. This kind of self-denial is what Johann Arndt called dying to the "external idolatries" of fornication, adultery, theft, gross materialism and other sins obvious to most observers.[9]

Another kind of self-denial is far more difficult: the denial of our natural tendency to exalt ourselves. This is impossible to practice unless the soul has seen the beauty of God's love and lives in response to that love. For it is the cheerful willingness to allow its own sufferings and achievements to go unnoticed. Arndt said this is "inner repentance,"[10] which is both deeper and higher than the outer repentance I described in the paragraph above. It is dying to one's pride—one's natural inclination to want to be noticed.

The unregenerate (those who have never been transformed by seeing the beauty of God's love) are often able to practice the first kind of self-denial but are totally incapable of the second. They can deny themselves the obvious sins of the flesh because they know that those sins will hurt them and ruin their reputations. But they don't have the foggiest notion of why anyone would reject self-promotion. Or, if they see that this is desirable, they cannot do it. Edwards observed that church history is full of such people. There have been hermits, for example, who gave up the pleasures of this world without giving up their pride. "They never denied themselves for Christ, but only sold one lust to feed another. [They] sold a beastly lust to pamper a devilish one; and so were never the better, but their latter end was worse than the beginning."[11]

Signs of False Humility

There are some people in our churches who frequently describe themselves as sinners, all the while expecting to be regarded as particularly spiritual persons. It is dangerous to suggest that they really are what they say they are (wicked sinners). If someone suggests that they are not good Christians, they are hurt. They may become angry and carry a grudge for a long time.

Why then do they keep testifying to their sinfulness? John of the Cross explained that they do this in order to silence their guilty conscience. Confessing their sinfulness in general gives them the (false) assurance that they can ignore their sins in particular. They are more interested in their own peace of mind than in God's glory and honor. And they don't realize that "if He should take their imperfections from them, they would probably become prouder and more presumptuous still."[12]

Some of these people are the loudest champions of "Christian truth." In fundamentalist and evangelical churches, they (rightly) condemn the doctrine that good works or intentions can save, or that social justice can ever substitute for justification by faith. In mainline and liberal churches, they (rightly) criticize faith that is not concerned about the poor and unfortunate. Both sets of champions have the right ideas but do not have true humility if they are not eager to confess their own unrighteousness. They are equally guilty of what Martin Luther called the final form of sin—the unwillingness to be regarded as sinners.[13]

Spiritual Pride

One form of false humility is perhaps the most insidious. This is the spiritual pride that is proud of its humility. Because it "is lurking at the door" (Gen 4:7) of all who yearn to be humble, it is worth exploring in some depth. There are several telltale marks of spiritual pride.

First, spiritual pride tends to admire its own spiritual experiences and consider itself spiritually superior to others. As the religious speaker in Isaiah 65:5 sneered, "Do not come near me, for I am too holy for you." The Pharisee in Jesus' parable (Lk 18:9-14) was less obnoxious but equally arrogant. He was impressed by his own spirituality and grateful that he was better than most other people. The tax collector, in contrast, mourned his sinfulness; he compared himself not to other people but to God and his righteousness. (In today's inversion of biblical values, we might chide the tax collector for his poor self-esteem and admonish him to learn proper self-acceptance from the Pharisee.)

Demanding to Teach

Second, spiritual pride is unhappy unless it can teach others. It is convinced that it is "a guide to the blind, a light to those who are in darkness, a corrector of the foolish, a teacher of children" (Rom 2:19-20).

I remember Larry, a young man in our church who was always chomping at the bit unless he could teach adults. Our church has a policy that a new member is not to teach until church leaders have had at least six months to get to know the person. Larry was impatient with this policy and continually asked the pastor and the other leaders for a teaching position. When he was finally granted one, he proceeded to attack the church and its leaders for not being Christ-centered. By that he meant that the pastor did not explain the plan of salvation in every sermon. Larry soon left the church, but not without teaching me that a person who demands to teach is not humble enough to teach properly.

True humility does not *demand* to teach. It knows that it knows very little, and that teachers in the church "will be judged with greater strictness" (Jas 3:1). It is therefore wary of asking for a position of influence or authority; as Teresa of Ávila warned, "Anyone who is to hold a position of authority should be very far from desiring or wishing for one, or at least from trying to obtain one."[14] Clearly Teresa is speaking hyperbolically; she is using overstatement to warn against vain ambition. There is nothing wrong with offering our gifts—whether they be gifts of teaching, administration, leadership or anything else— for the use of the church, particularly when the church plainly needs those gifts. Scripture commands us to use our gifts for the edification of the body (Rom 12:4-8). But there is a difference between *offering* our gifts and *demanding* that they be used. The first humbly offers to help where help is needed, but the second is never happy unless others are sitting at its feet.

Humility is more impressed by others' gifts than by its own. This is what Paul means when he says we should "regard others as better than [ourselves]" (Phil 2:3). Thomas à Kempis adds, "If you have any good qualities, believe that other people have better ones."[15]

The great masters of spirituality have always taught that humble souls are eager to listen and learn. James wrote, "Let everyone be quick to listen [and] slow to speak" (Jas 1:19). Thomas à Kempis advised, "Do not have too much confidence in your own opinion, but be willing to hear what others have to say."[16] And John of the Cross observed that humble souls "have a deep desire to be taught by anyone who can bring them profit."[17]

The spiritually proud admire their own spirituality, but humble saints are "poor in spirit" (Mt 5:3). They are convinced of their spiritual and moral bankruptcy. The more they see of God's holiness and beauty, and of the length and breadth and height and depth of Christ's love for sinners, the more persuaded they become of how far short they fall. Because they see better than the unregenerate how much they owe to their loving Savior—how great their love and devotion *ought* to be— they see more of their own sin than the unregenerate do. Therefore they regard what they have done for God as a tiny pittance, both in comparison to what they *haven't* done and in comparison to what God has done for them. Or they conclude, as did Thomas à Kempis, that whatever service they give God is their duty as unworthy creatures: "Is it a great thing to serve you, whom all creation is bound to serve?"[18]

It can be taken as an infallible rule that those who think they are more spiritual than others, are not. They are proud and self-righteous instead. In Paul's words, "Anyone who claims to know something does not yet have the necessary knowledge" (1 Cor 8:2). The author of Proverbs puts it succinctly: "Do you see persons wise in their own eyes? There is more hope for fools than for them" (26:12).

The Final Proof of Spiritual Pride
A third characteristic of spiritual pride is that it doesn't see its own sin. In Reinhold Niebuhr's monumental *Nature and Destiny of Man,* perhaps

the most profound analysis of sin written in the twentieth century, he suggested that "the final proof that man no longer knows God is that he does not know his own sin."[19] Ignorance of one's own sin is reliable evidence that a person's spiritual experience arises from darkness rather than light. Without knowledge of one's own fallen condition, it is impossible to see anything else at all, much less God.

True saints, on the other hand, see their sin *especially* when experiencing grace. In the midst of greatest spiritual delight, Teresa referred to herself as "the weakest and wickedest [of all who are born]" and "that sea of evil—myself."[20] I don't understand how Teresa could think of herself as the worst of all sinners, and I don't recommend that kind of severe piety for every saint today. But I do think that in this narcissistic and self-indulgent age, a jolting reminder of our own sinfulness may help restore balance to our distorted perspectives.

As I write this, I remember a time several weeks ago in our home Bible study when we were studying a passage in Isaiah that condemned the pride of Babylon. Milt, a godly engineer in his sixties who converted from Judaism some fifteen years ago, remarked that he saw the same pride in himself and marveled that God had saved him, a wicked sinner who deserved only hell. Milt was deeply grieved by his sinfulness because he had experienced the joy of God's grace. "It is this way with all the saints," Thomas à Kempis tells us. "The higher they are in glory, the more humble they are in themselves."[21]

Teresa compares this phenomenon to a glass of water held up to the light. When the sun shines on it, its impurities are visible as they had not been before.

> Just so the water in a vessel seems quite clear when the sun is not shining upon it; but the sun shows it to be full of specks. . . . Before the soul had experienced that state of ecstasy, it thought it was being careful not to offend God. . . . But once it reaches this stage, the Sun of Justice strikes it and forces it to open its eyes, whereupon it sees so many of these specks that it would fain close them again . . . it sees that it is wholly unclean. It remembers the verse which says, "Who shall be just in Thy presence?"[22]

Not only does an experience of grace especially show us our sin, but it also convinces us of our spiritual ignorance. After seeing God's glory, Agur confessed, "Surely I am too stupid to be human; I do not have human understanding. I have not learned wisdom, nor have I knowledge of the holy ones" (Prov 30:2-4).

The Bible cautions us against thinking that we know much about God and faith. Proverbs warns, "Do not be wise in your own eyes" (3:7). Isaiah addresses the proud as "you who are wise in your own eyes, and shrewd in your own sight" (Is 5:21). Paul cautions, "[Do] not . . . think of yourself more highly than you ought to think" (Rom 12:3).

A story is told of Karl Barth, the twentieth century's greatest theologian. After he had given a lecture at a distinguished American university, an admiring graduate student asked him to identify the greatest theological truth he had ever learned. Barth replied simply, "Jesus loves me, this I know, for the Bible tells me so." Barth refused to boast of great knowledge and was content to claim only the knowledge of a child.

When We Are Proud of Our Humility

A fourth mark of spiritual pride is thinking highly of our humility. Lewis's *Screwtape Letters* suggests that this is how the devil particularly tempts the saints. Screwtape (a senior demon) tells his nephew that a Christian's humility can easily be turned into a vice.

> Your patient has become humble: have you drawn his attention to this fact? All virtues are less formidable to us once the man is aware that he has them, but this is especially true of his humility. Catch him at the moment when he is really poor in spirit and smuggle into his mind the gratifying reflection, "By jove, I'm being humble," and almost immediately pride—pride at his own humility—will appear. If he awakes to the danger and tries to smother this new form of pride, make him proud of his attempt—and so on, through as many stages as you please.[23]

Although saints may be tempted to be proud of their humility, they are more apt to notice their pride. Toward the end of his life Niebuhr was interviewed by a journal editor about his distinguished career in ethics and public life. When the editor asked Niebuhr why he accepted so many speaking invitations that his schedule nearly crushed him, Niebuhr confessed, "Probably because of my pride."

Those who have never been touched by true spirituality, on the other hand, are usually not aware of their pride. They are quick to see the speck of dust in their neighbor's eye but oblivious to the logs in their own. Those with the most pride are most obsessed with the pride of others. They see pride everywhere, and it galls them. For them the old adage is true: "It takes one to know one." They tend to be far more disturbed by their neighbor's failings than by the filth of their own hearts.

Pride is a problem of groups, not just individuals. We can be self-righteously proud of our country, thinking that because we have more political and material blessings, we are somehow better than others. Or we can be so impressed by our own spiritual understanding that we don't seek to learn from others. After the fall of communism in 1989, many Christians in Eastern Europe complained that some missionaries from the West assumed they had little or nothing to learn from the churches in these formerly communist lands. Not only was this missionary pride offensive to these suffering Christians, but the missionaries lost a grand opportunity to learn from those who had walked with Christ amidst persecution and deprivation.

This is also a problem in our own churches. Many of us think of our churches or denominations as having a corner on the truth. This is not necessarily wrong, because most churches do have aspects of the truth that other churches don't share. But it becomes sinful pride when we consider those who don't share our theology or experience to be second-class Christians, or when we think we have nothing to learn from those who don't think like us.

True Humility Isn't Noisy
We've devoted considerable attention to pride. Now we will look more closely at the characteristics of true humility. According to Edwards, the first mark of genuine humility is that it isn't noisy. It tends not to talk about itself. Instead, it considers its sin and listens. Jeremiah taught, "It is good for one to bear the yoke in youth, to sit alone in silence when the LORD has imposed it, to put one's mouth to the dust" (Lam 3:28-29). The author of Proverbs gave similar advice: "If you have been foolish, exalting yourself, or if you have been devising evil, put your hand on your mouth" (30:32). Johann Arndt asked, "Why shall [a man] open his mouth? The best that a man can say with his mouth is to speak two words: I have sinned, be merciful to me."[24]

Humble saints are quiet for two reasons. First, they are listening for God's voice. "God is a hidden God (Is. 45:15), [and] the soul with which God is to speak must live in its secret depths (Ps. 85:9; 34:5-7; 5:4). The more the soul lives in its secret depths, the more it cuts itself off from the world. The patriarch Jacob drew away from his children and friends and spoke with God, and the angels spoke with him (Gen. 32:24ff)."[25]

The second reason the humble tend to be quiet is that they listen to others. They realize that God often speaks through people. In the months after her husband's death from cancer, Christian poet Luci Shaw discovered in her new loneliness that God sometimes manifests himself through people: "I find [God] in the light [moments of delight] but lose him in the dark. When I'm anxious and reach for him, I can't touch him or sense his reality. That's when he comes in the guise of other people."[26]

One of the benefits of silently listening for God is that we get to see God act as our defender. Richard Foster writes,

> One of the fruits of silence is the freedom to let one's justification rest entirely with God. We don't need to straighten others out. There is a story of a medieval monk who was being unjustly accused of certain offenses. One day he looked out his window and watched a dog biting and tearing on a rug that had been hung out to dry. As he watched, the Lord spoke to him saying, "This is what I am doing to your reputation. But if you will trust me, you will not need to worry about the opinions of others." Perhaps more than anything else, silence brings us to believe that God can justify and set things straight.[27]

True Humility Is Poor in Spirit

We have already seen that the truly humble realize their moral and spiritual bankruptcy. They can't help realizing this after seeing the beautiful holiness of Jesus. Bonhoeffer said this realization makes it impossible for the saint to think he is better than others: "If my sinfulness appears to me to be in any way smaller or less detestable in comparison with the sins of others, I am still not recognizing my sins at all. . . . Brotherly love will find any number of extenuations for the sins of others; only for my sin is there no apology whatsoever."[28]

Not only do the truly humble see their own smallness before the greatness of God, but everything they do reflects that awareness. Because they recognize their unworthiness, they aren't touchy; they refuse to hold a grudge, because they realize they have no right to. When someone suggests an idea that is better than their own, they cheerfully support it rather than stubbornly insisting on their own way because it is theirs. They aren't surprised when they are criticized, because they know they may well deserve it. They listen to rebukes meekly, realizing there is at least a grain of truth in every criticism. And they aren't offended when their accomplishments go unrecognized.

Humble saints know they don't know it all. They don't think they have the answer to everyone else's problems. And because they are so aware of their own limitations, they are slow to criticize others. The saint, said Bonhoeffer, "will be able to cease from constantly scrutinizing the other person, judging him, condemning him, putting him in his particular place where he can gain ascendancy over him and thus doing violence to him as a person."[29]

The Foundation of All Christian Virtue

The great saints of the church have often said that without humility no other Christian virtue is possible. As Teresa put it, "What I have learned is this: that the entire foundation of prayer must be established in humility, and that, the more a soul abases itself in prayer, the higher God raises it. I do not remember that He has ever granted me any of the outstanding favours of which I shall speak later save when I have been consumed by realizing my own wickedness."[30]

Teresa and the other masters of spirituality testify that if we don't see our own true condition, we can never see anything else in its true light. It is out of humility—a sense of inner brokenness—that every other Christian virtue flows. Just as Mary's translucent alabaster jar had to break before the fragrant ointment could flow out of it, our confidence that we can do something *for* God has to break before we can do a beautiful work *of* God.

This means that true Christian love springs from an awareness that in and of ourselves we are incapable of loving. True Christian desires arise from a recognition that we don't deserve what we desire. And true Christian joy, even when unspeakable, gushes up from a heart that mourns its wounds to Jesus' heart.

I will close this section with George Gwynn, the janitor I described at the beginning of the chapter. George is one of the best men I've ever known—generous, self-sacrificing, honest, compassionate. He is also more aware of his spiritual poverty, in the face of God's holiness, than anyone I've known. I have always seen in George a direct connection between these two things—his awareness of his smallness before God, and his greatness as a man. Without his humility, his generosity would be smug and his honesty harsh. His altruism and compassion would be pharisaic attempts to impress others. But George has none of these vices. It is clear to me, and to most who know him, that his spiritual greatness is a fruit of his humility.

How Do We Get Humility?

Perhaps you, like me, are daunted by the distance between this picture of humility and the pride of your heart. You wonder how on earth you can ever begin to approach this virtue. Following are a few tips from a fellow seeker.

First, the mere recognition that you have so far to go is a sign that you are on the right path. Those who think they have arrived wandered off the path long ago.

Second, start asking God for humility. Christians today rarely make such a request. Often they are afraid to, thinking—so very rightly—that this is a prayer God loves to answer and often answers in ways that crucify the flesh (deny our desires for pleasure and recognition). But the saints of old prayed this prayer with enthusiasm and regularity, knowing that such painful answers open doors to joy. They learned from experience that only through the death of pride are the delights of humility born. They knew that pride is a heavy burden from which Jesus wants to free us: "Take my yoke upon you, and learn from me; for I am gentle and humble in heart, and you will find rest for your souls. For my yoke is easy, and my burden is light" (Mt 11:29-30).

Finally, approach each day's events with openness to the humility that God may be wanting to work in you through those events. When you are criticized or overlooked, ask God to use that situation to work into you the humility of Jesus. Or when you experience *any* failure or weakness or even limitation, ask God to use the experience to open your eyes to see things as they really are.

13

. . . . .

The Seventh
Reliable Sign
A Change of Nature

NEITHER CIRCUMCISION NOR
UNCIRCUMCISION MEANS ANYTHING;
WHAT COUNTS IS A NEW CREATION.
PAUL

J AY IS A VIETNAM-ERA VETERAN WHO USED TO GET HIS KICKS BY ENTICING gay men to a hotel room with the implicit promise of a sexual encounter. Once there, he would mug the unsuspecting man and run off with his cash and valuables.

In the mid-1970s Jay had a powerful conversion experience. Some time ago he described it to me in a letter.

I didn't turn to Christ because of conviction of sin—that came later—but by extreme poverty of spirit. I was dead empty inside. I was tired of bars, drugs and the friends I did these things with. Life seemed to have no meaning or purpose.

One day, I remember, as I was driving to my construction job in Milwaukee, I felt like I didn't have the strength to live one more day. I drove by the job site to a park on Lake Michigan. I sat in the car, looking at the lake, not knowing what to do or where to go. Suddenly it occurred to me to take my new BMW motorcycle that I had just bought—the best that was then made—and head for South America.

That week, without going back to work, I started planning my trip, with no intention of returning. I figured I would probably die on the way. But God had other plans for me. A friend from Madison happened to drop by to give me a book entitled *Be Here Now.* This was something of a classic in the sixties and seventies. It was filled with sayings from religious teachers and philosophers, mostly from the East.

I took the book to my room the next day and started to read it. Something strange started happening: I felt my inner spirit being lifted or stirred. For the first time in years I felt a glimmer of hope. Then I came across the teaching of Jesus about not letting your left hand know what your right hand is doing. Nothing profound, but it triggered a battle in my soul. A voice inside me insisted, "This is what you need; Jesus is the way."

But other voices within me argued that I didn't want Jesus and offered several reasons why. The debate continued for quite a while and increased in intensity. While I sat on the edge of my bed, the call to follow Jesus got stronger and stronger, and I kept resisting harder and harder. Then I stood up and paced back and forth, from one end of my small room to the other. There was now a battle raging within my soul, with one part of me afraid to let go of my old life, and the other crying out for freedom. Finally I fell to my knees and shouted, "I give up!" In that split second of time my life changed. My soul and spirit were flooded with a peace and hope I had never felt before. The battle was won. I knew who I was going to live for the rest of my life.

True Spiritual Experience Is Transforming

Jay has grown in the Lord ever since. Now he is a deeply committed Christian who works with the youth ministry of his church whenever he can get time away from his job as a professional photographer. His experience is typical of the millions of true conversions that have occurred since the birth of the church two thousand years ago. There is a spiritual enlightening that transforms. It changes the nature of the soul, so that one's life is different ever after. The change is not always outwardly visible, at least for a while, but what happens on the inside changes one's very nature. Eventually the inner change will manifest itself in a different kind of life: a different pattern of thinking, feeling and acting.

The apostle Paul described this inner transformation in 2 Corinthians: "And all of us, with unveiled faces, *seeing* the glory of the Lord as though reflected in a mirror, *are being transformed* into the same image from one degree of glory to another; for this comes from the Lord, the Spirit" (3:18). Paul implies that the true Christian experiences a continual process of change. And he confirms what I have said throughout this book—that it is *seeing* the glory and beauty of Christ that starts the work of inner transformation. It was Jay's seeing something of Jesus' holiness, which is his glory, that led to his transformation.

Only God Can Change Our Inner Nature

Perhaps my claim strikes you as overreaching. After all, people change their lives all the time without any spiritual experience—much less seeing the beauty of God's glory. People go on diets and take up new hobbies and resolve to be better parents and friends. And often these changes are real and lasting.

People who are not necessarily Christians may be the ones who call for Christian changes. In the wonderful novel *To Kill a Mockingbird* one of the townspeople says of Atticus Finch (the lawyer defending a black man falsely accused of rape in a racist Southern town), "We're so rarely called on to be Christians, but when we are, we've got men like Atticus to go for us."[1] The townspeople on the jury convict the black man, despite clear evidence that he is innocent. They know what changes genuine Christians would make, but they also know that they aren't going to make them.

These are not the changes to which I refer. I am talking about a fundamental orientation of one's life, not simply changing a hobby or way of parenting, or recommending that someone else make changes. I mean changing from hating or ignoring God to loving God. Or from seeing life as empty, as Jay did, to seeing it as charged with beauty and hope. This kind of seeing changes our lifestyle. Rather than asking others to make changes, we are led to change our own lives.

This kind of fundamental change requires far more than willpower or a new way of thinking. It is possible only through a basic change of heart—a change of affections—that God alone can give.

Breaking the Power of Addiction

Those who have struggled with an addiction know what I am talking about. They know the need for fundamental change and the futility of New Year's resolutions and self-help formulas. So does Gerald May, a psychiatrist who started his career with the confidence that his psychiatric training would equip him to change lives. When the Vietnam War ended, he took a position as director of a community drug-abuse clinic, where he discovered that the best of human knowledge and effort was not enough.

"With all the energy that might be expected of a young doctor, I applied my best psychiatric methods to the treatment of addictions. None of them worked." Then May did some informal research. He identified a few people who had overcome serious addictions to drugs and alcohol and asked them how they did it. "All of them described some sort of spiritual experience," he reports. They said that they had gotten some professional help, but that this was not the source of their healing. "What had healed them was something spiritual. . . . It had something to do with turning to God."[2]

None of them pointed to anything but God: not willpower or self-discipline or meditation or using their own spiritual energy or self-esteem. All testified to a power that came from outside themselves, like the voice that came to St. Augustine when he was sitting in his Milan garden in the summer of A.D. 386.

The Demon of Lust

Augustine had battled the demon of sexual lust for years. He knew in his heart of hearts that sexual abstinence was right but was afraid that life without sex would be unlivable. Some years before his conversion he had prayed, "God, give me continence, but not yet!" Then one day, through a little child's voice, he was delivered. From a nearby house Augustine heard the words "Pick up and read, pick up and read." He picked up a New Testament lying nearby and read the first passage on which his eyes fell: "Make no provision for the flesh, to gratify its lusts"

(Rom 13:14). Through those words shone "a light of relief from all anxiety. . . . All the shadows of doubt were dispelled."[3] He was freed through the grace of God coming to him from outside himself. Augustine found that the joy of freedom far outweighed the pain of sexual deprivation.

For years Augustine had tried on his own to break the power of his sexual addiction but had failed. Only God by his grace was able to do it. Many addicts today say the same. " 'I was walking to the grocery store one day,' said one alcoholic man, 'and there, on the sidewalk, I discovered equanimity.' He had suffered from alcoholism for many years, and that particular day had seemed no different from any others. Yet in a simple, wondrous moment, his life was transformed. He hasn't had a drink since."[4]

The transformation that comes in true spirituality is a revolution from the inside out. The authors of Scripture make it clear that this inner revolution is the implantation of a new nature. They call it being "born again," becoming a "new creature," "rising from the dead," becoming "renewed in the spirit of your mind," "dying to sin and living to Christ," "putting off the old man and putting on the new man," being "ingrafted into new stock," having a "divine seed implanted in your heart" and being made "partakers of the divine nature."

True Grace Brings Lasting Change
If the inner transformation is real, it is lasting. But if the change is only temporary, it is not the result of genuine conversion. Many people dabble with various spiritualities before they are converted by the grace of Jesus. While experimenting with these spiritualities, they make some changes in their lifestyle and habits. But the changes are usually made with great effort. It is like pushing a boulder uphill or cutting wood against the grain. Their old nature tries to do something that only a new nature can do consistently and over the long haul. They may boast of the wonderful change they have made in their lives, but their change has been produced by human striving rather than God's grace. There has been no new creation.

And without that fundamental transformation of the heart, neither moral change nor religious activity has any lasting value: "Neither circumcision nor uncircumcision means anything," Paul says; "what counts is a new creation" (Gal 6:15 NIV).

Learning from a Pig

The change in nature that comes with true conversion is lasting because it produces a new desire for holiness. It doesn't just restrain the old desires for sin but imparts both the desire and power to live a different kind of life. Edwards explained this new nature through the analogy of a pig. A pig, he said, is filthy by nature. It loves to play and wallow in filth. A farmer may wash the pig one day and make it look clean on the outside. He may even tie a pink bow around its neck and make it look pretty. But that pig's true, inner nature is still filthy. As soon as it has a chance, it will roll around in the nearest pile of mud, getting as dirty as it can.

Similarly, we begin our lives with a natural predisposition to sin. We can try by our own efforts to avoid sin, and in some areas of life we can achieve success. We can live outwardly moral lives and be well respected in our community. But no matter how much we are esteemed for our morality and decency, we know (if we are self-aware) that we are self-obsessed. We know that self-interest controls the inner recesses of our psyche, hiding a labyrinth of lust, pride, greed, hatred and a host of other demons. We realize that we are like that washed pig—clean on the outside but disposed to filth in the inner self.

Change that pig's inner nature, however, and there's hope for the pig. Put a desire for cleanliness in that pig's little heart, and it will seek water rather than mud. Maybe it will even look for pink ribbons in the barn! In the same way, when a person's inner nature is transformed, her outer life will change as well. And because she has received a nature that will stay with her permanently, the changes in her life will last.

A Word of Caution

Don't feel condemned if you believe you have experienced genuine conversion but still struggle with demons of your own. True conversion doesn't usually change one's temperament or personality. And it doesn't eliminate the old temptations. If we battled lust or anger before, we'll probably continue to fight them. We'll have a new power to resist and a new motivation for resistance, but the temptations will still be there.

St. Augustine realized late in his life that true spirituality is never free from temptation. When he was a young Christian he imagined that the mature Christian wouldn't feel the desire for sin. But as an old man, he concluded that sin's attractiveness is never fully absent. It continues to allure—often because it looks like so much fun!—until the end of life. This doesn't mean, though, that the battle against sin is no different after conversion from what it was before. Augustine said that the regenerate have a new love (what I have called a new taste) that provides a new power for the fight. Before conversion, one cannot be anything but self-obsessed in the long run, but after conversion there is a divine enablement by (new) nature and by the help of the Holy Spirit to gradually move towards Christlike selflessness.

A Gradual Transformation

Notice the word *gradually.* The new nature changes us, and the change lasts. But the change usually does not occur overnight. For most of us old habits of selfishness are progressively weakened over years rather than weeks or months.

Mario is a pilot in his sixties who has been a Christian for two decades. From the very beginning of his Christian life he has recognized that anger is the sin that "so closely clings." But it has taken twenty years of trying, failing and seeking grace anew to come to some degree of victory. Now he counts to ten when one of his grown daughters says something that hurts—lest he explode at her in anger. By the time he reaches ten, he's had time to realize that a sharp retort will do more harm than good.

The Scriptures hint that change is gradual. Paul tells us that we are to be *continually* transformed by the renewing of our minds (Rom 12:2) and to *"keep on being* renewed in the spirit of [our] minds, putting on the new self which is created by God in righteousness and true holiness" (Eph 4:23-24, my translation). So the new self is not something we put on just once, but continually, as we are gradually and progressively transformed into the image of Christ.

Therefore no one has arrived. No one is perfect. But there is progress. There is gradual renewal that comes from a new nature. Hence Paul could write, "Even though our outer nature is wasting away, our inner nature is being renewed day by day" (2 Cor 4:16). Even after bemoaning the struggle against sin that he waged every day and his recurring failures (Rom 7), Paul rejoiced in the real and lasting change that was occurring over the long term: "Thanks be to God through Jesus Christ our Lord! . . . For the law of the Spirit of life in Christ Jesus has set me free from the law of sin and of death" (Rom 7:25; 8:2).

The Radiance of Holiness

When Moses met with God, God's holiness shone with such a dazzling radiance that Moses' face shone as well. When Moses came down from the mountain after meeting with God, his face continued to shine with that splendor of holiness (Ex 34:30-35).

The same thing will happen to us if we commune with Christ. After we have waited on God, seeking his holiness, our faces will radiate something of his presence. When we go out into the world, others will notice that there's something different about us. They will remark, as they did about the disciples, that we have been with Jesus (Acts 4:13).

14

· · · · ·

The Eighth
Reliable Sign
A Christlike Spirit

IN THE EVENING THEY WILL EXAMINE THEE IN LOVE.
JOHN OF THE CROSS

WHENEVER I TRY TO IMAGINE A CHRISTLIKE SPIRIT, I THINK OF Mary Friberg, who taught first grade in a Minnesota school I served as principal. She exemplified the best of Christian meekness. Although she had plenty to complain about (a tougher schedule and less money than others), she never did. Instead, she filled the air with a quiet but cheerful enthusiasm. Mary also knew how to forgive—both the disruptive students and the parents who neglected to do the work for which they had volunteered. But what really stood out about Mary was her love. She cared about her students and colleagues with a warmth and tender concern that were tangible. She spent hours after school planning special lessons to help slow learners, many of whom were difficult for others to like. She racked her brain thinking up creative ways to stimulate quick learners. When her students reached up to hug her and tell her with a grin that they loved her, I knew they meant it.

During the summers Mary used what little extra money she had to travel to Tibet to share the gospel with unbelievers. I was not surprised to learn that Mary was more effective than most missionaries: her love drew many to ask what filled this woman with such a beautiful spirit.

Little Christs

The New Testament indicates that every true believer will be something like Mary. Not that every Christian will have as dramatic an impact on others as Mary does, but every regenerate person will bear some resemblance to Christ. As Luther put it, the Christian is a "little Christ." Paul told the Corinthian church that all true Christians are being "transformed" gradually into Christ's "image" (2 Cor 3:18). He wrote the Romans that Christians are "predestined to be conformed to the image of his Son" (Rom 8:29). In his first letter to the Corinthians he put it this way: "As is the man of heaven, so are those who are of heaven" (1 Cor 15:48).

This should not surprise us. As we have already seen, the New Testament teaches that Christians are joined with the spirit of Christ. We are told that "God has sent the Spirit of his Son into our hearts" (Gal 4:6). "Anyone united to the Lord becomes one spirit with him" (1 Cor 6:17). "It is no longer I who live, but it is Christ who lives in me" (Gal 2:20). "Anyone who does not have the Spirit of Christ does not belong to him" (Rom 8:9).

Meekness

What does it mean to have the spirit of Christ, or, in Paul's words, to "put on the Lord Jesus Christ" (Rom 13:14)? In this short space it is impossible to do justice to this question. But I will describe briefly four qualities that the masters of spirituality have commonly associated with Christlikeness. The first is meekness.

Jesus said that he is meek and we should imitate his meekness: "Take my yoke upon you and learn from me, for I am meek and humble in heart" (Mt 11:29, my translation). Paul implied the same: "I myself, Paul, appeal to you by the meekness and gentleness of Christ" (2 Cor 10:1).

Meekness is not the subject of many sermons today. Perhaps this is because it seems to contradict the spirit of our age that tells us we should be assertive. We think that meekness means letting people walk all over us or acting like the comic-strip character Caspar Milquetoast, who was nice but had no convictions. But Jesus meant something entirely different.

Becoming Like Children

The best way to understand what Jesus meant is to realize that Jesus often taught his disciples to imitate the attitudes of children. He said that the kingdom of heaven belongs to people who are like children, and that people can't enter the kingdom of heaven unless they become like children (Mt 19:14; 18:3).

What is it about children that we are to imitate? From looking at both children and the Gospels, it seems to me that Jesus is pointing us to three characteristics, and all three are characteristics of meekness. First, children are willing to admit publicly that they are wrong. We adults are much more hesitant, fearing that such an admission could hurt us. The story is told of Count Nikolaus von Zinzendorf (1700-1760), founder of the Moravian Church, that he was worried that his parishioners thought too highly of him. So he instructed them from the pulpit one Sunday to be sure to point out his sins publicly.

Because children are more willing to admit their faults, they give up their resentments more easily. It has never ceased to amaze me how quickly my boys have become best buddies with children who seemed to be their worst enemies just days before. This flexibility of spirit—both to admit one's faults and to give up resentments—is a quality of meekness that Jesus would have us imitate.

Second, children are teachable. They are willing to listen in silence to others. Sometimes it is difficult for me to listen at any length to others. I am fidgety by nature and can't help thinking of all that I have to do. If I am hearing a teaching of some kind, I'm impatient if it's on a subject I think I already know. But as Bonhoeffer put it, "The silence of the Christian is listening silence, humble stillness."[1] It listens to what God may be saying to me through my brother or sister. It realizes that every other person has insights and gifts I do not have, and from which I can learn. And it listens to the still, small voice of God that may be speaking in the absence of any other voices.

Third, children tend to realize they deserve discipline after they have done wrong. Similarly, meekness involves a willingness to suffer (although much, perhaps most, suffering is not discipline for wrong-doing). For the spiritual masters, suffering is "the badge of true discipleship."[2] According to Bonhoeffer, "the disciple is a disciple only in so far as he shares his Lord's suffering and rejection and crucifixion."[3] Thomas à Kempis wrote, "If you will not suffer, you refuse to be crowned."[4] But Christians are willing to suffer because they realize that in the long run suffering brings Christlikeness and joy: "The desert can become a furnace of real repentance and purification where pride, complacency, and even some of the power of attachment itself can be burned away, and where the rain of God's love can bring conversion: life to the seeds of freedom."[5]

What About Holy Boldness?

Perhaps you are wondering if a willingness to suffer will open the door to people who are more than willing to take advantage of our meekness. Don't we need to be assertive? Aren't Christians supposed to confront evil boldly, as Jesus angrily challenged the moneychangers in the temple?

There is a place for righteous anger (Eph 4:26: "Be angry but do not sin"), and sometimes this means that Christians are called to boldly and firmly confront people who oppose the kingdom of God. For example, the Confessing Church in Germany in the 1930s was called by Christ to condemn Nazism as anti-Christian. Too often, however, Christians use Jesus' actions in the temple as a pretext for attacking with unholy emotion and self-righteous indignation those who oppose their political agenda.

True Christian courage has more to do with fighting the enemies within us than attacking other people. More often than not, Christian boldness means courageously maintaining an attitude of trust in God when all hell seems to be breaking loose around us. Or refusing to retaliate against those who have wronged us. Jesus showed his courage not by erupting in fiery passion or angry speeches but by submitting to his torturers and praying for their forgiveness. As Edwards put it, he shed not others' blood but his own.[6]

Christ showed us that ferocity and violence, more often than not, are signs of weakness rather than strength. Martin Luther King Jr. and his followers in the civil rights movement of the 1960s showed strength rather than weakness when they braved police sticks and dogs, and risked lynching and murder, without fighting back. Their courageous refusal to retaliate stirred the conscience of white America. Nonviolent prolife protesters show the same courage when they endure police brutality in their efforts to stir American consciences today. The tiny number of prolifers who endorse violence demonstrate weakness rather than strength and only perpetuate violence against the unborn.

Some of what claims to be holy boldness is a cover for pride or a desire for attention. True boldness often means humbly confessing one's own sins in the presence of one's enemies.

Christian Zeal

Like boldness, Christian "zeal" is often misunderstood. True Christian zeal is not the willingness to publicly denounce our opponents, but the burning desire to melt their hearts with the love of Christ. If there is righteous anger, it is directed not against persons but against things and practices. Carol Everett, the owner of several abortion clinics, was won both to Christ and to a prolife position by a man with true Christian zeal. Rather than attacking her for killing babies, a preacher named Jack Shaw touched Carol's heart by talking to her tenderly about her need for genuine love. He told her that we all search for love but often in the wrong places. He helped Carol realize that she was running abortion clinics for money that she could use to buy attention, respect and love from others. Jack led Carol in a prayer to receive Christ and his love for her.

Jack said nothing to Carol about killing babies. But shortly thereafter, as a result of Jack's love, Carol started seeing things differently. "Upon my return to the clinic," Carol remembers, "I noticed something was different. From my point of view, women had been dancing in through the front door, singing, 'I'm pregnant . . . Do my abortion . . .' But when I got back, I saw that all the women coming in the front door were crying. I'd never noticed that before."[7]

True Christian zeal treats its opponents not as enemies but as fellow sinners needing redemption. It is concerned first about its own sin and secondarily about the sins of others. Mahatma Gandhi was not a

Christian, but he used Christian principles which he learned from the Sermon on the Mount and Tolstoy's writings on suffering love. He told his followers who were fighting the British for Indian self-rule in the 1940s that in all their resistance they were resisting "loved ones." Gandhi refused to characterize his British opponents as enemies, even when they treated him and other Indians cruelly. For Gandhi, the British were loved ones, and the purpose of Gandhi's political efforts was to reform these loved ones by appealing to their consciences. He said his goal was the dissolution not of antagonists but of antagonism.[8]

Forgiveness

So far we have looked at meekness, the first quality that the spiritual masters have associated with Christlikeness. We have seen that meekness means admitting publicly that we have been wrong, being teachable and being willing to suffer. A second quality that is universally associated with Christlikeness is forgiveness. Jesus Christ himself, of course, is our example. He forgave his murderers even as they were murdering him. The New Testament tells us that we are to "forgive each other just as the Lord has forgiven" us (Col 3:13).

What does it mean to forgive? Jesus helped us understand by telling the parable of the slave who owed his king fifteen years' wages (Mt 18:23-35). The king forgave his debt. But this same slave refused to forgive another slave who owed merely a day's wage. Jesus condemned the unforgiving slave and said God will not forgive us if we don't forgive those who sin against us.

Corrie ten Boom's experience is a powerful illustration of how the Spirit enables a Christian to forgive even in the most difficult circumstances. She and her sister Betsie had been thrown into Nazi concentration camps because they had tried to save Jews from the Holocaust.

It was at a church service in Munich that I saw him, the former S.S. man who had stood guard at the shower room door in the processing center at Ravensbruck. [With the other guards, he had run his hands over their naked bodies and responded callously to their requests for assistance.] He was the first of our actual jailers that I had seen since that time. And suddenly it was all there—the roomful of mocking men, the heaps of clothing, Betsie's pain-blanched face. [Betsie died at the Ravensbruck death camp.]

He came up to me as the church was emptying, beaming and bowing. "How grateful I am for your message, *Fraulein,*" he said. "To think that, as you say, He has washed my sins away."

His hand was thrust out to shake mine. And I, who had preached so often to the people in Bloemendaal the need to forgive, kept my hand at my side.

Even as the angry, vengeful thoughts boiled through me, I saw the sin of them. Jesus Christ had died for this man; was I going to ask for more? Lord Jesus, I prayed, forgive me, and help me to forgive him.

I tried to smile, I struggled to raise my hand. I could not. I felt nothing, not the slightest spark of warmth or charity. And so again I breathed a silent prayer. Jesus, I cannot forgive him. Give me your forgiveness.

As I took his hand the most incredible thing happened. From my shoulder along my arm and through my hand a current seemed to pass from me to him, while into my heart sprang a love for this stranger that almost overwhelmed me.[9]

Love

The third quality of Christlikeness is the most important of all: love. In a sense, it includes the other three. That is, all the qualities of a Christlike spirit can be thought of as different aspects of love.

The sign of true spirituality most insisted on in the New Testament is love. Jesus said that "by this everyone will know that you are my disciples, if you have love for one another" (Jn 13:35). John wrote, "We know that we have passed from death to life because we love one another. Whoever does not love abides in death" (1 Jn 3:14). In the same epistle he warned that without love for others we cannot love God: "Those who say, 'I love God,' and hate their brothers and sisters, are liars; for those who do not love a brother or sister whom they have seen, cannot love God whom they have not seen" (1 Jn 4:20).

The great saints have said the same. According to John of the Cross, "In the evening they shall examine thee in love."[10] Johann Arndt wrote, "Great intelligence is common to pagans and Christians, and great works are common to believers and unbelievers. Love alone is the proper test of a Christian and distinguishes false Christians from true

Christians, for where there is no love, there is no good thing, even if it is costly and seems to be great."[11]

Jesus referred to the law of love as something peculiarly his own. "*I* give you a *new* commandment," he said, "that you love one another" (Jn 13:34). "This is *my* commandment," he went on, "that you love one another as I have loved you" (Jn 15:12). Jesus taught that the presence or absence of love is a barometer of both our own spirituality and the spirituality of others.

But there is a problem with love. Everyone seems to mean something different by the word. What did Jesus and the authors of Scripture mean by it? Without going into a technical study of how the word is used in the Bible, let me say this: for the authors of Scripture, and for Jesus, love is not a feeling. It will sometimes involve feelings, but in its essence it transcends feeling. Love is a commitment to *do* what is good for another. In other words, biblical love is practical. "The Lord is among the saucepans," said St. Teresa of Ávila.[12]

If love is all-important because it is the sum of Christlikeness, it is also the measure by which we will be judged. In Mother Teresa's words, "It is not how much we do, but how much love we put into it. When we do little things with great love, they become great."[13] Thomas à Kempis explained it like this: "God places more importance on how much love you put into your work than how much work you actually do."[14]

The Acid Test

Those who test for gold use nitric acid to determine if a rock is truly gold. So the term *acid test* has come to mean a conclusive way of determining if something is genuine. Jesus indicated that the acid test of Christian love is the way we treat our enemies. Loving those who love us, Jesus implied, is relatively easy. It comes naturally, both for the Christian and the non-Christian, the regenerate and the unregenerate. But distinctively *Christian* love begins when we do what is unnatural and extraordinary by going the second mile or offering our left cheek to our enemy after he has slapped the right. According to Bonhoeffer, it is "not only to refrain from treating [our enemy] as he treats us, but actively to engage in heart-felt love towards him."[15]

A lawyer asked Jesus, "Who is my neighbor?" Perhaps we need to ask, Who is my enemy? Bonhoeffer, who was murdered by his enemies, provides an answer: "By our enemies Jesus means those who are quite intractable and utterly unresponsive to our love, who forgive us nothing when we forgive them all, who requite our love with hatred and our service with derision."[16]

Bonhoeffer adds something that has helped me deal with my enemies—the notion that my enemy *needs* my love. No one, he wrote, needs our love more than our enemy. "The more bitter our enemy's hatred, the greater his need for love."[17]

There was a story in *Guideposts* some time ago about Elizabeth Morris, a woman whose only child, an eighteen-year-old boy, was killed by a drunk driver.[18] This mother was filled with unspeakable pain and grief. She was also full of venomous hatred for Tommy Pigage, the twenty-four-year-old warehouse worker who had killed her son. Nothing seemed to heal the pain. It felt even worse when Tommy was given probation rather than a prison sentence for killing her boy.

Some months later Tommy broke the terms of his probation and was sent to jail. Elizabeth felt compelled to visit him. As they talked Tommy suddenly burst out, "Mrs. Morris . . . I'm so sorry. Please forgive me." It had seemed impossible to forgive until this point, but for the first time Elizabeth saw Tommy not as the murderer of her son but as a person in need of love and guidance. She forgave Tommy and asked him to forgive her for hating him. Tommy was baptized at the Morrises' church by Elizabeth's husband, Frank, and the couple petitioned the judge to let them pick him up for church every Sunday. Soon he was spending every Sunday in their custody, having lunch in their home after church and then discussing the Bible most of the afternoon before being driven back to jail. At last report Tommy was on probation again and hadn't had a drink since his release.

Because of this woman's love for an enemy, a young man came to terms with his sin. Elizabeth's son was not restored, but another life was, because she had loved her enemy.

Helping the Poor
A fourth quality of Christlikeness is concern for the poor and unfortunate. According to the Scriptures, this is an indispensable sign of Christian love. Not only does true spirituality love its enemies, but it also cares for the poor and unfortunate. From Genesis to Revelation,

the Bible insists on charity to the needy as an essential mark of the true Christian. The psalmist tells us that "the righteous are generous and keep giving. . . . They are ever giving liberally and lending. . . . [They] have distributed freely, they have given to the poor" (Ps 37:21, 26; 112:9).

Proverbs is filled with passages such as the following: "Those who oppress the poor insult their Maker, but those who are kind to the needy honor him. . . . All day long the wicked covet, but the righteous give and do not hold back" (14:31; 21:26). In a verse that will startle those who think charity has nothing to do with being a Christian, the prophet Jeremiah wrote, " 'He defended the cause of the poor and needy, and so all went well. Is that not what it means to know me?' declares the LORD" (Jer 22:16 NIV).

The New Testament is equally clear. James insists, "Religion that is pure and undefiled before God, the Father, is this: to care for orphans and widows in their distress, and to keep oneself unstained by the world" (Jas 1:27). John asks, "How does God's love abide in anyone who has the world's goods and sees a brother or sister in need and yet refuses help?" (1 Jn 3:17). In Christ's description of the Day of Judgment (Mt 25), we are judged by how we treated those who need food and clothing and those in prison. Christ indicates that in some sense he is in them: "Just as you did it to one of the least of these who are members of my family, you did it to me" (Mt 25:40).

"On the last day," Johann Arndt reflects, "God will not ask how learned you were in the arts, in languages and in great knowledge, but how you practiced love by faith. *I was hungry and you fed me*, and so forth."[19]

My father has always been a great example to me in this area. In the last twenty years he has never had a reliable income and has often suffered financial distress. But at the same time he has been more generous than many affluent Christians. I have lost count of the number of times he has donated part or all of his savings to someone in desperate need of food or money. Like Christ, he cares for the poor.

Some of us may need to think of the *corporate* dimension of helping the poor. That is, what is our church doing to help the poor in our city or around the world? Sometimes more can be done when talents and resources are mobilized by a group than by individuals working on their own. Should our church build a Habitat for Humanity house in our town? Or enable a refugee family to move into our community? Or act publicly to combat racism against an ethnic group that because of its poverty is unable to defend itself effectively? In the kingdom of God churches are asking these questions so that they can demonstrate *corporately* the love of Jesus Christ.

Caution: Warning Ahead

I will close this chapter with two words of caution. First, don't be alarmed if you don't feel that you are meek, forgiving, loving or concerned about the poor. The mere fact that you are alarmed and *want* to grow into these is a sign that the spirit of Christ is working in you. Turn back to chapter six. Recall from there that we all are sinners who, like Paul, often despair because of the power of sin that we see in our lives. None of us has arrived; we are all very imperfect sinners who see more and more of our sin as we draw closer to Jesus. In fact, if you see more of your sin as time goes on, it is a good sign that the spirit of Christ is working within you. His light will illumine what was previously hidden by darkness.

My second warning is to pastors and other spiritual counselors. Those who boast of wonderful spiritual experiences but don't show *anything* of this grace of Christ—this change in the "spirit of the mind" to *want* to be meek, forgiving, loving and generous to the poor, and to be grieved when they are not—should not be encouraged that they have been converted. Scripture knows nothing of true Christians who are miserly, hateful, habitually unforgiving and self-righteously arrogant.

15

. . . . .

The Ninth
Reliable Sign
Fear of God

*FEAR OF THE LORD
IS THE BEGINNING OF WISDOM.*
P R O V E R B S

It WAS THE SUMMER AFTER MIKE'S SOPHOMORE YEAR IN COLLEGE. HE WAS intrigued by the new preacher who had come to his country church. This earnest man had a deep faith in God and preached from the Bible as if he believed every word. For the first time in his life, Mike was afraid for his soul. But he was also relieved when he heard this preacher say that belief in Christ would save from damnation. Mike felt that he was safe because he believed that Jesus had died for his sins. He didn't think that he needed to make any drastic changes in life, as long as he believed.

When Mike returned to college in the fall, he paid less attention to the state of his soul. He didn't think much about whether he was committing sin, and he rarely read the Bible. When he did, he found it difficult to understand; frankly, it bored him. He didn't go to church very often because he stayed out so late on Saturday night and often woke up the next morning with a hangover. When he was able to drag himself into church, he was sermon-proof. The pastor always seemed to be preaching about someone else's sin. If the sermon sometimes bothered his conscience, Mike figured it must be the devil. Occasionally he felt guilty because he had fallen back into his old habit of reading pornography. But then he reassured himself that he was saved because he still believed.

Fear Without Conversion

Mike is like many people who have unreliable religious affections. You may remember from the first chapters of this book that these are spiritual experiences without true conversion. Mike understood a part of what is involved in faith, that is, believing the facts of the gospel, but he never repented of his sin and so was never converted. He believed intellectually but did not trust with his heart.

People like Mike are not willing to be disciples of Jesus. They don't want to carry the cross. They insist on continuing to indulge their favorite lusts. For them, Christ is the Savior *of* their sins, not the One who saved them *from* their sins. Instead of using Christ to defend them against their spiritual enemies, they use Christ to defend their spiritual enemies. Christ becomes for them a spiritual narcotic that allows them to sin in good conscience, without fear of God. They are like the false teachers who, according to Jude, "pervert the grace of our God into licentiousness" (Jude 4).

A Fear That Softens

Saving grace, in contrast, imparts fear of God. Instead of hardening the heart, as happened to Mike, saving grace softens the heart. It makes us afraid to sin, not because we're afraid of hell but because we don't want to hurt the beautiful Savior whom we love. This is the difference between proper and improper fear of God. Improper fear is servile, the abject terror of the doomed grasping at anything that will save them from their destruction. Proper fear of God is reverence—a loving eagerness to please one's heavenly Father. It will want to change whatever is displeasing by asking the Spirit for the power to change.

This was Rick's attitude after a conversion experience in his freshman year at college. As a child he had been afraid of going to hell, but when he came home on spring break he went to a prayer meeting where he was overwhelmed by the beauty of Jesus' suffering love for his own sin-sick soul. This experience left him with a fear not of eternal damnation but of wounding the heart of the beautiful Savior who had suffered for him.

A whole new world opened up for Rick. He was struck by God's beauty in the sunrise and sensed God speaking to him in a myriad of voices—convicting him of sin in sermons, imparting wisdom through the counsel of friends and unveiling himself through the words of Scripture.

Rick read the Bible most nights after he got home from work that first summer and was amazed to discover that this book, which once had seemed incomprehensible and rather dry, had become a delightful treasure. He couldn't seem to get enough of it. The more he read, the more love he felt for this glorious God who had saved him. And the more distressed he felt when he sinned. When a new Christian friend told Rick that the pictures of nude women that decorated his room were "not of the Spirit," Rick was quick to take them down. When Rick's roommate at college complained that he was too noisy at night and rarely showed interest in him, Rick asked his forgiveness and asked God for sensitivity. Rick also started to realize that his fear and dislike of African-Americans was sinful racism. He asked the Spirit to cleanse him of these attitudes and to help him to see people as individuals whom he was called to love.

In other words, Rick had the fear of God. He was anxious to please God and fearful of offending him, not because he feared punishment from God but because he loved him.

Fear That Springs from Love

The other day my twelve-year-old son Ross reminded my wife to buy me some Fig Newtons, my favorite snack, when she went to the store. Last week when he had forgotten his daily chore (emptying the garbage) for the second day in a row, Ross panicked when he saw me coming home from work. He wasn't afraid of punishment (simply forgetting doesn't usually merit discipline in our house) but fearful that he might disappoint me. As soon as I stepped inside the door, Ross called out cheerfully, "I'm going to do the garbages, Dad." Ross did what he did because he loves me. He was delighted to please me with the Fig Newtons and distressed to realize that he hadn't done what I had asked.

This is something like what the Bible means by fear of God. It is anxious to know what pleases God and pained when it realizes it has displeased him. According to Scripture, fear of God softens the heart so that it is easily wounded by sin. Like bruised flesh that is tender and easily hurt, the saint's heart hurts with godly sorrow when it displeases God. As David wrote, "The sacrifice acceptable to God is a broken spirit; a broken and contrite heart, O God, you will not despise" (Ps 51:17). Speaking through Isaiah, God says, "I dwell in the high and holy place, and also with those who are contrite and humble in spirit" (Is 57:15). God looks for the one who "trembles at my word" (Is 66:2).

Shouldn't We Be Bold Before God?

Perhaps you're wondering how boldness fits into this. Does fear of God mean that the Christian cannot enter God's presence with confidence? Aren't we supposed to pray with boldness, knowing that the blood and righteousness of Christ enable us to stand free of sin with full access to God's love and attention?

Of course we should. The problem is that sometimes we forget our real situation. We forget that it is only by Christ's blood and righteousness that we have any right to stand before God. Instead we tend to think, like the Pharisee, that God is fortunate to have such a good person working for him: "He trusted in [himself] that he was righteous" (Lk 18:9).

I've heard Christians address God as if he were the neighborhood ice-cream man, only bigger. Or something like the Wizard of Oz, a being who has extraordinary power but is not essentially unlike us (I've heard some call God "the big man"). Yet God *is* essentially unlike us. He is holy and we are unholy. Our best intentions and deeds are only "filthy rags" when seen in the blinding light of his pure love.

We should approach God with the same awe and (proper) fear as the biblical saints displayed. Elijah was intimate with God, yet when he talked with God on the mountain he dared not show his face but "wrapped his face in his mantle" (1 Kings 19:13). Moses spoke with God face to face, as one speaks to a friend (Ex 33:11). Yet when he was nearest to God, on Mount Sinai, Moses "quickly bowed his head toward the earth and worshiped" (Ex 34:8). Even the spotless and glorious angels cover their faces before God's throne (Is 6).

Why was it that nearly every biblical saint who was approached by the presence of God fell to the ground in terror? Because of the holiness of God. They had the sense of something radically different, something totally other, a Being who could destroy them in an instant and not be unjust in destroying them. In comparison to the absolute purity of this Being, they were filthy. God's fearsome otherness has a way of destroying all our pretensions and opening our eyes to what is really Real. As R. C. Sproul puts it, "When we encounter Him, the totality of our creatureliness breaks upon us and shatters the myth that we have believed about ourselves that we are demi-gods, junior-grade deities who will try to live forever."[1]

Jesus commended the tax collector for his fear of God. Because he knew his own moral filth, the tax collector dared not lift his eyes to heaven but beat his breast and cried, "God, be merciful to me, a sinner" (Lk 18:13). The woman "who was a sinner" (Lk 7) felt unworthy to come before Jesus, so she "stood behind him at his feet, weeping," bathing his feet with her tears, drying them with her hair, kissing them and anointing them with ointment. There is perhaps no other portion of Scripture that so beautifully illustrates proper fear of God: sorrow for sin and desire to please that flow from love.

The Telltale Mark

Jonathan Edwards said that the telltale mark of proper fear of God is conviction of sin. True grace promotes it, making the heart more tender. Rick is a good example of this. When he sensed from Scripture, a sermon or others' advice that he was displeasing God, he was quick to repent, seek forgiveness and ask the Spirit for the power to change. Rather than defend himself, Rick agreed with the Spirit that was convicting him of sin.

False spirituality, on the other hand, doesn't admit to sin. Like Mike, the college student described at the beginning of this chapter, it rushes to defend itself or point the finger elsewhere when the Spirit exposes its sin. The result is a hardened heart that resists the Spirit's work within.

Is Fear Compatible with Assurance of Salvation?

Fear of God is a delicate subject. Several points need to be made for the sake of clarity. The first has to do with fear. In this day when we are discovering more about the nature and extent of child abuse, some have concluded that the Christian concept of fear of God reflects unhealthy parent-child relationships in the premodern world. But as I have tried to show, proper fear of God is not the child's servile fear of a capricious and domineering parent. Instead, it is the eagerness of a child who loves its daddy (an accurate translation of *abba*, the Aramaic word Jesus used for God) and wants to please him.

Another misunderstanding is that the fear of God is rooted in a fear of hell. But the Bible is clear that proper fear of God springs from assurance of salvation. The psalmist writes, "Truly the eye of the LORD is on those who fear him, on those who *hope* in his steadfast love" (Ps 33:18). For the biblical authors, hope is not an uncertain wish but a confident expectation. So to "hope in his steadfast love" is to trust that God *will* save me. We find the same notion in Psalm 147:11: "The LORD takes pleasure in those who fear him, in those who hope in his steadfast love."

Proper fear of God is always allied with assurance of salvation. It is a "trembling with joy" (Ps 2:11). In fact, the more we are assured of salvation, the greater we will fear displeasing our Lord and the more tender our consciences will become. Why? Because as we grow in assurance, we will grow in love for the Assurer and thus grow more anxious not to hurt his heart.

At the same time we will grow in holy boldness. We will be more confident to come before God because of Christ's blood and righteousness, but less confident in ourselves. For the more assured we are of salvation from hell, the more we will feel worthy of hell.

Paradoxically, then, we grow stronger as we feel weaker. Our fear (of sinning against God) increases as we become more and more confident of our protection (from sin and hell). As Edwards put it, "The saint has the firmest comfort, but the softest heart: richer than others, but poorest of all in spirit: the tallest and strongest saint, but the least and tenderest child amongst them."[2]

Fear of God and Social Justice

I need to sound one more note before closing this chapter. Fear of God is concerned not only with personal sin but with social sin as well. True saints are awestruck by the demands of God's law as they pertain to society, not just personal morality. They are eager to honor God's holiness by seeking God's justice for their neighbors as well as themselves. Like Amos, they will speak out against those who "trample on the needy, and bring to ruin the poor of the land" (Amos 8:4). They will realize that it is not just kings, princes and judges but every believer who is to "do justice" (Gen 18:19; Ps 119:121; Prov 1:3). They will see that to "do justice" is particularly expected of those who "fear God" (Lk 18:2).

Reinhold Niebuhr was a young pastor in Detroit in the 1920s. He could have remained contented with building his little church from 65 members to 653 over the course of a little more than a decade. But he could not shake the feeling that God's holy law was calling him to work for social justice. Niebuhr took on Henry Ford, one of the most powerful industrialists in the United States. In an attempt to raise the low living standard of Ford assembly-line workers, Niebuhr published his findings that inflation had resulted in a significant loss of real income, despite Ford's claim that his workers were well paid.

Niebuhr also struggled to expose the problems faced by black citizens of Detroit. He served as the leader of a citywide committee on race problems. In a national journal he itemized the problems black Detroiters faced: housing discrimination by banks and white neighborhoods, police brutality, exclusion from entire professions and the failure of white churches to help black congregations of their own denomination. He called on his readers to fight for racial justice.[3]

We may not be able to serve on citywide committees or write for national journals. But we all can hear the voice of the Hebrew prophets urging us to "do justice, love kindness and walk humbly" with our God (Micah 6:8). Jesus reminds us that if we fail to listen to the cries of the hungry and the thirsty, the stranger and the prisoner, we are ignoring the voice of Jesus himself (Mt 25:31-46). Then it will be clear that we fear not God but our own discomfort.

16

. . . . .

The Tenth
Reliable Sign
Balance

ANOTHER THING WHEREIN THOSE AFFECTIONS
THAT ARE TRULY GRACIOUS AND HOLY,
DIFFER FROM THOSE THAT ARE FALSE, IS BEAUTIFUL
SYMMETRY AND PROPORTION.
JONATHAN EWARDS

TRUE SPIRITUALITY IS A MATTER OF BALANCE. IF THERE IS PROFESSION
of faith with the lips, there is also walking the faith out with the feet.
Believers who love God love their neighbors as well. They follow Christ
in both good times and bad.

Not that there is perfection in the lives of saints. Far from it. The
saint's sense of balance is always imperfect owing to imperfect teaching,
personality quirks or errors in judgment.

Assurance and Fear
But the saint's life doesn't have the enormous imbalance that commonly characterizes false spirituality. Think, for instance, of Mike from
the last chapter. He professed Christ and believed that he was saved,
yet neglected church, prayer and the Bible, continued to get drunk

regularly and ignored the needs of those around him. Mike had enormous imbalance in his life—assurance of salvation but no fear of God. Talk about the Spirit without any fruit of the Spirit!

Anita, on the other hand, balances assurance of salvation with fear of God. A forty-one-year-old wife and mother, Anita came to Christ as a teenager and now tries to serve the Lord through her church and family. "I serve the Lord because I love him," she told me recently, "but I also fear his discipline. I know that if I give in to my natural tendency to laziness, his rod of correction will get me back on the straight and narrow path.

"This may sound strange, but God's discipline makes me feel secure. My parents raised me in the sixties and, perhaps because of the permissiveness of that era, never gave me the discipline I needed. So I grew up as a wild and rebellious young woman. As a result, it's been very hard for me to discipline my life in the way that I think the Lord wants. But fearing his corrections—and some of them may simply be natural consequences of my sin, I don't know for sure—helps keep me close to him."

Joy and Mourning

Like the two women who left Jesus' tomb "with fear and great joy" (Mt 28:8), Anita balances joy and fear. She also balances joy with mourning. Her joy is still the joy of salvation, but her mourning is over her sins. Jesus indicated that true saints will continue to mourn in repentance for their sins: "Blessed are those who mourn, for they will be comforted" (Mt 5:4).

The masters of spirituality have said the same. Johann Arndt wrote that saints will mourn both their own and others' sins.

If a man looks at himself, he finds more reason to sorrow than to be joyous. If he properly looks upon other people's lives, he finds more reason to weep for them than to envy them. Why did the Lord weep over Jerusalem, which persecuted him and killed him? Your sin and blindness were the cause of his weeping (Lk 19:42). Thus, the greatest reason for weeping should be our sins and other people's unrepentance.[1]

Thomas à Kempis adds that godly grief comes from honest self-examination: "The more closely [a saint] examines himself, the more he grieves. The grounds for our just grief and remorse are our faults and sins."[2]

The true saint therefore balances assurance of salvation with fear of God and mourning for sin.

Love for God and Love for Others

Some people profess great love for God and Christ but are filled with grudges and envy and frequently fight with others. I remember the leading family of a church I attended as a boy. They were very active in the church, and the mother impressed many as particularly holy because she was always the first to go to the Communion rail, with great solemnity. Yet she led the faction that drove a new priest out of the church. His offenses? He recited the liturgy with great feeling and extended the sermon from its traditional ten to twenty minutes. In this woman's words, "He changed the way we do things here." Perhaps she and her followers felt targeted by the priest's sermons about the difference between external religiosity and inner piety. By the time this man left, she and her followers had come to speak of him with hatred in their voices.

The apostle John wrote, "Those who say, 'I love God,' and hate their brothers or sisters, are liars; for those who do not love a brother or sister whom they have seen, cannot love God whom they have not seen" (1 Jn 4:20). With these words John makes clear that *a true Christian maintains a balance between love for God and love for others, particularly those with whom we disagree.*

Love for Friends and Strangers

Some people have great affection for their friends or family or like-minded neighbors but hate those who are different. Many Americans before the Civil War, for instance, were active church members who preached love for neighbor but held their black neighbors in chains. Some white Americans claimed that they loved their black slaves, but keeping them in bonds against their will is a strange kind of love. The slaves undoubtedly experienced this professed love as hatred.

Most of us know people, like the woman I described above, who praise God in church while hating fellow church members with whom they disagree. They agree with the minister when he preaches love for neighbor but refuse to fellowship with those of another faction and enjoy spreading bad reports about their opponents in the church.

Jesus said that Christians are to love their enemies, the persons who are different and have different opinions.

If you love those who love you, what credit is that to you? For even sinners love those who love them. If you do good to those who do good to you, what credit is that to you? For even sinners do the same. If you lend to those from whom you hope to receive, what credit is that to you? Even sinners lend to sinners, to receive as much again. But love your enemies, do good, and lend, expecting nothing in return. (Lk 6:32-35)

True saints therefore have balance; they love not only their friends but also their enemies and those who are different.

Love for Neighbor and Family

Some people love their neighbors but are mean and unloving to their own family. Leslie is a sixty-year-old woman who has cut herself off from her sisters and brother for more than twenty years. She never was easy to get along with, but the final rupture came when mother died and the adult children tried to settle the inheritance. Leslie's brother Freeman, who had reluctantly agreed to serve as executor of their mother's estate, tried to be fair. Leslie, however, decided that Freeman had not given her as much as she deserved. After cursing the hapless Freeman for his "insensitivity" to her, she told him she would not speak to him or her sisters ever again.

Leslie has kept her word. She refuses to take her siblings' calls. When one of Freeman's children stopped by Leslie's house to say hello, Leslie answered the door icily and made it clear she didn't want to talk. Freeman, who tried hard to be fair, is devastated. Both sisters are heartbroken. Yet Leslie is a faithful churchgoer and is regarded as a good neighbor.

Sometimes the toughest place to love is home. There we feel free to "be ourselves," dropping the courtesies and discretions that we customarily show outside the home. There it becomes plain that there is a gap between what we profess and who we really are. We tend to take our loved ones for granted and fail to show them the appreciation that we would give to a guest. As a friend once told me, we should treat our family like guests and our guests like family.

I don't know any Christian parents who don't love their children. But I do know some Christian parents who have never communicated their love to their children because of their legalism. Rather than concentrating on how to let their children know they are loved, these parents have been primarily concerned with what others think, or they have majored on minors. Their years with their teenagers were dominated by fights over hair length, clothing and whether they could attend a dance or go to the movies. They were concerned more with keeping rules than with demonstrating the love of Christ. It's no wonder that some of their children want nothing to do with Christianity.

Pastor George and his wife, Ann, were different. Their three boys knew that their dad would interrupt his work at any time to talk if they really needed to see him. That is, they knew that George was more concerned about his relationship with them than about what people in the church thought. George and Ann were strict with their boys, but honesty and respect counted more in their home than length of hair or wearing jeans to church.

True spirituality is balanced between love for neighbor and love for family.

Love for Body and Soul

Some church people are greatly concerned to feed the poor and clothe the naked but consider evangelism unimportant. To them, it is culturally arrogant to think that we have a religious message that can benefit someone from a culture that does not know of Christ.

Other church people today are so offended by this mentality that they think all Christian energies and monies ought to be directed to evangelism. Efforts to help the poor ought to be left to the government, they say, while the church redoubles its effort to get the gospel to those who haven't heard it.

Jesus did both. Mark describes a situation in which Jesus wanted to be alone with his disciples. But then he saw a crowd following him. "He had compassion for them, because they were like sheep without a shepherd; and he began to teach them many things" (Mk 6:34). The day grew late, and Jesus noticed that the crowd was hungry. So he multiplied bread and fish to feed more than five thousand. Jesus cared for both body and soul; he neglected neither evangelism nor social action.

Isn't this why Mother Teresa has won the respect of both liberals and conservatives, Protestants and Catholics, believers and unbelievers? She feeds the hungry and clothes the naked while at the same time telling them that only Jesus has the love they desire. Her selfless work for the poorest of the poor has enabled her to talk about Jesus to those who would not listen otherwise. And her bold proclamation of the gospel has pricked the consciences of church people who had previously thought they were not their (poverty-stricken) brother's keepers. Mother Teresa illustrates *the balance of the Christian faith as it feeds both body and soul and leads other Christians to do the same for others.*

Concern for My Own Sins as Well as Others'
Some of us are obsessed with the sins of others but don't see our own. Edwards said that false zeal is easy to spot: it is outraged by the sins of others but oblivious to its own.[3]

In a delightful passage from *The Screwtape Letters,* Uncle Screwtape tells his nephew (a junior devil in training) that human beings have a tendency to overlook their own faults and suggests the ridiculous lengths to which this can go.

> Aggravate that most useful human characteristic, the horror and neglect of the obvious. You must bring him to a condition in which he can practice self-examination for an hour without discovering any of those facts about himself which are perfectly clear to anyone who has ever lived in the same house with him or worked in the same office with him.[4]

Jesus told us that citizens of his kingdom, however, will mourn their sins (as we saw above) and will be aware of their spiritual poverty: "Blessed are the poor in spirit, for theirs is the kingdom of heaven" (Mt 5:3). According to Jesus, therefore, *true spirituality demonstrates a balanced concern for one's own sins and the sins of others.*

Trusting God for Salvation and Provision
Some church people say they trust God completely but are not willing to give money to help the poor or spread the gospel. They say they trust God with their souls but don't trust him to be Lord over their bank

accounts. But if we truly believe Jesus is Lord, we should also believe him when he says that "all these things [material provisions for life] will be given to you as well" (Mt 6:33). In this same passage Jesus says that it is non-Christians who worry incessantly about money; his disciples need not worry. For they should know that God cares about them, far more than he cares about the birds of the air and the lilies of the field, for which he provides richly.

Dick is a sixty-eight-year-old man who has had very little money for the last twenty-five years. Once a corporate executive, he lost his job at the age of forty-four when he disagreed with the president of the firm. He was never able to get a decent job after that. In the years since, he has worked for others and himself, never earning more than a small fraction of the salary he commanded as a young man. He lost his savings and his house and has learned to live a frugal life.

Yet in all these years of scarcity Dick has become known as a very generous man. He has always given a minimum of ten percent of his income to the church and to the poor, and often substantially more. I have lost count of the times Dick has given away a good part of his savings to someone he thought needed it more. Like the poor widow in the Gospels, Dick gives not out of his plenty but out of his scarcity. He would be the first to tell you that he gives because he knows that God supplies his needs. *Christians, then, are balanced: they trust God not only for salvation but also for financial provision.*

For Better or for Worse

Some people are spiritual only intermittently—when everyone else is or when a revival comes to town. They are like the rocky-soil hearers who rejoice in the gospel when they first hear it but fall away "when trouble or persecution arises on account of the word" (Mt 13:21). Or they are like the thorny-soil people whose faith was choked by "the cares of the world and the lure of wealth" (Mt 13:22). Both sorts of people stick with the gospel only as long as it doesn't make things difficult for them.

I remember the large number of teenagers who joined our prayer meetings in the early 1970s because they were exciting. People were getting healed and having dramatic spiritual experiences. But most of the joiners stopped coming when they realized that the Christian life involves discipline and self-denial. As far as I know, many of these people are still living secular lives and have never committed themselves to a community of believers. Thomas à Kempis described them well when he said, "Many follow Jesus up to the breaking of the bread, but few as far as drinking from the chalice of his Passion."[5] Jude said they are like comets that appear for a while with a huge blaze of light and then disappear (Jude 13).

True disciples, however, don't give up. They will have their ups and downs and perhaps even backslide for a time. But they will repent, pick themselves up off the ground and ask the Spirit for strength to carry on. Jesus said that within a saint will be a well of water continually "gushing up to eternal life" (Jn 4:14). It will never be depleted. Jeremiah wrote that a true saint is "like a tree planted by water, sending out its roots by the stream. It shall not fear when heat comes, and its leaves shall stay green; in the year of drought it is not anxious, and it does not cease to bear fruit" (Jer 17:8).

The disciple of Jesus therefore loves Jesus in good times and bad. In Johann Arndt's words, "a Christian . . . is pious, both in good and evil times, and loves God at both times in fortune and misfortune, in ownership and loss, in need and superfluity."[6]

Doug Howe showed his true colors when his thirty-four-year-old wife Judy, mother of five children, died of cancer. Doug missed Judy deeply and was suddenly faced with caring for young children for whom Judy had met nearly every need. Doug was overwhelmed. Yet through his faith, Doug managed to endure.

I'll always remember a conversation I had one day with Doug about the huge medical bills he faced because of Judy's hospitalization. I remarked on how discouraged I would be if I faced such huge bills. Doug replied with a smile of confidence that I'll never forget, "Gerry, it's only money." Doug was saying that monetary problems don't compare with the loss of a loved one. He was also saying that he knew the same Jesus who had given him the grace to endure Judy's death would help him pay his bills.

Doug somehow managed to both pay the bills and regain his bearings after his terrible loss. But he didn't accomplish this by his own strength. He reached down deep for the waters of Jesus' consolation and found them because of the deep well that the Spirit had previously dug in his heart. Doug is an illustration that *Jesus' disciples follow him both in good times and in bad.*

Public Worship and Secret Prayer

Others have strong religious affections in public or with other believers but little or nothing of true spirituality in private. Some of them are consumed with telling others about Jesus but know nothing of secret prayer.

The Bible, however, says that true spirituality disposes a person to spend time alone, in solitary places, for meditation and prayer. As the psalmist wrote, "My soul is satisfied as with a rich feast, and my mouth praises you with joyful lips when I think of you on my bed, and meditate on you in the watches of the night" (Ps 63:5-6).

The Scriptures indicate that God particularly manifested himself to his people when they were alone. He revealed his promises and kindnesses to Abraham, for example, when he was alone. Isaac received his special gift (Rebecca) when he was walking alone, meditating in a field. Jacob was alone in prayer when the angel of the Lord came to him and wrestled with him. God revealed himself to Moses in the burning bush when Moses was in a solitary place in the desert. On the mountain God revealed his glory when Moses had been alone for forty days and nights. God came to Elijah and Elisha primarily when they were alone.

It was Jesus' habit to get alone to pray to his Father. He started his ministry by spending forty days alone in the desert. Before choosing the Twelve he spent an entire night alone in the desert hills (Lk 6:12). After feeding the five thousand, he dismissed his disciples and the crowd and "went up the mountain by himself to pray" (Mt 14:23).

Even in the midst of an exhausting schedule Jesus blocked out time to pray. Mark tells us that in Capernaum he spent a good part of a sabbath teaching and casting out demons. Then he healed Peter's mother. At sundown "the whole city" brought to him "all who were sick or possessed with demons." He cured many and cast out many demons (Mk 1:32-34). After such an exhausting day, most of us would welcome the chance to sleep in, to restore our strength. But Mark tells us that next morning before dawn Jesus "got up and went out to a deserted place, and there he prayed" (Mk 1:35). And Jesus was transfigured when he was apart from the crowd, with only his closest disciples, and in prayer at night.

We find a similar pattern in the lives of other saints of the New Testament. When the angel Gabriel appeared to Mary, she seems to have been alone. When John received his revelations, he was alone on the island of Patmos.

This pattern can also be seen in the lives of great saints in church history. As Thomas à Kempis wrote, "The greatest saints guarded their time alone and chose to serve God in solitude."[7] The story is told of Martin Luther that one day he faced so much work that he felt it necessary to spend three hours in prayer. It must also be said, however, that in times of crushing workload Luther would "stack up" his prayers over several weeks and then devote whole days to solitary prayer and meditation to make up for time lost. Jonathan Edwards habitually rose before dawn (4:00 a.m. in summer and 5:00 a.m. in winter) to spend unhurried time in prayer and adoration before he began his day of study.

Thomas à Kempis advised, "Seek a quiet place for yourself and love to linger there alone. Do not look for idle chit-chat, but pour forth devout prayers to God."[8] True saints try to follow Thomas's advice. As they grow in grace, they enjoy such quiet times more and more. *They balance public worship with times of private prayer* in which they "listen to the thunder of God's silence."[9]

At the same time that we need to be reminded of the urgency of private prayer, we also need to recall the indispensability of corporate worship. Too many Christians think Sunday worship is optional. Our society's disenchantment with organized religion has encouraged some of us to consider private prayer an acceptable substitute for corporate worship. "I can worship God better alone on a hilltop than at church," some of us say.

We forget, however, that participation in regular corporate worship is one of the Ten Commandments (and that we usually don't take the time on Sundays to worship at the hilltop anyway). The church has always understood "Keep the sabbath holy" to mean that we are *obliged* to join together with other believers at least weekly to worship, pray, listen to the Word and, for most of the world's Christians, receive the sacraments.

It is also a time to build one another up. Too many of us evaluate church by what we get out of it. But the Scriptures talk more about our duties: to worship God and to "encourage one another" (Heb 10:25). We encourage one another by weeping with those who weep and rejoicing with those who rejoice, by exhorting and loving, hugging and listening, ministering the Word and receiving the Word, and simply by our presence. If we think like consumers who are simply out for a bargain, how will the kingdom of God grow? Who will do the works of faith and love required to build the church on earth? We must ask not what the church can do for us, but what we can do for the church.

Regular participation at worship is not only a Christian duty, however. It is also a gift. If we decline to take the gift regularly, we will suffer in a number of ways. First, we will lose spiritual life. The fire of a coal separated from a pile of other burning coals will soon die. So will our love for God diminish if we remove ourselves from regular participation in a local expression of the body of Christ. This last image is telling: as Christians, we are members of Christ's body (Rom 12:4-5; Eph 1:22-23). If we stay away from church, we are cutting ourselves off from Christ himself, whose body is the church.

Second, we will lose the benefit of discipline. My brothers and sisters in Christ at my church keep me accountable. When I stray from the narrow way, particularly in ways that I do not recognize, they let me know. I am thankful for their correction and reproofs because they warn me when I am beginning to cut myself off from the life that feeds me.

Third, we miss out on the encouragement that comes from the rest of the body. We all go through dark periods when we need to be reassured that God and others still care for us. If we are not plugged into a body of believers, we will stand alone.

Barbara, a member of our church, is dying of cancer. She receives enormous strength and encouragement from church members who spend time with her at the hospital and at home. But they are also refreshed and encouraged by Barbara's shining faith. Little of this would be happening if Barbara and her friends were not active members of a church.

Finally, we miss out on the special graces that are given through Bible preaching and the sacraments. Using Romans 10:14-17, which suggests that Christ speaks through preachers of his Word, the great Reformers Luther and Calvin taught that the Spirit of Christ communicates through Bible preaching in a way that is different from what happens in personal Bible study. I cannot count the times I have sat under Bible preaching that made a passage come alive in a way that was completely new and compelling to me, even after I had studied that same passage privately. I seemed to be hearing God himself speak to my heart through the words of the preacher, even if the sermon was otherwise mediocre.

And for many Christians, corporate worship is their only time to receive the Eucharist, the real presence of the body and blood of Christ. For these believers this is the most precious time of their week, when they receive the person and life of Christ in a way not available to them outside the Lord's Supper. Because of the sacraments, they are grateful for the gift of corporate worship.

In summary, true spirituality is balanced between assurance and fear of God, joy and mourning, love for God and love for others, love for both friends and strangers, love for neighbor as well as family, and concern for others' bodies as well as souls. It is concerned for our own sins and not just others', it trusts God for both salvation and financial provision, and perseveres in the faith through trials and troubles. Finally, it is regular at public worship as well as secret prayer.

17

· · · · ·

The Eleventh
Reliable Sign
Hunger for God

*MY SOUL LONGS, INDEED IT FAINTS
FOR THE COURTS OF THE LORD.*
THE PSALMIST

FOR A LONG TIME ANNA EDSON PUZZLED ME. SHE WAS IN HER LATE SIXTIES at the time I knew her, when I belonged to a Christian community in Indiana. I was fresh out of college, anxious to learn more about life and what it means to be a Christian. I eagerly attended seminars and studies on the Bible and Christian theology because I wanted to prepare myself for a life of Christian service. But Anna, nearing the end of her life, was every bit as attentive and inquisitive as I was. She sat in the front row, avidly taking notes, asking keen questions.

One day I tried to figure out why Anna was working so hard to learn in the twilight years of her life. If I were her age, I thought, I wouldn't work so hard to learn new things. So I asked her if she liked the seminars, hoping to get an inkling of her motivation. "Gerry," she replied, "I love these seminars. Don't you think they're wonderful?"

"Yes, but don't you know this stuff already?" I was determined not to let her go until she told me why she was so determined.

"Oh, no. There's a lot I don't know. And much of what I do know I haven't put into practice. But when I hear these things taught in new ways, it helps me to put them in my heart and then experience them. Don't you think these teachers' stories are fascinating?"

I admitted that they were interesting but pressed her again. This time I asked her if sitting through all these teachings didn't tire her.

"Sure, it's a bit tough at my age. But I've got so much to learn. When I listen to these teachings on the nature of God, I feel like a baby who has just started out in life. I feel like I'm just beginning to know what it means to love him."

A Divine Discontent

True spirituality hungers for more and more of God. Anna was hungry to experience more of God, even though she had been a dynamic Christian for more than forty years. False spirituality, in contrast, is content with what it has. It figures that it already knows enough of God and has no desire to go deeper.

Like Anna, true saints want more. The more they love God, the more they want to love him, and the more distressed they are by how little they love him. The more they hate sin, the more they want to hate sin, and the more disturbed they are by how much they love sin. The more they mourn their sins, the more they want to mourn; the more their hearts break, the more they wish their hearts would break continually; the more they thirst and long for God, the more they want to thirst and long to long.

We Are Beggars

There are several reasons that saints are not satisfied with where they are and what they have spiritually. First, they realize that in comparison to what they want to be, they are "like newborn infants" (1 Pet 2:2). Paul compares our spiritual experience on this side of heaven to childhood experiences of thinking, reasoning and talking (1 Cor 13:10-11). Even our deepest spiritual experiences and thoughts are childish in comparison to the maturity we will reach in heaven. Now, Paul says, our vision is "partial"; then it shall be "complete" (1 Cor 13:10). On this side of the veil we see through a mirror dimly, but in eternity we will see face to face (1 Cor 13:12).

The saint recognizes that, as Martin Luther put it on his deathbed, "we are beggars." In comparison to the infinite riches of grace that we can experience, we have next to nothing. Our greatest spiritual treasures are but tiny foretastes of the gargantuan glory awaiting us. The indwelling Spirit in our hearts is only "a first installment" (2 Cor 1:22; 5:5; Eph 1:14) or down payment on the heavenly realities in store for us. Realizing this makes us hunger for more.

Therefore saints press forward, never content with the paltry spirituality that they have. Though Paul had seen more of God than most of us ever hope to see, he said, "Forgetting what lies behind and straining forward to what lies ahead, I press on toward the goal for the prize of the heavenly call of God in Christ Jesus" (Phil 3:13-14). Like Paul, the saint is never complacent or self-satisfied.

Because the taste of God's holiness and glory is sweet—and the holier the saint, the sweeter the taste—the saint always hungers for more. Teresa of Ávila's autobiography is filled with descriptions of rapturous ecstasies in which she felt overwhelming joy in the presence of God. But instead of making her content to live with their memory, they inspired fresh hunger for more of God and his holiness.

Part of the saints' ever-growing hunger is fed by their growing realization of the depth of their sin. As they see more of their sin, they plead all the more for grace to forgive and overcome their sin. Their prayer is that of the father whose son had an evil spirit: "I believe; help my unbelief!" (Mk 9:24).

How Can Grace Satisfy?

Perhaps you are wondering how grace can be satisfying if the saint is never satisfied. Admittedly, there is a bit of a paradox here. But it can be better understood if we ask ourselves how, or in what respects, grace satisfies. Edwards suggested four ways.

First, those who have grace want no other kind of satisfaction. Having tasted the soul-satisfying delights of grace, they realize that nothing else comes close to providing the profound peace and joy that come by grace. Augustine discovered this at his conversion at the age of thirty-two. After living for years as a sex addict and fearing that he could not be happy without sex, he realized instantly upon conversion that he would always be happy with grace and that never again would he need sex for happiness.

Second, only grace fulfills one's expectations. The things of this world never quite live up to our hopes. I realized this when I was nine years old. For months I had been lusting for a simulated fighter jet cockpit. I begged my parents to get it for me for Christmas. When Christmas finally arrived and I breathlessly ripped the paper off a large package, I was overjoyed to discover that I had what I wanted. But several hours later I was depressed. The thrill was gone. Now that I had used it for a while and performed all the operations it was capable of, it was no longer fun. Never again would I experience the excitement of that first hour or two. Even the months of hopeful anticipation had been better than what I now felt as I played with it.

In a childish but nevertheless genuine manner, I realized that the greatest earthly joys would never be all that great. But I have discovered since my conversion that the joys of grace are far greater than anything this earth can provide, and that they always point beyond themselves to something better. They fulfill expectation and then some.

Third, the pleasure of grace is permanent. Worldly pleasures satisfy only for a time. Afterward one feels empty. Like saltwater, they never truly refresh. The joy from spiritual pleasures, on the other hand, remains. Although one tastes only a tiny fraction of the riches available, that tiny fraction leaves a permanent residue. It is something like a great work of literature. After you have read it, you can enjoy the memory, and perhaps the new vision it provided, for the rest of your life.

Finally, spiritual pleasure is boundless. It's an "infinite ocean."[1] The only thing that keeps us from receiving more is our small capacity. If we aren't satisfied, the problem is with us. As Edwards put it so pithily, "We don't open our mouths wide enough."[2]

If worldly things don't satisfy us, the problem doesn't usually lie with us. Sex, money and power (and food!) can never finally and permanently satisfy because of what they are—worldly things that do nothing to quench our spiritual thirst. Nothing of this world will ever be able to satify that part of us that is not of this world. Trying to get these things to satisfy us is like trying to fit a round peg in a square hole.

Now we can understand better why grace alone ultimately satisfies, yet the saint always wants more. The saint desires more not because grace has not been satisfying but precisely because grace *has* been satisfying. Joy in God makes us want to know more of God.

Seeking and Striving

It is very different for the unregenerate. When they have intense religious affections (see chapter three), their hunger for grace dies.

Eddie, a college student, was terrified of going to hell. His roommate convinced him to go to church one Sunday. The Baptist minister preached an evangelistic sermon, and Eddie felt emotionally moved to accept Christ. Because of his emotional experience, Eddie felt that he had been saved. He had no more longing for grace and holiness, because he believed he was no longer in danger of going to hell. He no longer thought of himself as spiritually bankrupt, but as spiritually prosperous. Now, he thought, he was a spiritual person. He didn't read the Bible or go to church, and he prayed only occasionally. These omissions didn't bother him, because he was convinced that his memorable emotional experience made him a spiritual person, destined for heaven.

Eddie is typical of many unregenerate persons who have had spiritual experiences but not genuine conversions. They trust in their emotional experiences or their baptisms and conclude that their spiritual work is done. They consider holiness to be something they did in the past.

The Bible, however, portrays the regenerate as persons who continue to seek God. They are saints who "seek him, who seek the face of the God of Jacob" (Ps 24:6). The psalmist writes, "Do not let those who seek you be dishonored because of me, O God of Israel" (Ps 69:6); "You who seek God, let your hearts revive" (Ps 69:32); and "Let the hearts of those who seek the Lord rejoice" (Ps 105:3). Jesus said, "Blessed are those who hunger and thirst for righteousness" (Mt 5:6).

According to Scripture, the seeking of the saint takes place primarily *after* conversion, not before. Conversion is only the beginning of the saint's seeking and striving. Biblical writers speak of Christians running the race that is set before them, striving and agonizing, wrestling, fighting, putting on the whole armor of God, standing, having done all to stand, pressing forward, reaching forth, struggling in prayer and crying to God day and night.

A Burning Desire

If the unregenerate keep on seeking, they do so for some benefit they think it brings them: because others then think of them as "spiritual," or because they like feeling religious, or because it quiets their conscience when they suspect they have not been regenerated and may indeed have nothing of true spirituality.

But for the saint, hungering and thirsting for God and holiness come naturally. There is an "inward burning desire . . . a holy breathing and panting after the Spirit of God, to increase holiness, as natural to a holy nature, as breathing is to a living body."[3]

The saint is more interested in holiness itself than in the benefits that accrue from it. For holiness is as much the saints' food and drink—the object of their spiritual appetite—as it was Jesus' food and drink: "My food is to do the will of him who sent me and to complete his work" (Jn 4:34). Mother Teresa tells the world that there is infinite joy in loving and surrendering everything to Jesus. In other words, holiness is its own reward.

True saints desire God's Word, not so much to discover how much God loves them as to grow in holiness. Their treasure—their most precious possession—is grace: "the fear of the LORD is [their] treasure" (Is 33:6). The profit they seek is not material gain or fame but godliness (1 Tim 6:6).

Therefore what distinguishes saints from the rest of the world is not their revelations from God or experiences of his love or desire for heaven but their longing for holiness. Unlike the rest of the world, they hunger and thirst to have a holier heart and to live a holier life. They refuse to be content with their spiritual status quo.

18

· · · · ·

The Twelfth Reliable Sign *Christian Practice (Surrender & Perseverance)*

SURELY WHEN THE DAY OF JUDGMENT COMES,
WE SHALL NOT BE ASKED
WHAT WE HAVE READ BUT WHAT WE HAVE DONE,
NOT HOW WELL WE HAVE SPOKEN
BUT HOW DEVOUTLY WE HAVE LIVED.
THOMAS À KEMPIS

THE LAST TIME I SAW MO THAT YEAR, HE WAS BEING CARRIED OUT OF A bar, feet first, by Virginia Beach's finest. Mo's tanned, muscular body was contorted with rage. He was cursing the officers and shouting something about the other guy starting the fight.

"So I had a difficult time believing it was the same Mo whom I saw just six months later, fully clothed and in his right mind. He was the picture of serenity. After exchanging a hug and the usual greetings, I asked Mo what in the world happened to him. He looked so different.

"Mo said that he'd become a Christian. He didn't try to convert me, but the change I saw in him made me think long and hard about the life I was leading."

My pastor, who told me this story, was transformed by Jesus a few months later, in part because of the change he saw in his friend Mo. Mo abandoned the hedonistic, uncommitted lifestyle he had flaunted for years and settled down to a disciplined pursuit of holiness. Instead of chasing women, he gave himself faithfully to his wife, children and church. In the years since his conversion, Mo has become a physician with a difference. He takes extra time with his patients rather than rushing them through in order to make more money. He waives his fees if he knows a patient is destitute. And he cares about them after they finish treatment. He sees his patients, in other words, not as diseased organs or sources of income, but as fellow creatures of God whom he is privileged to serve.

A New Lifestyle

Mo is a living illustration of the twelfth and last reliable sign: Christian practice. True saints are people whose lifestyles are distinctive. They practice the principles of the kingdom of God.

Another way of explaining what Mo illustrates is to say that God saves us because he has a job for us to do. He regenerates us in order to prepare us for a life of service. "For we are what he has made us, created in Christ Jesus *for good works,* which God prepared beforehand to be our way of life" (Eph 2:10).

Martin Luther wrote that true faith will always result in good works because it is the nature of true faith to work. "O, it is a living, busy, active, mighty thing, this faith, and so it is impossible for it not to do good works incessantly. It does not ask whether there are good things to do, but before the question arises it has already done them and is always at the doing of them."[1] True faith naturally puts into practice what it believes.

Redemption is not simply a ticket to heaven. Its purpose is to enable us to live a transformed life here on earth. As Paul put it two thousand years ago, "He it is who gave himself for us that he might redeem us from all iniquity and purify for himself a people of his own who are zealous for good deeds" (Tit 2:14). To the Corinthians he wrote that we are redeemed so that our motivation might change: "And he died for all, so that those who live might live no longer for themselves, but for him who died and was raised for them" (2 Cor 5:15). Our new motivation leads to a holy life: "And you who were once estranged and hostile in mind, doing evil deeds, he has now reconciled in his fleshly body through death, so as to present you holy and blameless and irreproachable before him" (Col 1:21-22). In the inspired words of Zechariah the priest, "That we, being rescued from the hands of our enemies, might serve him without fear, in holiness and righteousness before him all our days" (Lk 1:74-75).

Christian practice is not only the purpose of redemption but also the purpose of election. That is, even before we were redeemed God chose us for himself. And the purpose of that choice was that we might bear holy fruit. Jesus said, "You did not choose me but I chose you. And I appointed you to go and bear fruit, fruit that will last" (Jn 15:16). Paul said that God "chose us in Christ before the foundation of the world to be holy and blameless before him in love" (Eph 1:4). So a true Christian is a person whose life bears fruit in holiness.

Total Surrender

This twelfth sign, Christian practice, has three important implications. The first is that true saints will be committed to the lordship of Christ over every part of their lives. Second, they will make service to God their number-one priority. And third, they will persevere in Christian practice until the end of their lives.

Let's look first at the principle of total surrender. This means that true Christians don't save one area of life as their secret sin. They don't protect one sin from the searing light of God's holiness. They allow the Holy Spirit's searchlight to expose and deal with all of their sins.

A pastor friend of mine is a good example of total surrender. He meets regularly with a Christian friend to confess his sins, particularly those that spring from his greatest weakness. He has shared quite frankly with his prayer partner about this weakness and has agreed to confess to his friend every time he succumbs to it. Another friend of mine knows that the "sin which doth so easily beset" him (Heb 12:1 KJV) is sexual lust. When he goes out of town he makes a point of telling the hotel clerk that he is a Christian and asks to have the X-rated videos turned off in his room. This helps protect him from yielding to lust after a tiring, lonely day of work.

Scripture indicates that true disciples try to crucify their favorite sins. The author of Hebrews exhorts, "Therefore, since we are surrounded by so great a cloud of witnesses, let us also lay aside every weight and the sin that clings so closely, and let us run with perseverance the race that is set before us" (Heb 12:1). James reminds us that we shouldn't be satisfied if we are dealing with most of our sins but neglecting a favorite sin. For "whoever keeps the whole law but fails in one point has become accountable for all of it" (Jas 2:10). So, as Paul put it, "those who belong to Christ Jesus have crucified the flesh with its passions and desires" (Gal 5:24).

Saul was commanded to kill all the Amalekites. As far as he was concerned, he did just that. But he saved Agag, his favorite. Saving Agag proved to be Saul's ruin. Similarly, saving our favorite sin—though we obey in all other areas—will ruin us spiritually.

Just a Little Sin?

The sin we save doesn't need to be a big one. After all, a tiny leak can sink a big ship. A man I know died after being shot by one bullet from a .22 rifle. It was a relatively small wound, and the bullet missed vital organs. But because he was on a fishing trip far from a hospital, he bled to death before he could get help.

It is not the size of the sin that matters, but the attitude of heart. I know a man who drove his wife to a nervous breakdown because he left his guns around the house.[2] He bought and sold guns for a hobby and tested them with live ammunition. But he was very forgetful and often left them lying out, despite his wife's pleadings that their young children could misuse them and get killed. The children never had an accident, but this man's unloving neglect eventually drove his wife to a nervous condition that plagued her for years. To him it seemed trivial, but to her it was a loud reminder that he didn't care. The persistence of a "little" sin can signal the presence of a big problem—a stubborn contempt for God's call to holiness.

Herod loved to hear John the Baptist preach because he believed John was from God. But Herod didn't like to hear John talk about Herod's favorite sin—his illicit love for Herodias, who had been married to Herod's brother Philip. We don't remember Herod for his love of good preaching or his fascination with biblical prophecy. Instead we remember Herod for the great crime that was stimulated by a "little" vice—lust for another man's wife. Herod is an illustration of Jesus' warning that allowing one part of the self to remain corrupt can carry the whole self into hell (Mt 5:29-30).

Missing Out on the Love of Jesus

There is another reason we must crucify our favorite sin(s). If we do not, Jesus won't reveal his love to us. He told his disciples, "Those who keep my commandments love me; I will love *them* and reveal myself to *them*" (see Jn 14:21).

Joseph refused to reveal himself to his brothers until Benjamin, the baby of the family and most precious to their father Jacob, was handed over (Gen 42—43). In similar fashion, Jesus will not reveal the fullness of his love to us until we part with our favorite lusts.

Are We like Pharaoh?

The problem is that sometimes we want to serve God and enjoy our lusts as well. Perhaps we are like Pharaoh. He was willing to let Moses and his people sacrifice to God within the land of Egypt, but he would not let the people leave the country. Moses insisted that the Israelites be permitted to take a three-day journey into the wilderness to offer sacrifice. Pharaoh replied, "OK, but don't go too far." Don't we often do the same with our sins? We are willing to quit for a while but not to abandon them completely. We pray prayers similar to Augustine's: "Lord, give me chastity, but not yet!"

Later Pharaoh said, "I'll let you go to the wilderness, but only if you leave the women and children behind." Again Moses refused to budge. He asked God to send more plagues. After Pharaoh had his fill of locusts and darkness, he told Moses and the Israelites they could go if they left their cattle behind (Ex 10:24). Are we sometimes like that? Do we repent of some of our sins, but not all of them? Do we repent of our most obvious sins, but not of our inner lusts or the less visible indulgences of those lusts?

Finally Pharaoh repented and let all the Israelites go, along with everything they had. But he wasn't sincere in his repentance. He soon changed his mind and chased the Israelites into the Red Sea. Why was Pharaoh so perversely fickle? Because he had never really crucified his lusts. And it was those lusts that finally destroyed him.

So it is with some of us. We repent of sin, even our favorite sin. But our repentance is shallow. We return like a dog to its vomit. We are like the disciples who traveled with Jesus for a while but ran away when discipleship became costly.

Why Some Find It So Hard to Believe

This is why some people have such a hard time believing with any degree of certainty: they refuse to surrender unconditionally to Jesus. According to Bonhoeffer, they will never be able to acquire a firm faith until they commit themselves to obey.

> Are you worried because you find it so hard to believe? No one should be surprised at the difficulty of faith, if there is some part of his life where he is consciously resisting or disobeying the commandment of Jesus. Is there some part of your life which you are refusing to surrender at his behest? Some sinful passion, maybe, or some animosity, some hope, perhaps your ambition or your reason? If so, you must not be surprised that you have not received the Holy Spirit, that prayer is difficult, or that your request for faith remains unanswered. Go rather and be reconciled with your brother, renounce the sin which holds you fast—and then you will recover your faith! If you dismiss the word of God's command, you will not receive his word of grace. How can you hope to enter into communion with him when at some point in your life you are running away from him? The man who disobeys cannot believe, for only he who obeys can believe.[3]

Serving the Lord with Zeal

A second implication of this twelfth sign—Christian practice—is that true Christians live their lives with all of their hearts. God has first priority for them, which means that Jesus is Lord over their professional and private lives.

When I want to understand how a Christian can submit to Jesus at work, I think of my friend John Childress. John has a high-stress management position for a national copy-machine corporation. He's not afraid to advertise and lead a company Bible study one morning each week before work. When others fudge the numbers to meet their quotas or twist the rules to get ahead, John is scrupulously honest.

Consequently John's performance figures are not as high as some, but all who work with him know that he has always maintained his integrity. At our church men's retreat this past fall John said something that I've been thinking about since: "My number-one priority at work is to honor the Lord in what I do. I'm more concerned about the Lord's opinion than about the opinion of my human superiors."

John knows that he cannot serve two masters. Like Paul, he submits all he does to one overriding objective: "This one thing I do" (Phil 3:13). And he struggles, with God's grace, to fulfill that objective.

The New Testament describes the Christian life as just that sort of struggle. It characterizes the life of a disciple as running, wrestling and fighting. It admonishes Christians to fight the good fight of the faith and declares that all true Christians are good and faithful soldiers of Jesus Christ. It warns that slackers never win the race. We are told to watch and pray always, put on the whole armor of God, forget the things that are behind and lay aside every sin that clings so closely.

Persevering to the End

A third implication of this twelfth sign is that Christians don't give up. They don't turn around after beginning the race. They persevere in following Jesus until the end of their lives.

True Christians may well stumble and fall. They may lose their way for a while. They may have times of despair. In the words of the Westminster Confession, they may "fall into grievous sins; and for a time continue therein: whereby they incur God's displeasure, and grieve his Holy Spirit; come to be deprived of some measure of their graces and comforts; have their hearts hardened, and their consciences wounded; hurt and scandalize others, and bring temporal judgments on themselves."[4]

But true saints never grow so weary of the life of faith that they habitually dislike and neglect it. If they fall, they get back on their feet, ask for forgiveness and seek the grace to continue. Like Job, they refuse to finally turn away from God even if they angrily question God for a time. Unlike those who have a spiritual experience but never truly repent, genuine Christians show a genuine difference in lifestyle after their conversion. And even if they falter for a part of the journey, they keep on keeping on until they finish the trip.

Last week a retired engineer told me how his seventeen-year-old epileptic son drowned just as they were on the verge of seeing significant improvement in his condition. This broken man cried and argued with God, then gave up on God when he couldn't seem to get any answers. But as some of the wounds healed, he came back to God. Now, he says, he loves God with a deeper love than before.

This man's faith could not die because it was real. Real faith in a Christian always reasserts itself, even after a dark night of the soul. Christians have been so touched by grace that they are new persons, new creations, not only on the inside but in their behavior as well. They are sanctified in spirit, soul and body. Old things are passed away; all things have become new. They have new hearts, new eyes, new ears, new tongues, new hands and new feet. They walk in newness of life. Those who fall away after an apparent conversion and never again walk as Christians may never have risen with Christ in the first place.

I know: these are hard words. Because they are controversial, permit me to show now that they are anchored in Scripture. Consider all the different ways Scripture teaches this principle of perseverance. Jesus said that "the one who endures to the end will be saved" (Mt 10:22; 24:12-13). In his parable of the sower and the seed, only the seed that endured through trouble, persecution, the cares of the world and the lure of wealth was pronounced "good" (Mt 13:4-8). In another parable Jesus declared, "Blessed are those slaves whom the master finds alert when he comes" (Lk 12:37). And in John's Gospel Jesus teaches, "If you *continue* in my word, you are truly my disciples" (8:31).

Paul is just as emphatic. To the Romans he wrote, "Note . . . God's kindness toward you, *provided* you continue in his kindness; otherwise you also will be cut off" (Rom 11:22). In Colossians we read, "You . . . he has now reconciled . . . *provided that* you continue securely established and steadfast in the faith, without shifting from the hope promised by the gospel that you heard" (1:21-23).

Perseverance is taught even more explicitly by the author of Hebrews. "We are [God's] house *if* we hold firm the confidence and the pride that belongs to hope. . . . For we have become partners of Christ, *if only* we hold our first confidence firm to the end" (3:6, 14). In Revelation Jesus adds, "To everyone who conquers and *continues to do my works to the end,* I will give authority over the nations" (2:26). It seems clear that true spirituality perseveres until the end.

The Most Important Sign of All

So far we have seen that true spirituality always puts its faith into practice. It will slip and fall (every day!), but over the long haul there will be clear signs of a lifestyle that aims to imitate Jesus. Now we need to see the importance of this last reliable sign. It is the last because it is the most important of all. In Edwards's words, it is the "chief of all the marks of grace, the sign of signs, and evidence of evidences, that which seals and crowns all other signs."[5]

Practice is the most important of all the signs of grace. Practice is where the rubber meets the road. If a person identifies her faith in God as the source and meaning of life, one would expect to see that faith affect her daily practice. If a person says he intends to go to college in the fall but doesn't apply to a college in the spring of that year, one would doubt his intention. People can talk about loving God as much as they want. But if they don't show in some practical way that they love God, we can reasonably conclude that their love for God is just talk.

Our Only Way to Judge Others

Christian practice is evidence of true spirituality in two ways. It is the principal evidence about others and ourselves. That is, it is the best way that we can recognize others as Christians, and it is the best way that we can determine what is in our own hearts.

Let's consider the first way—that it is evidence of grace in others. Jesus made this very clear. Twice he said of false prophets that we would know them by their fruits (Mt 7:16, 20). Then he said that a person's heart is manifested by his or her practice: "Either make the tree good, and its fruit good; or make the tree bad, and its fruit bad; for the tree is known by its fruit" (Mt 12:33; see also Lk 6:44).

Jesus never said that we could know a tree by its leaves or flowers— that is, by people's talk or the dramatic stories they tell of their spiritual experiences, or by their eloquence or sincerity. Nor did he say that we could sense their spirituality by the emotion with which they speak or the feelings they stir in us.

Christian practice is the only criterion Jesus gave us by which to distinguish true believers from false. "Let your light shine before others," he taught, "so that they may see your good works and give glory to your Father in heaven" (Mt 5:16). The author of Hebrews notes sadly those who "tasted the heavenly gift, and have shared in the Holy Spirit, and have tasted the goodness of the word of God and the powers of the age to come," yet have fallen away (6:4-5). They are compared to ground that produces thorns and thistles; their end "is to be burned over" (Heb 6:8).

But then he tells his readers, "We are confident of better things in your case, things that belong to salvation" (Heb 6:9). How does the author know that the others were not saved but these Hebrew readers were? He knew their "work and the love that [they] showed for his sake in serving the saints, as [they] still do" (6:10). In other words, it was the first group's lack of Christian practice that indicated their unregenerate state, and this group's demonstration of Christian practice that confirmed their regeneration.

The Most Reliable Evidence

John and James tell a similar story. According to his third epistle, John was overjoyed when Gaius's friends testified that he was faithful to the truth. How did John know that Gaius was indeed being faithful? Because "you walk in the truth. . . . You do faithfully whatever you do for the friends, even though they are strangers to you" (3 Jn 3, 5). John then warned against Diotrephes, a false worker, explaining that we can always tell false workers by their practice: "Whoever does good is from God; whoever does evil has not seen God" (11).

James asked, "What good is it, my brothers and sisters, if you *say* you have faith but do not have works? . . . But someone will say, 'You have faith and I have works.' Show me your faith apart from your works, and I by my works will show you my faith" (Jas 2:14, 18). According to James, therefore, there are two ways to show our neighbor what is in our hearts—by our words and deeds. Jesus, James and John obviously prefer deeds as the most reliable evidence of grace.

Words are cheap. They are easier to produce if you want to counterfeit true spirituality. Deeds are more difficult because they cost something. They usually demand some kind of self-denial. Therefore it is far easier for counterfeit Christians to talk a good game than to walk like a disciple of Jesus.

I am reminded of Jack McSherry, my freshman English teacher in high school. From the time that he called me up after class to commend one of my papers and challenge me to write more, I sensed there was something different about him. Because I was not a Christian, I didn't know what it was at the time. But the love that he continued to show the next few years kept me hunting for something more in my life, which I knew I had found when I was confronted by Christ as a freshman in college. Jack never shared the gospel with me, and he never told the class (as far as I can remember) that he was a Christian. But I knew by the ways that he gave of his time and heart to his students that he had something special. When I finally met Christ, I realized that he had been the special presence in Jack's life. It was Jack's deeds rather than his words that showed me Christ.

What About Works Without Faith?
Does this mean that it doesn't matter what you believe as long as you live a Christian lifestyle? Our friend Annie is the daughter of a Jewish rabbi. She believes in God but not in Jesus as the incarnation of God. Annie is one of the best mothers and kindest persons we have ever known. My wife and I often feel guilty because she does far more for us than we are able to do for her. As parents of three active boys, we treasure our few opportunities to be alone together for more than a few hours. Several times Annie has cared for two or three of our boys when my job permitted Jean and me to get away for a weekend. Though we have offered, schedules have never permitted us to do the same for Annie and her husband, Steve (they have two boys). But Annie doesn't seem to care. She loves to give of herself in service to her friends.

Does what I have said mean that Annie is a disciple of Jesus because her life seems more illustrative of Christian practice than many Christians'? Not quite. Annie herself would tell you that she does not consider herself a Christian in a way that would distinguish her from a Jew. She makes no pretense of believing the doctrines of orthodox Christianity.

This last and most important sign (Christian practice) is not a rule by which to determine the spiritual state of morally good people (good as far as observation can tell) who don't claim to be following Christ.

Instead, it enables us to distinguish between professing Christians. By it we can tell the difference between hypocrites (those who claim to be Christians but do not practice their faith) and sincere believers (those who do practice their faith).

Jesus made it clear that this rule was to help us distinguish among those who profess faith in Christ. He said that Christian practice is the way to recognize a false prophet—that is, teachers who claim to follow Christ but really don't. He applied the same rule to ordinary church people active in Christian work. Some, he said, will call him "Lord, Lord" on the Day of Judgment. That is, they will claim to be following him. But Jesus will deny them because they were "evildoers" who heard his words but did not "act on them" (Mt 7:21, 23). Christian practice, then, is the rule for determining the sincerity of those who claim to follow Christ.

If someone says she is not a Christian and does not believe in Christ as Messiah and God incarnate, her good life does not oblige us to call her a sincere Christian. We can admire her morality and even be stimulated by her to a better Christian life, but we don't need to call her a Christian. Fruit must be joined to flowers—action to profession.

Not Just a Law-Abiding Citizen

If Annie is not a Christian because she doesn't believe Jesus was the Christ, what about my students who do? What does "Christian practice" really mean? Is it enough to obey the laws of the land and agree with the rest of the population that child abuse and terrorism are terrible? Most of my students feel morally outraged about these things. They also say they don't go out of their way to hurt other people. Does this mean they illustrate Christian practice?

Hardly. Christian practice means letting your light shine before others so that they will recognize that you love your Father in heaven. It is a labor of love for Christ's name that will convince others of your love for Christ. In other words, it is not just refraining from acts that will ruin your reputation, but a willingness to act in ways that may hurt your reputation by associating you with Jesus. It is not simply the absence of the negative but the presence of the positive.

It involves such things as total surrender to the lordship of Christ, the fear and love of God, love for saints and one's enemies. It means forgiving those who have hurt us, showing mercy to the hurting and being concerned for others' interests and not just our own. It includes denying ourselves by bridling our tongues and being willing to suffer for Christ.

A Caveat

I must close this chapter with a warning. Although Christian practice is our most reliable sign of grace in another, it can never give us certainty. We can never be certain about the spiritual state of anyone else's heart, because no external acts are infallible evidences of grace. Only the internal exercises of the soul reveal with certainty a person's true nature. And only God can see into the soul.

So we are obliged to welcome as saints those who profess Christ and demonstrate Christian practice. We are obliged to love them and rejoice in them as children of God. We are to work together with them as colaborers in the kingdom. But we can never know with certainty the state of their souls before God. We can observe neither their hearts nor all of their behavior, much of which is secret and hidden from others.

One more thing. An implication we should *not* draw from this rule is that we are to be spiritual sleuths searching for signs of hypocrisy in our fellow Christians. The Scriptures give the rule to protect us from false prophets and to motivate us to let our light shine. It was not meant to make us suspect the sincerity of people in our church. We should beware of thinking we know what goes on inside anyone. Our primary concern should be to see that our own walk looks something like our talk.

19

. . . . .

The Twelfth
Reliable Sign
*Christian Practice
(Suffering & Obedience)*

N OW WE TURN TO THE SECOND WAY IN WHICH CHRISTIAN PRACTICE IS the best evidence of true spirituality—one's own conscience. We saw in the previous chapter that practice is the most reliable way to discern false prophets. This chapter will show that practice is also the best way to tell if we are fooling ourselves when we say that we follow Jesus.

Bob, a close friend, knows that he has truly experienced conversion, because he sees a real change in his life. Since turning to Christ, he has found himself dropping the cursing and swearing that had been a regular part of his speech. He now sees pornography as degrading to women and personally demeaning. He no longer has the desire to get drunk. He also has entirely new desires—to hear good preaching, read the Bible (though he's not always faithful), pray (though it's often very imperfect at that). Although he had never been concerned in the past, now he is anxious to contribute to organizations that feed the hungry and bring the gospel to people who haven't heard it. Despite the fact that he feels woefully unfaithful in many ways, he sees genuine change in both his behavior and desires. Because of this new pattern of practice, he is convinced in his own conscience that Christ has truly invaded his life.

"Let the Little Brute Wallow in It"

This kind of Christian practice is very different from the spiritual experience I described in the first five chapters of this book. Christians are to look at themselves not in search of visions or voices or spiritual feelings but to see if they are practicing the Christian virtues. If inner experiences don't result in action or even the attempt to act, they are unreliable signs of grace. As Screwtape advised his demonic nephew,

The great thing is to prevent [the new Christian convert's] doing anything. As long as he does not convert it into action, it does not matter how much he thinks about this new repentance. Let the little brute wallow in it. Let him, if he has any bent that way, write a book about it; that is often an excellent way of sterilizing the seeds which the Enemy plants in a human soul. Let him do anything but act. No amount of piety in his imaginations and affections will harm us if we can keep it out of his will. As one of the humans has said, active habits are strengthened by repetition, but passive ones are weakened. The more often he feels without acting, the less he will be able ever to act, and, in the long run, the less he will be able to feel.[1]

It is therefore ridiculous to claim to have a good heart while leading a life of self-indulgence. As we saw in chapter two, our actions flow from our affections, which are the strong inclinations of the soul or heart. If the affections of our hearts are good, our lives will show evidence of it.

There is plenty of evidence in the New Testament that Christian practice is the best evidence of grace to one's own conscience. At the end of the Sermon on the Mount, for example, Jesus distinguishes true from false disciples by their practice: "Everyone then who hears these words of mine and acts on them will be like a wise man. . . . And everyone who hears these words of mine and does not act on them will be like a foolish man" (Mt 7:24, 26). So we can know what kind of disciples we are by looking at our practice.

In John's Gospel, Jesus teaches the same: "If you love me, you will keep my commandments. . . . Those who love me will keep my word. . . . Whoever does not love me does not keep my words. . . . My Father is glorified by this, that you bear much fruit and become my disciples. . . . You are my friends if you do what I command you. . . . If you continue in my word, you are truly my disciples" (Jn 14:15, 23-24; 15:8, 14; 8:31).

In his first letter John picks up this theme: "Now by this we may be sure that we know him, if we obey his commandments. . . . Little children, let us love, not in word or speech, but in truth and action. And by this we will know that we are from the truth and will reassure our hearts before him" (1 Jn 2:3; 3:18-19). James proclaims that only the ones who care for orphans and widows in their distress and keep themselves unstained by the world can claim to have true religion (Jas 1:27).

Not surprisingly, when the New Testament refers to hypocrisy (false spirituality), it nearly always points to false practice. Paul told the Corinthians that people who claimed to be Christians but continued to practice fornication, idolatry and other gross sins would not inherit the kingdom of God (1 Cor 6:9-10). In Ephesians he reiterated this point: "Be sure of this, that no fornicator or impure person . . . has any inheritance in the kingdom of . . . God" (5:5-6). In his first letter John wrote, "Whoever says, 'I have come to know him,' but does not obey his commandments, is a liar, and in such a person the truth does not exist" (1 Jn 2:4). "If we say that we have fellowship with him while we are walking in darkness, we lie and do not do what is true" (1:6). In Revelation he wrote, "But nothing unclean will enter [the temple in the New Jerusalem], nor anyone who practices abomination or falsehood" (21:27). James also linked hypocrisy to practice: "If any think they are religious, and do not bridle their tongues but deceive their hearts, their religion is worthless" (Jas 1:26).

Evidence for the Judgment

The New Testament also makes plain that Christian practice will be the grand evidence used on the Day of Judgment. In Bonhoeffer's words, "God will not ask us in that day whether we were good Protestants, but whether we have done his will."[2] The purpose of that judgment will not be to tell God something he doesn't already know but to manifest the justice of God's judgments to the world.

John says that the judgment will be based on works: "And the dead were judged according to their works, as recorded in the books. And the sea gave up the dead that were in it, Death and Hades gave up the dead that were in them, and all were judged according to what they had done" (Rev 20:12-13). Paul echoes this theme: "For all of us must appear before the judgment seat of Christ, so that each may receive recompense for what has been done in the body, whether good or evil" (2 Cor 5:10).

The Judge on that fateful day won't ask people about their spiritual insights or their conversion stories. Instead their works, both open and secret, will be brought forward as evidence of what they are: "For God will bring every deed into judgment, including every secret thing, whether good or evil" (Eccles 12:14).

A Different Kind of Practice

The practice that is the chief evidence of grace to others is different from this practice that is the best evidence of grace to ourselves. Others can see what we do, but only we know what is in our hearts. While external acts are the best evidence of grace to others, the inner exercises of the heart are the best evidence to ourselves about the state of our souls. We can determine whether or not we have been the recipients of grace by looking at what is going on in our hearts. For the heart is the self in the sight of the Lord. "The LORD does not see as mortals see; they look on the outward appearance, but the LORD looks on the heart" (1 Sam 16:7).

Bob was convinced that he had received grace by noticing a change in his desires. He no longer *wanted* to do the things he formerly enjoyed, and he now wanted to do things related to God and the Christian life. Getting drunk was no longer fun, but sitting around with his new Christian friends and talking about the Lord was.

Notice what Jesus says in the passage just quoted from the Sermon on the Mount. "Everyone then who hears these words of mine and acts on them" is wise (Mt 7:24). Which words is he talking about? The words of the Sermon on the Mount, which refer in large part to new attitudes, not simply new actions: Blessed are the poor in spirit, those who mourn, the meek, those who hunger and thirst for righteousness, the merciful and the pure in heart. The Sermon goes on to discuss anger, lust and love for enemies—all of which are more matters of the heart than ways of behaving.

Jeremiah reports God saying something very similar: "I the LORD test the mind and search the heart, to give to all according to their ways, according to the fruit of their doings" (Jer 17:10). Notice that Jeremiah implies that behavior is a manifestation of heart attitude.

In words that paraphrase the Jeremiah passage, Jesus says in Revelation, "I am the one who searches minds and hearts, and I will give to each of you as your works deserve" (2:23). Once again, works are linked to the exercises of the heart. So Christians gain assurance of their salvation by looking not just at their outward actions but also at the motivations of their hearts.

Christian Practice and Suffering

There is an interesting connection between practice and suffering that can help us better endure our suffering. Scripture indicates that God uses suffering as a trial to "prove" our practice. That is, he permits suffering to come our way in order to test our determination to obey. He allows difficulties to come into our lives that force us to make a clear choice between God and other things. Scripture calls these difficulties "trials" or "proofs" (2 Cor 8:2; Heb 11:17; 1 Pet 1:7; 4:12).

An earlier chapter of this book discussed the day when Satan challenged God. He told God that Job was faithful only because God had bribed him. After all, God had blessed Job with a wonderful family and more riches than any other man in the East. Satan implied that Job would forsake God if those blessings were taken away. So God agreed to permit Satan to kill Job's children and destroy his wealth (and health), if only to prove that there was a man on earth who "fears God and turns away from evil" (Job 2:3). Job was forced by his trial to choose between despair and God. Though he angrily argued with God and probably was self-righteous, Job never gave up on God, as his wife had suggested he do. His trial proved that Job finally chose God above everything else.

God gave a similar trial to Israel in the wilderness. "Remember the long way that the LORD your God has led you these forty years in the wilderness, in order to humble you, testing you to know what was in your heart, whether or not you would keep his commandments" (Deut 8:2). He used the same strategy after they reached the Promised Land. "In order to test Israel, whether or not they would take care to walk in the way of the LORD as their ancestors did, the LORD had left those nations, not driving them out at once, and had not handed them over to Joshua" (Judg 2:22-23). Peter said God was doing the same to his church: "For a little while you have had to suffer various trials, so that the genuineness of your faith—being more precious than gold that, though perishable, is tested by fire—may be found to result in praise and glory and honor when Jesus Christ is revealed" (1 Pet 1:6-7).

What's the Point?

Perhaps you're wondering why God has to test us. Doesn't he already know what is in our hearts? Of course he does. He tests us not so much for his sake as for ours. We need to know what makes us tick. Often we are not aware of our deepest affections. Only the crucible of suffering is able to show us who we really are. Perhaps you recall Malcolm Muggeridge's observation that the only worthwhile lessons he learned in life came from suffering.

The rich young man of Matthew 19 is a good example of how God uses a test to show a person what is in his heart. When this religious man asked Jesus what good things he had to do to earn eternal life, Jesus saw through his question. According to Bonhoeffer, he recognized it to be "the question of a piety shaped by and centered in the self."[3] So despite the young man's claim to be obeying all the commandments, Jesus challenged him to give away all of his possessions. This was a test to prove whether he was willing to choose God over the world. As Jesus knew he would, he flunked the test.

The disciple who promised that he would follow Jesus to the ends of the earth was given a similar test. Jesus told him, "Foxes have holes, and birds of the air have nests; but the Son of Man has nowhere to lay his head" (Mt 8:20). This test enabled another would-be disciple to see that he preferred the comforts of this world to following Jesus.

The parable of the sower and the seed indicates that God sends us tests in the course of daily life. The seed was sown in different kinds of soil—beaten down, thorny, rocky and good—and in most of the soils it looked the same after it first sprang up. But when it was tested (tried, if you will) by the burning heat of the sun, differences began to appear. So too, many conversions look similar in the beginning. But the tests of suffering show believers whether their experiences of spirituality were true or counterfeit.

A building's strength is tested by a strong wind or, if it is in California, by an earthquake. A soldier's mettle becomes known only in battle. A car's safety and strength are revealed in a collision. To determine if a walking stick is strong or rotten in the middle, we put weight on it and watch what happens. To see the condition of our souls, we should observe ourselves during and after suffering. God may be testing our practice to show us where we stand.

The Sign of Signs

In sum, Christian practice is the best evidence of saving faith, both to others and to ourselves. A fig tree either does or does not bear figs. A man may learn of a great treasure that can be had at the end of a long and arduous journey. He may think he is willing to make the trip when he first hears about the treasure, Edwards argues, but the best evidence of his willingness to go is his actually making the trip. Similarly, if a Frenchman promises an American woman that he will marry her in France, the best evidence of her willingness to marry him is that she actually travels to France.

According to Edwards, Christian practice is the crown of all the other signs. We can see that by looking at its relation to classical Christian virtues. Practice is the best evidence of knowledge of God. As Paul wrote, "They profess to know God, but they deny him by their actions" (Tit 1:16).

Practice is also the best evidence of repentance. John the Baptist told the Jews that only practice proved the sincerity of their repentance: "Bear fruit worthy of repentance" (Mt 3:8).

Practice is the best evidence of coming to Christ. When Christ called Levi, Levi actually "got up, left everything, and followed him" (Lk 5:27-28). If Levi had stayed, there would be no evidence that he came to Christ, even if he had told himself that he was following Christ in his heart.

Practice is the best evidence of faith. Because Abraham had faith in God, he left his own country. Because Moses had faith in God, he refused to stay in the luxury of Pharaoh's palace, choosing instead to suffer with God's people (Heb 11:25-26). Because others had faith in God, they were stoned, sawn in two, executed by the sword, mocked and tortured, thrown in prison, and forced to wander about in animal skins, poverty and torment (Heb 11:32-38).

Martin Luther used a nautical analogy to explain how true faith leads to practice. The person who doesn't have faith, he said, "is like someone who has to cross the sea, but is so frightened that he does not trust the ship. And so he stays where he is, and is never saved, because he will not get on board and cross over."[4] Just as this person doesn't have faith in the ship unless he gets on board, true faith is not merely believing something but putting that belief into practice.

Practice is the best evidence of love, as we've seen from the many places in Scripture where Jesus said that only those who keep his commandments actually love him.

Practice is the best evidence of humility. We learn from the classic text in Micah that humility is a walking: "He has told you, O mortal, what is good; and what does the LORD require of you but to do justice, and to love kindness, and to walk humbly with your God?" (Mic 6:8).

Finally, practice is the best evidence of fear of the Lord. The author of Proverbs explains that by the fear of the Lord we *avoid* evil (16:6). A good illustration of this is a pastor friend who once told Jean and me, "May the Lord take me before I do something that dishonors him." Skip's fear of the Lord has been shown clearly in many difficult choices he has made. He has chosen, for example, not to strike back when accused unjustly and to give large portions of his small savings when he felt called by the Spirit to help people in desperate need. He has also adopted a self-denying lifestyle in order to keep in check desires that he knows could undermine his Christian witness. Skip's practice is clear evidence of his fear of the Lord.

Is This Legalistic?

Perhaps this chapter's emphasis on practice has made you uneasy. Does it imply that we are saved by our good works? Or, if it doesn't go that far, does it encourage saints to place too much confidence in their works? If so, this robs glory from Christ, who gives us grace and saves us freely. Perhaps it also seems inconsistent with the doctrine of justification by grace through faith alone.

I don't think that this or the previous chapter teaches or implies anything close to salvation by works. I will give two reasons for my contention.

1. These chapters *would* be inconsistent with the idea of God's grace being free if they taught or implied that works earn us God's favor. But these chapters teach nothing of the kind. They say something very different—that works are the sign of God's favor, not the price of God's favor.

If I give a student a dollar bill (I sometimes do this to teach this very point) simply because I feel like it, she will look at the dollar in her hand as a sign of my generosity. She knows that she has done nothing to earn that dollar. Her possession of the dollar says nothing about her. I could have given it just as easily to the student sitting beside her. And it says nothing about her character—whether she is studious or lazy, friendly or obnoxious. But it does say something about me. It says that either I am generous or I just wanted to make a point to my class that day. Similarly, the presence of works in believers' lives does not mean that they are better than unbelievers or more deserving, or that those works have earned them a place in God's kingdom. It simply indicates that God has freely poured his grace on them. The result of that grace is works (Christian practice). For God's grace is always active and will always produce Christlike character.

In theological terms, this is the idea of justification without works. We are justified (accepted by God and received into his kingdom) only by the righteousness of Christ, not by our own righteousness. In other words, we are saved by Christ's works, not by our own. But once we are saved, we are filled with the Holy Spirit, who inevitably does works through us.

Faith, then, cannot be separated from obedience. To emphasize the fact that we are saved by a free gift, we say that we are saved by faith and not by works. But as these chapters have shown, all true faith produces works (practice). If faith does not produce works, it is not true faith. Bonhoeffer explained, "From the point of view of justification it is necessary thus to separate [faith and obedience], but we must never lose sight of their essential unity. For faith is only real when there is obedience, never without it, and faith only becomes faith in the act of obedience."[5]

2. If justification by grace through faith alone and the doctrine of free grace are contradicted by the importance of holy practice as a sign of grace, then they are also contradicted by the importance of *anything* as a sign of grace: joy, love, gratitude, a softened heart, conviction of sin or any kind of holy practice. Any of these can be regarded as human works that earn salvation. But just as a saint typically will see these spiritual experiences as signs of (not payments for) grace, the saint when properly instructed will see practice as a sign of grace.

Practice and Free Grace Go Hand in Hand

Scripture commonly presents both together—the notion that grace is free and unearned and the exhortation to practice. Revelation 21:6-7, for example, suggests that grace is absolutely free: "To the thirsty I will give water as a gift from the spring of the water of life." The passage goes on to indicate that only those who practice their faith will take this gift: "Those who conquer will inherit these things, and I will be their God."

Revelation 22:14-17 shows the same pattern, but in reverse order. First we read of practice as if it is a condition: "Blessed are those who wash their robes, so that they will have the right to the tree of life and may enter the city by the gates. Outside are the dogs and sorcerers and fornicators." Then we see the offer of a free gift: "Let everyone who is thirsty come. Let anyone who wishes take the water of life as a gift."

The pattern appears again in Revelation 3:20-21. This time the free gift is first: "Listen! I am standing at the door knocking; if you hear my voice and open the door, I will come in to you and eat with you, and you with me." The (implied) exhortation to practice is second: "To the one who conquers I will give a place with me on my throne."

It isn't just John, the writer of Revelation, who presents this pattern of both free grace and the command to practice. Jesus does the same. "Come to me," he says, offering free grace, "all you that are weary and are carrying heavy burdens, and I will give you rest." But directly following the invitation is a commandment: "Take my yoke upon you, and learn from me" (Mt 11:28-29). Practice—taking on his yoke—is necessary for us to receive his rest.

Isaiah makes a very similar promise and appeal. "Ho, everyone who thirsts, come to the waters; and you that have no money, come, buy and eat! Come, buy wine and milk without money and without price" (Is 55:1; this entire chapter is a magnificent portion of Scripture and richly rewards careful study). But verse 7 suggests that only those who repent will be able to receive that gift: "Let the wicked forsake their way, and the unrighteous their thoughts; let them return to the LORD, that he may have mercy on them."

Putting the Two Together

How is it that these two elements do not contradict each other? How can a gift be free if you have to earn it? As I have pointed out repeatedly, all these reliable signs of grace are just that—*signs* of grace, not *prices* to pay to get grace. As Augustine observed, we can't receive a gift unless we empty our hands.

Let's say someone offers us a box of cookies while we are already holding a pile of books. We must put down the books in order to receive the gift of cookies. We are not so foolish as to think that putting the books down has earned us the right to get cookies. It was simply part of the process of *receiving* the gift. So too, when one first becomes a Christian, one has to put down, as it were, certain attitudes and habits perhaps that get in the way of receiving the gift of salvation. This is repentance. The putting down is not a price to be paid but part of the act of receiving.

The same principle applies to the Christian life after conversion. Once we have taken the gift of cookies, we enjoy it by eating them. We would never consider our eating to be a payment for them, but simply the way we enjoy them. Similarly, the practice of the Christian life is not what we do to earn our salvation, but the way we use and enjoy the gift of grace we have already received.

20

. . . . .

Are You
Overwhelmed?

"I DO BELIEVE," THE BOY'S FATHER BURST OUT.
"HELP ME TO BELIEVE MORE!"
MARK'S GOSPEL

ARE YOU FEELING DISCOURAGED? ARE YOU SO DAUNTED BY THE GAP between the twelve reliable signs and your own spiritual development that you wonder if you even want to go on? Perhaps you know that you are saved because of God's manifest workings in your life. But reading about the twelve reliable signs makes you feel that you don't measure up to any of them. You feel like a spiritual failure. Seeing the huge gap between where God wants you to be and where you are makes you unsure about whether you want to go on. You feel overwhelmed.

If this describes your situation, consider the four admonitions below before you throw in the towel. They may show you that you are overwhelmed because you are looking at spirituality from the wrong perspective. Changing your perspective can change your attitude toward God and following Jesus.

Don't Rely on Feelings

You may have misunderstood the second chapter's definition of the affections, concluding that you must have spiritual feelings to be really spiritual. But the affections are not feelings (you may want to look again at the chart at the end of chapter two for the differences between affections and emotions). So being spiritual (having true religious affections) does not mean *feeling* spiritual. Many Christians have become discouraged because they equate spirituality with feelings and consider themselves unspiritual or even damned because they feel sinful rather than spiritual.

True spirituality means being aware of our sins. So being spiritual means feeling that we are sinful—because we are! If we recognize that we are sinful, we can be sure that we are being influenced by the Spirit. For the Spirit shows us the truth, and the truth is that "nothing good dwells within me, that is, in my flesh" (Rom 7:18).

Remember that we are to "walk by faith, not by sight" (2 Cor 5:7). If we always feel spiritual, or always feel the presence of the Spirit within us, we are walking by sight, not by faith. Don't assume that because you don't feel the presence of the Spirit every moment, the Spirit must not be there. That assumption means that you have forgotten to walk by faith.

God often calls us to walk in the "darkness" (Lam 3:2), where we cannot see or sense his presence with us. Scripture is full of the cries of saints who walked in the darkness, crying out for some sign of God's presence. At one point Jeremiah thought that God wasn't even listening to his prayers: "Though I call and cry for help, he shuts out my prayer" (Lam 3:8). David pleaded, "How long, O LORD? Will you forget me forever?" (Ps 13:1).

The saints of church history have testified of times when they did not *feel* God's presence or guidance or love. They knew God was there by faith only. They learned not to trust their feelings. That is, they learned not to conclude that they were unspiritual because they couldn't feel God's presence—and not to think that God didn't love them because he hadn't revealed himself recently.

Don't Be a Perfectionist

After reading the last chapter, you may wonder if you are regenerate because your practice is so defective. Remember that even Paul lived with spiritual failure. "I do not understand my own actions. For I do not do what I want, but I do the very thing I hate" (Rom 7:15). He too was distressed by the gap between his performance and the ideal. But rather than despairing of his salvation, he trusted in what Christ had done to atone for his sins: "Thanks be to God through Jesus Christ our Lord! . . . There is therefore now no condemnation for those who are in Christ Jesus" (Rom 7:25; 8:1).

Christian practice does not mean never falling. Instead, it means getting back up after falling and continuing on. In other words, the Christian life is a life of sin (John says that if we say we have no sin, we deceive ourselves), receiving God's forgiveness for our sins and asking for God's grace to live the life of the Spirit.

As we saw earlier, the greatest saints have always said that the closer they drew to God, the more they saw of their own sin and the more they noticed that they were sinning. So if you are dismayed because you notice that you sin so frequently, you are probably on the right track. Those who think they are doing just fine (perhaps even feeling grateful that they have achieved victory over sin) may be in trouble. For Jesus said that heaven belongs to those who realize their spiritual poverty: "Blessed are the poor in spirit, for theirs is the kingdom of heaven" (Mt 5:3).

True spirituality is not moral perfection. It is recognizing that we are imperfect and looking to grace for forgiveness and power to carry on.

What Is the Unpardonable Sin?

I haven't talked much in this book about the devil. But at this point it needs to be said that the devil will work harder to bring you down if you begin to seek God with greater determination. And one of his most potent weapons against the saints is the thought that they have committed the unpardonable sin—the sin against the Holy Spirit. Satan enjoys terrifying God's saints by planting the notion in their brains that they are beyond hope since they have committed this sin. Because of it, they think, God will never forgive them. There is perhaps no torment greater than this—thinking that one faces eternal damnation and that there is no way out.

I have known people who were convinced that they had committed this sin. Their emotional pain was monstrous. But talking to them convinced me that none of them was guilty of this sin. The best proof of their innocence was that they truly wanted God and Jesus, and were horrified by the thought of having committed this sin.

Let me explain why their desire for God was proof that they were not guilty of this sin. Jesus referred to this sin just after he had healed a blind and deaf man (Mt 12:22). The Pharisees had attributed his healing miracle to the power of Beelzebul (Satan). Jesus was addressing the Pharisees' statement when he talked about the sin that will never be forgiven (Mt 12:24). Therefore the sin against the Holy Spirit is saying that Jesus is from the devil, meaning that Jesus is evil, in league with the prince of darkness. Thus we can see that the unpardonable sin is to refuse to accept the Holy Spirit's testimony about Jesus, which is that Jesus is from God—in fact God's Son and Messiah.

People guilty of the sin against the Holy Spirit are people who want nothing to do with Jesus and God. They choose life without God, which is a way of describing hell. By persisting in this attitude throughout life, they wind up in the only place where that attitude reigns—hell. Here there is no forgiveness. This is why Jesus said the sin against the Holy Spirit is unpardonable. Those who want nothing to do with Jesus and God don't want forgiveness and will never get it. God will not pardon them because they never ask for it. And to pardon them would admit them to a realm they would hate—because there God and Jesus are worshiped and served.

This is also why desire for God and Jesus is proof that one has not committed this sin. This sin involves rejection of Jesus and everything that he stands for. Those who want to be with Jesus but are afraid they have been shut out from his presence are just the opposite. Hence they cannot be guilty.

People who fear they have committed the unpardonable sin need to be reminded that anyone who asks forgiveness for unbelief and reaches out for Jesus as Savior *will* be pardoned. Jesus promised, "Anyone who comes to me I will never drive away" (Jn 6:37). It doesn't matter if they have rejected Jesus before. After all, that was the condition of all of us at one time. We were all "children of wrath" (Eph 2:3) before we were pardoned. And God will continue to pardon us, even after we turn away from him again. For when we ask God to forgive us through what Jesus did on the cross, we are accepting the Holy Spirit's testimony about Jesus. Hence we cannot be guilty of the sin against the Holy Spirit, which is rejecting that testimony.

Don't Be Surprised If God Seems Silent

Several years ago I teamed up with a Christian oncologist friend to write a book about God and cancer.[1] As part of my research, I interviewed many cancer patients and their families and read books by both cancer patients and other saints who have suffered great trauma. I was surprised to discover a dominant pattern in the lives of most of these people. Nearly all of them had been devout believers, for whom the sense of God's presence and love had been strong and vivid. But when they faced a life-threatening illness or other trauma, most of them spent some time in spiritual desolation. The God who had been real to them for years suddenly seemed to have abandoned them. He had become strangely silent.

This was also true for the great figures of the Bible. Throughout the psalms, David cries out, "How long, O Lord? How long? Why have you abandoned me?" As we have already noted, Job utters the same lament. So does Jeremiah in Lamentations. Even God's own Son felt abandoned on the cross: "My God, my God, why have you forsaken me?" (Mt 27:46).

Great saints have experienced the same. In 1944 C. S. Lewis wrote a marvelous book, *The Problem of Pain*, that he and many others thought did a fine job of solving the riddle of why a good and all-powerful God would permit terrible suffering. But in 1961, when his own wife was dying from cancer, the answers he had proposed seventeen years earlier no longer made sense to Lewis. The God who had been so intimate and sustaining now seemed to have abandoned him. Lewis was frustrated and angry. He called God a "cosmic sadist" and doubted everything he had ever believed about God.

Then one morning Lewis woke up to find that both the grief and doubt had vanished. From this bewildering and painful experience he learned a lesson: "You can't see anything properly when your eyes are blurred with tears."[2]

Like Lewis, David and Jeremiah found that the sense of God's presence and love returned. Most of David's psalms of lament end on a note of reassurance, and Jeremiah reminds his readers that "the steadfast love of the LORD never ceases, his mercies never come to an end; they are new every morning" (Lam 3:22-23).

The saints have found the same. God may appear to have abandoned us, they say, but the truth is that he is always near. If we wait for him with trust and perseverance, our experience of his presence and love will return.

What If . . . ?

What would happen if more of today's church understood the difference between the reliable and unreliable signs of true spirituality? Would this really change things? Or would it simply be additional head knowledge?

I think a true understanding of the contents of this book would make a profound impact on today's church. Let me suggest what could happen. Those who are now in the church but are deceived by sub-Christian and non-Christian spiritualities would recognize their errors and come to true grace. It would prevent the deception of those who have discovered an interest in Christ but have not yet become true disciples. It would tend to clear up confusion about how to get true faith and then how to continue in it.

It would counteract many current heresies. One of these claims is that a person can be saved without submitting to Christ's lordship. Understanding this book would show that it is the nature of true faith to submit to Jesus as Lord. It would tend to prevent professing Christians from neglecting holiness and promote their devotion to Christ and holy practice.

Wide understanding of this book would promote a Christian walk as well as spiritual talk. We would devote more energy to our service to God and our generation than to flapping our tongues about our spiritual experiences. As Edwards put it, tongues would run behind, not before, hands and feet.

Perhaps most important, a true understanding of the principles of this book would lead to less pride and greater humility. If, as Scripture suggests, pride is our greatest danger and humility is the prerequisite to true faith, the church would be strengthened immeasurably.

Finally, the twelve unreliable and reliable signs have corporate implications that, if understood, point to the importance of the *church* as the location of true discipleship and the best instrument of evangelism. Only active participation in the body can ensure access to the grace necessary to grow in the twelve reliable signs. And only the body as a whole can effectively show the world what the kingdom of God looks like. When churches of true saints practice their faith by serving others, the world will stand up and take notice. When believers work together to combat not just personal sins that prevent their own personal fulfillment but also the problems of the poor and oppressed outside their own neighborhoods and churches, the gospel of Jesus will become persuasive to those whose hearts had previously been hardened. Our witness will convince many of the reality of Jesus and the beauty of Christian holiness. Then our light will so shine before the world that "they will see [our] good works and give glory to [our] Father in heaven."

Appendix

. . . . .

The Unreliable & Reliable Signs of Grace

Unreliable Signs of Grace
1. Intense religious affections
2. Many religious affections at the same time
3. A certain sequence in the affections
4. Affections not produced by the self
5. Scriptures coming miraculously to mind
6. Physical manifestations of the affections
7. Much or eloquent talk about God and religion
8. Frequent and passionate praise for God
9. The appearance of love
10. Zealous or time-consuming devotion to religious activities
11. Being convinced that one is saved
12. Others being convinced that one is saved

Reliable Signs of Grace
1. A divine and supernatural source
2. Attraction to God and his ways for their own sake
3. Seeing the beauty of holiness

4. A new knowing
5. Deep-seated conviction
6. Humility
7. A change of nature
8. A Christlike spirit
9. Fear of God
10. Balance
11. Hunger for God
12. Christian practice

Study Guide

· · · · · · · · · · · · · · · · · ·

This guide is suitable for individual study or group discussion.

Chapter 1

1. Consider the four cultural trends outlined at the beginning of the chapter. Do you think they accurately depict American society as you know it? Why or why not?

2. Some would say that the "Sheila mentality" and the relativism described by Allan Bloom are infecting today's churches. Do you agree? If so, describe how one or both of these have affected a church you know.

3. The author claims that these four trends have contributed to a sense of spiritual confusion today. Do you feel confused about how to discern true from false religion?

Options for Group Discussion

A. Break the group up into pairs. Let each person explain to a partner why she or he is a Christian rather than something else—such as a Buddhist or atheist. Then let each one explain why he or she has chosen this particular Christian denomination. After the large group re-forms, talk about whether this experience has increased or reduced a sense of spiritual confusion.

B. Discuss as a group: How do we know that Christianity is true? Or that our denomination is preferable to others? Does our culture make it hard to answer these questions?

C. Invite individuals to share why they chose Christianity over other religions, or this denomination over others. The group might then discuss: does the modern proliferation of religious choices contribute to a sense of spiritual confusion?

4. Do you find it hard to criticize a spiritual leader or a religious group? When it is right to judge? When is it wrong?

5. Paul complained that the Galatian church had been "bewitched" (Gal 3:1). Have parts of the American church been bewitched? In what ways?

Chapter 2

1. Can you or anyone else in the group describe a time when your faith progressed from lifeless formality to true affections with feeling?

2. What groups around you show feeling in their worship? What are the strengths and weaknesses of their worship?

3. What groups around you focus on understanding in worship? What are the strengths and weaknesses of their worship?

4. After reading this chapter, a woman suddenly realized that her faith consisted of head knowledge only and that she didn't have the affections that lie at the heart of true spirituality. What should she do to find holy affections?

5. If you had more holy affections, how would your prayer life be different? Your relationships with friends? Family? How would your church be different if its worship flowed out of affections rather than just emotions or just beliefs?

6. Use the tables at the end of the chapter to try to distinguish between an emotion and an affection in your own life. Tell the group about the difference.

7. Look at table 4, "Examples of Affections." Discuss how holy affections are manifested at home, the workplace and church. Then do the same for unholy affections.

8. "If people are in the kingdom of God, they will be moved by spiritual conviction that affects all they are and do: their feelings, their thinking and their actions." Does this statement change your evaluation of your own life? Your church? Religious leaders or groups you know?

Chapter 3

1. Which unreliable signs involving religious experience have you previously accepted as reliable? Have you now changed your mind? Why or why not?

2. Can you think of people in the news or your own experience who

have wrongly thought they were saved because they had intense religious affections or a large number of affections?

3. What religious affections (such as love, sorrow for sins, worship or something else) have you seen counterfeited? Describe them.

4. Does the man with many false affections whom Edwards described in the second section ("many religious affections at the same time") sound familiar?

5. How is the sequence described in the third section ("a certain sequence in the affections") different from a true, godly sequence? Do our churches sometimes encourage the idea that the right sequence is proof of true faith?

6. Describe a person you know or know of who has had spiritual experiences originating outside the self but who was not a Christian. Did this happen to you before you became a Christian?

7. Does it surprise you that the Holy Spirit can influence non-Christians? If so, how does this change your view of your non-Christian friends?

8. Describe physical manifestations of spiritual activity that you have seen in both Christians and non-Christians. Is there a difference between the two? Are the motivations different?

9. How does this chapter change your understanding of the way God works in and through people? Does it change your view of your friends? Your relatives?

Chapter 4

1. "Much or eloquent talk about God and religion": try to demonstrate the truth of Edwards's claim that this is an unreliable sign by describing Christians and non-Christians alike who manifest this sign.

2. A loud and showy evangelist has come to town. Friends tell you that many have been saved and healed through his ministry. You are encouraged to sit under his teaching. What should you do? If you accept the invitation to attend, how do you try to evaluate his ministry?

3. Do you agree with Bonhoeffer that hypocritical praise is more of a problem today, when faith is sometimes fashionable? Why or why not?

4. Recall the differences between true and counterfeit love identified by Foster. Do they make sense to you? How might they help you purify your own love?

5. Do we tend to measure our maturity by the time we spend at church

or our involvement in church affairs? What are other ways in which we measure our spiritual maturity?

6. Where did Donna go wrong? How can we avoid her predicament? How can we help our children avoid it?

Chapter 5

1. Review the four ways people may be deceived about their own salvation. Which one has been present in your own life or the life of someone you know?

2. Is cheap grace a problem in your church or among Christians you know? If so, why do you think it is so attractive?

3. If you took Bonhoeffer's words seriously, what difference would it make in your life or in your church?

4. What lessons can be learned from Bill and Sally? How can you apply these lessons to your life? To your church?

5. According to this chapter, how should you treat someone who applies for membership in your church or fellowship, claiming that she (or he) is born again? What attitude should you take toward this person?

Chapter 6

1. What tips does this chapter give to help you gain assurance of salvation or confirm your assurance of salvation?

2. Are you doomed if sin is the only thing you see in your life? Why or why not?

3. How would you encourage someone reading this book who feels condemned because her life doesn't seem to match the twelve reliable signs?

Chapter 7

1. Recall the author's filthy mouth and how the Holy Spirit cleaned it up. Has the Spirit ever communicated his holiness to you in a way that didn't require much effort on your part?

2. Describe how everything looked to you after your conversion, specifying the differences.

3. What would you say about a person who has attended church all her life and professes Christian doctrine but has little or no love for others? Or the person who has heard voices and seen visions but is uninterested

in spiritual growth or loving the saints?

4. In what way can this new spiritual sense change one's marriage? How has it affected your marriage? Other relationships?

Chapter 8

1. How much of your own love is like the love of pagans?

2. Is it wrong to love God because of what he has done for us? How is this different from loving God because of what he is in himself?

3. If Edwards is right, much of today's preaching misses his point. How would Edwards change the focus of today's preaching?

4. What is the difference between enjoying God's graces and being obsessed with our spiritual experiences?

5. According to Calvin, the human mind is a factory of idols. What idols are being fashioned in the American church today?

6. This chapter argues that true faith is drawn to God primarily because of who he is rather than the benefits that he bestows. If this were more true in your life, how would it affect your prayer life? Your worship? Your work in the church? Your life at home? At work?

Chapter 9

1. The author tells the stories of Lin Yutang, Sojourner Truth and Marie of the Incarnation, all of whom were drawn to Christ because of the beauty of his holiness. Tell your own story of being drawn to Christ. What drew you? Which of Christ's attributes attracted you?

2. Try to distinguish God's natural attributes from his moral attributes in prayer and praise—either with the group or by yourself. Spend time praising him for his natural attributes and then for his moral attributes.

3. Isaiah says, "For as the heavens are higher than the earth, so are my ways higher than your ways and my thoughts than your thoughts" (Is 55:9). How does this verse help us understand God's holiness, which is an infinite "cut above" ours?

   Options

   A. Spend some quiet time meditating on God's infinitely pure holiness.

   B. Read Psalm 99 out loud and then spend time praising God's holiness in song or prayer.

4. Describe a "beautiful person" you know, focusing on how God's

holiness radiates from him or her.

5. Let different members of the group relate how seeing the beauty of God's holiness gave them power to change their lives.

Chapter 10

1. Did you see things differently after you found Christ? Try to explain how the world looked different to you.

2. We know that we are to walk by faith and not by sight, and that experience is not always a reliable guide to faith. Nevertheless, this new knowing involves experience. Tell the group about a time that your new knowing was also an experience.

3. The author describes how he saw the beauty of God in a leaf. Try something like that yourself. Go for a walk in a park or sit in your yard and study a part of the creation. Focus on the order and complexity and beauty of the natural world. Then thank God for it and praise him for what it shows you about him.

4. If there is an artist in the group, let that person talk about art as a way of seeing. Let the group try to relate what was said to the new seeing in Christ.

5. George Gwynn had a way of understanding how Christian principles applied to complex situations. Has Christ given you such spiritual vision in a difficult situation? Share the situation with the group.

Chapter 11

1. Perhaps you have heard non-Christians contemptuously refer to faith as a blind leap in the dark. Respond to this claim, using the material outlined in this chapter. If you're in a group, try out your answer on the group.

2. What would you say to an unbeliever who asks:

A. How can we be certain of anything?

B. How can we know if there is a God? Or that Jesus is the way to God?

For the group: let different members try out their answers on each other.

3. Can you remember a time when, as for C. S. Lewis, an intellectual conclusion turned into a heartfelt conviction (in other words, when the Holy Spirit added supernatural enlightening to the rational con-

clusions of your mind)?

    A. Share that experience with the group.

    B. Pray as a group for more of the reality of God and Christ to supernaturally enlighten your hearts. Or ask the Holy Spirit to bring that revelation to your non-Christian friends and relatives.

4. Refer to the last part of the chapter to consider how you would help a friend who fears he is losing his faith because he has doubts. Discuss this as a group.

Chapter 12

1. What part of this chapter especially spoke to your heart? Share this with the group.

2. What does false or counterfeit humility look like? How can we recognize it in ourselves?

3. Identify several ways spiritual pride can infect a Christian. How is it manifested in the life of the church? At home? On the job?

4. If you're in a group, consider two options, both of which require humility and courage (you may also do these alone):

    A. Confess how pride has infected your own life.

    B. Pray for humility.

5. What experiences has God used in your life to break you of pride? Is he doing this right now? How?

Chapter 13

1. Describe the difference between a change in lifestyle made through your own strength and a fundamental change in orientation of heart made by the Spirit.

2. Have you tried to break a habit without the power of the Spirit? Describe the result.

3. What has changed in you since the life of Christ has indwelt you?

4. Are there some changes that you know Christians should make but haven't made yourself?

5. Have you been freed from an addiction by the power of God? Describe the experience.

6. Are you discouraged by your own struggle against sin? Perhaps you are underestimating your progress because it has been gradual. Spend a few moments recalling the changes God has made in your life since

you first came to know him.

Chapter 14

1. The author says that Christian meekness means admitting our faults, being teachable and being willing to suffer. Are you meek? In what areas of your life is Jesus calling you to deeper meekness?

2. Jack Shaw reached abortionist Carol Everett through love. How can you show love to someone now living in darkness?

3. What can we learn from Corrie ten Boom's experience with the Nazi guard? How can you apply that lesson to your own life?

4. Who is *your* enemy? What would it mean for you to love that person? If this seems impossible, have the group ask God to give you grace to do the impossible.

5. What can you do to help the poor in your neighborhood? In your town? In your church?

6. Consider the suggestions at the end of the chapter for ways your church can help the poor. Which would be most feasible for you?

Chapter 15

1. Do we sometimes think that Jesus is the Savior *of* our sins? Is there a sin in your life that you are protecting?

2. Compare proper fear of God with the proper love and respect a child should have for parents. How are they similar? How are they different?

3. The author argues that fear of God softens the heart, opening it to conviction of sin. How can we allow our hearts to be softened?

4. If you had greater fear of God, how would your devotional life (prayer and Bible reading) change? Your family relationships? Your work?

5. Reinhold Niebuhr's fear of God led him to work for social justice. In 1995 the leaders of white charismatic and Pentecostal denominations were led by the fear of God to repent publicly for racist attitudes and actions against their brothers and sisters in black denominations. Is the Spirit speaking to you about racism or any other aspect of social justice? What can you do to please the Lord in this area?

Chapter 16

1. Review all the points of balance by reviewing the last paragraph in

the chapter. On what points are you in balance? On what points are you out of balance?

2. Which balance do you think is the hardest to keep? Why?

3. Is it more difficult to love family or neighbors? Why? What can you do to restore balance in this area?

4. Do you find it difficult to trust God for finances? Recall a time when God proved to you the truth of Matthew 6:33. Share that experience with the group.

5. Do you have a regular time alone with God each day? If so, share with the group strategies you have used to maintain this discipline.

6. "There is no such thing as a Lone Ranger Christian in the New Testament." What are the implications of this statement? Have you been negligent in this regard?

Chapter 17

1. How can we become more hungry for God? Tip: this chapter provides clues.

2. Recall the four ways in which, according to Edwards, grace satisfies. Which of these ways has been most meaningful to you? Share such an experience with the group.

3. Identify concrete ways we can draw closer to God. Share them with the group.

Chapter 18

1. What is your favorite or secret sin? What can you do to begin crucifying it?

2. Are you doing something that continually irritates your spouse or some other loved one? Ask God right now for help to start dealing with this problem.

3. Are you like the person Bonhoeffer described? That is, are you having doubts because you have never surrendered unconditionally to Jesus? If so, ask God for grace to repent and surrender fully. If you're in a group, discuss the relationship between doubt and failure to surrender unconditionally.

4. Does this emphasis on Christian practice as the most important sign change your view of your own faith? Of the spiritual claims made by others? Does it change the way you evaluate Christian teachers and

teachings? How?

5. If practice is the most important sign of true faith, what does this mean for your witness to non-Christian neighbors or colleagues at work? Do you need to change something about your life with them?

Chapter 19

1. Edwards claims Christian practice is the best evidence of grace to our own conscience. How do you measure up? Can you see grace in your own heart and life? Is there a difference since you first came to know Christ?

2. Think of an experience of suffering that taught you something new about your own heart. Share that experience with the group.

3. The author claims that this understanding of practice is not legalistic. Do you agree? Why or why not?

4. Meditate on the fact that grace is free. Spend time in thanksgiving, either by yourself or with the group.

5. Martin Luther said the person without faith is like someone who has to cross the sea. What makes you afraid at those times? You may want to ask the group to pray for you regarding this issue.

6. Practice, according to the author, is the best evidence of faith, love, repentance, humility and the fear of the Lord. What practice is God calling you to now? You may want to share this with the group.

Chapter 20

1. Do you feel overwhelmed after reading the book? Which of the four admonitions in this chapter helped you? Why?

2. How do *you* overcome perfectionism?

3. What advice would you give to someone who fears she has committed the unpardonable sin?

4. Does God seem silent to you now? What consolation does this chapter offer you?

5. What have you learned about Christian spirituality from this book? How will this understanding change your life?

6. What have you learned about discerning true religion from false? How will it change your life?

Notes

Chapter 1: Spiritual Confusion

[1]Robert N. Bellah et al., *Habits of the Heart: Individualism and Commitment in American Life* (Berkeley: University of California Press, 1985), p. 221.

[2]Allan Bloom, *The Closing of the American Mind* (New York: Simon & Schuster, 1987), p. 26.

[3]Cited by Martin Marty, *Context* 25 (October 15, 1993): 4-5.

[4]This book will not deal directly with the question of how Christians should regard non-Christian religions. However, it should provide indirect help by outlining both unreliable (chapters three through five) and reliable (chapters seven through nineteen) criteria for evaluating any religious experience. For more direct treatment of the truth of other religions, see Harold A. Netland, *Dissonant Voices: Religious Pluralism and the Question of Truth* (Grand Rapids, Mich.: Eerdmans, 1991); John Sanders, *No Other Name: An Investigation into the Destiny of the Unevangelized* (Grand Rapids, Mich.: Eerdmans, 1992); Clark H. Pinnock, *A Wideness in God's Mercy: The Finality of Jesus Christ in a World of Religions* (Grand Rapids, Mich.: Zondervan, 1992); J. N. D. Anderson, *Christianity and World Religions: The Challenge of Pluralism* (Downers Grove, Ill.: InterVarsity Press, 1984).

[5]The best version of this in print is edited by John E. Smith and published by Yale University Press. It is an expensive hardcover volume but well worth the investment.

[6]Roland Bainton, *Here I Stand: A Life of Martin Luther* (Nashville: Abingdon, 1950), p. 275.

Chapter 2: Feelings, Beliefs & the Affections

[1]I choose not to use the word *heart* because in today's English it is too narrowly associated with feelings and too dissociated from thinking. The affections as I define them motivate thinking just as much as they motivate feeling.

[2]Jonathan Edwards, *Religious Affections* (New Haven, Conn.: Yale University Press, 1959), p. 99. Hereafter referred to as *RA*.

[3]My translation.

[4]*RA*, p. 101.

[5]*RA*, p. 108. Emphasis added.

[6]Edwards's claim that love is the preeminent source of all the other affections is grounded in Scripture. When the lawyer asked Jesus to identify the greatest

commandment, Jesus replied, " 'You shall love the Lord your God with all your heart, and with all your soul, and with all your mind.' This is the greatest and first commandment. And a second is like it: 'You shall love your neighbor as yourself.' On these two commandments hang all the law and the prophets" (Mt 22:37-40). Paul was just as emphatic. He told his churches that "the one who loves another has fulfilled the law," and that "the whole law is summed up in a single command-ment, 'You shall love your neighbor as yourself' " (Rom 13:8, 10; Gal 5:14). Indeed, "love that comes from a pure heart" is the aim of Christian education (1 Tim 1:5). In his magnificent tribute to love (1 Cor 13) Paul warned that without love, the greatest knowledge and service to the church are as nothing. Giving all we have to the poor or dying a martyr's death will not make up for a lack of love. Even doing miracles and being a channel for the Holy Spirit's prophecies will count for nothing in the absence of love.

[7]My translation.

[8]*RA*, p. 266.

[9]*RA*, p. 111.

[10]*RA*, p. 120.

Chapter 3: Unreliable Signs Involving Religious Experience

[1]Thomas à Kempis *Imitation of Christ* 3.25.2.

[2]John of the Cross, *The Dark Night of the Soul*, ed. and trans. E. Allison Peers (Garden City, N.Y.: Image Books, 1959), pp. 40, 153.

[3]*RA*, p. 162.

[4]According to Acts 11:18, Cornelius experienced "repentance." In view of the narrative in Acts 10 his repentance may have involved primarily a "change of mind" about Jesus (rather than grief for his sins), which is the literal meaning of *repentance (metanoeō)*.

[5]John of the Cross, *Dark Night of the Soul*, p. 186.

[6]*RA*, p. 142.

[7]Jan Shipps, *Mormonism: The Story of a New Religious Tradition* (Urbana: University of Illinois Press, 1985); Klaus J. Hansen, *Mormonism and the American Experience* (Chicago: University of Chicago Press, 1981).

[8]Marc Breault and Martin King, *Inside the Cult* (New York: Signet, 1993).

Chapter 4: Unreliable Signs Involving Religious Behavior

[1]Important Christian thinkers have said the same. Justin Martyr (c. 100-165, an early apologist who was beheaded by the Romans) wrote, "The reality of our religion consists not of words but of deeds." Johann Arndt (1555-1621), a Lutheran mystic who inspired German Pietism, taught that "where Christ's life is not, Christ is not, even if one speaks many words concerning faith and doctrine." Dietrich Bonhoeffer (1906-1945), the German Lutheran theologian who was murdered by the Nazis, said that merely human love can speak "the Christian language with overwhelming and stirring eloquence." The Justin Martyr quote is from Philip Jacob Spener, *Pia Desideria*, ed. and trans. Theo-dore G. Tappert (Philadelphia: Fortress, 1964), pp. 104-5. The other quotes are from Johann Arndt, *True Christianity*, ed. and trans. Peter Erb (New York:

(New York: Paulist, 1979), p. 60; Dietrich Bonhoeffer, *Life Together* (London: SCM Press, 1954), p. 21.

[2]Luther, "Lectures on Psalms of Degrees," American ed. of *Works*, 40:361, quoted in Spener, *Pia Desideria*, p. 100.

[3]Dietrich Bonhoeffer, *The Cost of Discipleship* (New York: Macmillan, 1959), p. 79.

[4]The Shepard quote is from Edwards, *RA*, p. 137, n. 3.

[5]Bonhoeffer, *Cost of Discipleship*, pp. 214-15.

[6]*RA*, p. 146.

[7]For an evaluation of nontraditional cancer therapies, see "What About Coffee Enemas?" in William A. Fintel and Gerald R. McDermott, *A Medical and Spiritual Guide to Living with Cancer* (Dallas: Word Books, 1993).

[8]*RA*, p. 146.

[9]Bonhoeffer, *Life Together*, p. 21. Of course, Bonhoeffer was referring to counterfeit love, not members of the Unification Church.

[10]Bonhoeffer, *Cost of Discipleship*, p. 216.

[11]Richard Foster, *Celebration of Discipline* (San Francisco: Harper & Row, 1978), pp. 112-13.

[12]C. S. Lewis, *The Screwtape Letters*, in *The Best of C. S. Lewis* (Grand Rapids, Mich.: Baker Book House, 1969), p. 90.

[13]Ibid., p. 31.

[14]Bonhoeffer, *Life Together*, p. 21.

[15]Ibid., p. 22.

[16]Spener, *Pia Desideria*, p. 65.

Chapter 5: Unreliable Signs Involving Assurance of Salvation

[1]Canons and Decrees of the Council of Trent, sixth session, chaps. 9, 12.

[2]Thomas Aquinas *Summa Theologiae* 2a.24.

[3]Gerald May, *Addiction and Grace: Love and Spirituality in the Healing of Addictions* (San Francisco: Harper & Row, 1988), p. 45.

[4]Quoted in Heiko Oberman, *Luther: Man Between God and the Devil* (New Haven, Conn.: Yale University Press, 1989), pp. 105-6.

[5]Edwards, "Personal Narrative," in *Jonathan Edwards: Representative Selections*, ed. Clarence H. Faust and Thomas H. Johnson (New York: Hill and Wang, 1962), p. 70.

[6]Dietrich Bonhoeffer, *The Cost of Discipleship* (New York: Macmillan, 1959), pp. 47-48, 53.

[7]This does not mean that we make no distinctions in the work of the church. The Scriptures command us to distinguish between those fit and those unfit for ordination and leadership in the church (for example, 1 Tim 3:1-13). They also tell us to discipline those guilty of serious sin (Mt 18:15-18). But my point is that even while making these distinctions we cannot presume to know with absolute certainty the eternal destiny of most people. Some church people whose visible behavior obligates us to receive them in charity as brothers and sisters in Christ may be revealed at the Judgment as hypocrites (Mt 7:21-23). Other people whose faith we suspect may be revealed as shining lights.

[8]I do not mean to imply that all true Christians can point back to an emotional

experience at which point they repented and began to trust in Christ. Some
wonderful Christians, raised in Christian homes, have never known times when
they didn't love Jesus. The lack of a crisis experience is not important; all that
matters is that they trust Christ now and sense the Holy Spirit working in and
through them now.

[9]Bill's situation may be described by the Westminster Confession, which says of the
saints, "Nevertheless they may, through the temptations of Satan and of the world,
the prevalency of corruption remaining in them, and the neglect of the means of
their preservation, fall into grievous sins; and for a time continue therein: whereby
they incur God's displeasure, and grieve his Holy Spirit; come to be deprived of
some measure of their graces and comforts; have their hearts hardened, and their
consciences wounded; hurt and scandalize others, and bring temporal judgments
upon themselves." Westminster Confession 17.3, in *Creeds of the Churches,* ed. John
H. Leith (Garden City, N.Y.: Anchor Books, 1963). I am indebted to the Reverend
Dr. Greg Scharf for this observation.

Chapter 7: The First Reliable Sign: A Divine & Supernatural Source
[1]Augustine, *The Confessions,* ed. and trans. Henry Chadwick (Oxford: Oxford
University Press, 1991), p. 155.
[2]My translation.
[3]Edwards, "Personal Narrative," in *Jonathan Edwards: Basic Writings,* ed. Ola
Winslow (New York: Penguin, 1966), p. 85.
[4]Ibid., pp. 83-84.
[5]Charles Finney, "Baptism of the Holy Ghost," in *American Christianity: An Historical
Interpretation with Representative Documents,* ed. H. Shelton Smith, Robert Handy
and Lefferts Loetscher (New York: Charles Scribner's Sons, 1963), 2:23.
[6]Nathan Cole, "Spiritual Travels," in *Voices from the Heart: Four Centuries of American
Piety,* ed. Mark Noll and Roger Lundin (Grand Rapids, Mich.: Eerdmans, 1987),
p. 85.

**Chapter 8: The Second Reliable Sign: Attraction to God & His Ways for Their Own
Sake**
[1]Jonathan Edwards, *Some Thoughts Concerning the Revival,* in *Works of Jonathan
Edwards,* ed. C. C. Goen (New Haven, Conn.: Yale University Press, 1972), 4:331-32.
Emphasis added.
[2]Ibid., p. 337.
[3]C. S. Lewis, *The Screwtape Letters,* in *The Best of C. S. Lewis* (Grand Rapids, Mich.:
Baker Book House, 1969), p. 31.
[4]Thomas à Kempis *Imitation of Christ* 2.11.
[5]John of the Cross, *The Dark Night of the Soul,* ed. and trans. E. Allison Peers (Garden
City, N.Y.: Image Books, 1959), pp. 56-59.
[6]*RA,* p. 250.

Chapter 9: The Third Reliable Sign: Seeing the Beauty of Holiness
[1]My information comes from Marc Breault and Martin King, *Inside the Cult* (New
York: Signet, 1993).

[2]Ibid., p. 123.

[3]Ibid., pp. 158-59.

[4]Quoted in Hugh T. Kerr and John M. Mulder, eds., *Conversions: The Christian Experience* (Grand Rapids, Mich.: Eerdmans, 1983), pp. 208-9.

[5]Sojourner Truth, *Narrative of Sojourner Truth: A Bondswoman of Olden Time*, in *Conversions*, ed. Kerr and Mulder, pp. 115-16. Emphasis added.

[6]Quoted in Mark Noll and Roger Lundin, eds., *Voices from the Heart: Four Centuries of American Piety* (Grand Rapids, Mich.: Eerdmans, 1987), p. 26.

[7]Calvin, *Institutes of the Christian Religion* (Grand Rapids, Mich.: Eerdmans, 1960), 1.1.3.

[8]Edwards, "The Excellency of Christ," in *The Works of Jonathan Edwards* (Edinburgh: Banner of Truth, 1974), 1:681-82.

[9]C. S. Lewis, *The Great Divorce*, in *The Best of C. S. Lewis* (Grand Rapids, Mich.: Baker Book House, 1969), p. 181.

[10]Ibid., p. 180.

[11]Edwards, "Personal Narrative," in *Jonathan Edwards: Basic Writings*, ed. Ola Winslow (New York: Penguin, 1966), pp. 87, 93.

Chapter 10: The Fourth Reliable Sign: A New Knowing

[1]Edwards, RA, p. 266.

[2]Ruth Tucker, *Another Gospel: Alternative Religions and the New Age Movement* (Grand Rapids, Mich.: Academie Books/Zondervan, 1989), pp. 120-21.

[3]C. S. Lewis, *Surprised by Joy: The Shape of My Early Life* (London: Geoffrey Bles, 1955), pp. 170-71.

[4]Nathan Cole, "Spiritual Travels," in *Voices from the Heart: Four Centuries of American Piety*, ed. Mark Noll and Roger Lundin (Grand Rapids, Mich.: Eerdmans, 1987), pp. 84-85. Author's emphasis.

Chapter 11: The Fifth Reliable Sign: Deep-Seated Conviction

[1]Nancy Cartwright, *How the Laws of Physics Lie* (Oxford: Clarendon, 1989).

[2]My thinking in this section is largely indebted to Alister McGrath, *Intellectuals Don't Need God and Other Modern Myths* (Grand Rapids, Mich.: Zondervan, 1993).

[3]See, for example, N. R. Hanson, *Perception and Discovery* (San Francisco: Freeman and Cooper, 1969).

[4]McGrath, *Intellectuals*, p. 165.

[5]Material from the previous two paragraphs is taken from Thomas V. Morris, *Making Sense of It All: Pascal and the Meaning of Life* (Grand Rapids, Mich.: Eerdmans, 1992), pp. 79-80.

[6]See Lewis, *Mere Christianity*, bk. 2, chap. 3. Some have charged that Lewis omits another possibility—that while the New Testament writers presented Jesus as divine, Jesus did not think of himself in that way. For Lewis's own reply to this sort of biblical criticism in general, see his "Modern Theology and Biblical Criticism," in *Christian Reflections*, ed. Walter Hooper (Grand Rapids, Mich.: Eerdmans, 1967), esp. pp. 157-58. For more recent reflection on Jesus' messianic consciousness, see Larry Hurtado, "Christ," in *Dictionary of Jesus and the Gospels*, ed. Joel Green, Scot McKnight and I. Howard Marshall (Downers Grove,

Ill.: InterVarsity Press, 1992), pp. 106-17.

[7]This arrangement of evidence is taken from C. Stephen Evans, *The Quest for Faith: Reason and Mystery as Pointers to God* (Downers Grove, Ill.: InterVarsity Press, 1986), pp. 73-74.

[8]Quoted in Evans, *Reason and Mystery*, p. 74.

[9]C. S. Lewis, *Surprised by Joy: The Shape of My Early Life* (London: Geoffrey Bles, 1955), p. 211.

[10]Ibid., p. 223. Emphasis added.

[11]Luci Shaw, *God in the Dark: Through Grief and Beyond* (Grand Rapids, Mich.: Zondervan, 1989), p. 240.

Chapter 12: The Sixth Reliable Sign: Humility

[1]Thomas à Kempis *Imitation of Christ* 1.1.

[2]Teresa of Ávila, *The Life of Teresa of Jesus: The Autobiography of St. Teresa of Ávila*, ed. and trans. E. Allison Peers (Garden City, N.Y.: Image Books, 1960), p. 159.

[3]Calvin, *Institutes of the Christian Religion* (Grand Rapids, Mich.: Eerdmans, 1960), 2.2.11.

[4]Augustine *The City of God* 12.13.

[5]*RA*, pp. 311-12.

[6]Ibid.

[7]Teresa of Ávila, *Life of Teresa of Jesus*, p. 280.

[8]C. S. Lewis, *The Best of C. S. Lewis* (Grand Rapids, Mich.: Baker Book House, 1969) p. 55.

[9]Johann Arndt, *True Christianity*, ed. and trans. Peter Erb (New York: Paulist, 1979), p. 43.

[10]Ibid.

[11]*RA*, p. 315.

[12]John of the Cross, *The Dark Night of the Soul*, ed. and trans. E. Allison Peers (Garden City, N.Y.: Image Books, 1959), pp. 41-42.

[13]Martin Luther, *Superbus primo est excusator sui ac defensor, justificator*, in Weimar ed. of *Works*, 3:388; quoted in Reinhold Niebuhr, *The Nature and Destiny of Man* (New York: Scribner's, 1943), 1:200.

[14]Teresa of Ávila, *Life of Teresa of Jesus*, p. 394.

[15]Thomas à Kempis *Imitation of Christ* 1.7.

[16]Ibid., 1.9.

[17]John of the Cross, *Dark Night of the Soul*, p. 43.

[18]Thomas à Kempis *Imitation of Christ* 3.10.

[19]Niebuhr, *Nature and Destiny of Man*, p. 200.

[20]Teresa of Ávila, *Life of Teresa of Jesus*, pp. 108, 177.

[21]Thomas à Kempis *Imitation of Christ* 4.58.

[22]Teresa of Ávila, *Life of Teresa of Jesus*, pp. 201-2.

[23]C. S. Lewis, *The Screwtape Letters*, in *The Best of C. S. Lewis* (Grand Rapids, Mich.: Baker Book House, 1969), p. 54.

[24]Arndt, *True Christianity*, p. 102.

[25]Ibid., p. 122.

[26]Luci Shaw, *God in the Dark: Through Grief and Beyond* (Grand Rapids, Mich.:

Zondervan, 1989), p. 240.

[27]Richard Foster, *Celebration of Discipline* (San Francisco: Harper & Row, 1978), pp. 88-89.

[28]Dietrich Bonhoeffer, *Life Together* (London: SCM Press, 1954), p. 74.

[29]Ibid., p. 71.

[30]Teresa of Ávila, *Life of Teresa of Jesus*, p. 215.

Chapter 13: The Seventh Reliable Sign: A Change of Nature

[1]Harper Lee, *To Kill a Mockingbird* (London: Penguin, 1960), p. 219.

[2]Gerald May, *Addiction and Grace: Love and Spirituality in the Healing of Addictions* (San Francisco: Harper & Row, 1988), pp. 6-7.

[3]Augustine *The Confessions* 8.29.

[4]May, *Addiction and Grace*, pp. 152-53.

Chapter 14: The Eighth Reliable Sign: A Christlike Spirit

[1]Dietrich Bonhoeffer, *Life Together* (London: SCM Press, 1954), p. 60.

[2]Dietrich Bonhoeffer, *The Cost of Discipleship* (New York: Macmillan, 1959), p. 100.

[3]Ibid., p. 96.

[4]Thomas à Kempis *Imitation of Christ* 3.19.

[5]Gerald May, *Addiction and Grace: Love and Spirituality in the Healing of Addictions* (San Francisco: Harper & Row, 1988). p. 137.

[6]*RA*, p. 351.

[7]Carol Everett with Jack Shaw, *Blood Money: Getting Rich off a Woman's Right to Choose* (Sisters, Ore.: Multnomah Press, 1992), pp. 150-56; the quote is from pp. 155-56.

[8]Gandhi's statement that the British were loved ones does not mean, of course, that everything he did, or even intended, was good for the British. His exhortation to Indians to make their own cloth on spinning wheels helped foster economic independence for Indians but wasn't particularly helpful to British millworkers.

[9]Corrie ten Boom, *The Hiding Place* (Old Tappan, N.J.: Spire Books, 1971), p. 238.

[10]Quoted in Kenneth Leech, *Soul Friend: An Invitation to Spiritual Direction* (San Francisco: HarperSanFrancisco, 1992), p. 150. Love is necessary, but not sufficient, to be a Christian. Every true Christian will love, but simply loving does not make one a Christian. Gandhi loved his enemies. This is a Christian virtue, but it doesn't mean that Gandhi was a Christian.

[11]Johann Arndt, *True Christianity*, ed. and trans. Peter Erb (New York: Paulist, 1979), p. 124.

[12]Quoted in Leech, *Soul Friend*, p. 150.

[13]From *Mother Teresa*, a 1986 video produced by Petrie Productions and distributed by Today Home Entertainment.

[14]Thomas à Kempis *Imitation of Christ* 1.15. My translation.

[15]Bonhoeffer, *Cost of Discipleship*, p. 165.

[16]Ibid., p. 164.

[17]Ibid.

[18]*Guideposts*, January 1986.

[19]Arndt, *True Christianity*, p. 134.

Chapter 15: The Ninth Reliable Sign: Fear of God
[1]R. C. Sproul, *The Holiness of God* (Wheaton, Ill.: Tyndale House, 1988), p. 65.
[2]*RA*, p. 364.
[3]For more on Niebuhr's struggle for social justice, see Richard Fox, *Reinhold Niebuhr: A Biography* (San Francisco: Harper & Row, 1987).

Chapter 16: The Tenth Reliable Sign: Balance
[1]Johann Arndt, *True Christianity*, ed. and trans. Peter Erb (New York: Paulist, 1979), pp. 106-7.
[2]Thomas à Kempis *Imitation of Christ* 1.22.
[3]*RA*, p. 371.
[4]C. S. Lewis, *The Screwtape Letters*, in *The Best of C. S. Lewis* (Grand Rapids, Mich.: Baker Book House, 1969) p. 21.
[5]Thomas à Kempis *Imitation of Christ* 2.11.
[6]Arndt, *True Christianity*, p. 72.
[7]Thomas à Kempis *Imitation of Christ* 1.20.
[8]Ibid., 3.53.
[9]Richard Foster, *Celebration of Discipline* (San Francisco: Harper & Row, 1978), p. 94.

Chapter 17: The Eleventh Reliable Sign: Hunger for God
[1]*RA*, p. 379.
[2]Ibid.
[3]Ibid., pp. 382-83.

Chapter 18: The Twelfth Reliable Sign: Christian Practice (Surrender & Perseverance)
[1]Martin Luther, Works, 35:370; quoted in Philipp Jacob Spener, Pia Desideria, ed. and trans. Theodore G. Tappert (Philadelphia: Fortress, 1964), pp. 64-65.
[2]I don't mean to imply that the breakdown was inevitable or that she had no responsibility for it. But he seemed to bear more of the blame because he stubbornly refused to respond to her (justified!) concerns.
[3]Dietrich Bonhoeffer, *The Cost of Discipleship* (New York: Macmillan, 1959), pp. 72-73.
[4]Westminster Confession 17.3, in *Creeds of the Churches*, ed. John H. Leith (Garden City, N.Y.: Anchor Books, 1963), p. 212.
[5]*RA*, p. 443.

Chapter 19: The Twelfth Reliable Sign: Christian Practice (Suffering & Obedience)
[1]C. S Lewis, *The Best of C. S. Lewis* (Grand Rapids, Mich.: Baker Book House, 1969), p. 53.
[2]Dietrich Bonhoeffer, *The Cost of Discipleship* (New York: Macmillan, 1959), p. 215.
[3]Ibid., p. 79.
[4]Quoted in Alister McGrath, *Christian Theology: An Introduction* (Cambridge, Mass.: Blackwell, 1994), pp. 127-28.
[5]Bonhoeffer, *Cost of Discipleship*, p. 69.

Chapter 20: Are You Overwhelmed?

[1] William A. Fintel and Gerald R. McDermott, *A Medical and Spiritual Guide to Living with Cancer* (Dallas: Word Books, 1993).

[2] See C. S. Lewis, *A Grief Observed* (New York: Seabury, 1961).